THE CANONICAL HISTORY OF IDEAS
The Place of the So-called Tannaite Midrashim:

*Mekhilta Attributed to R. Ishmael, Sifra,
Sifré to Numbers,* and *Sifré to Deuteronomy*

SOUTH FLORIDA STUDIES IN THE HISTORY OF JUDAISM

Edited by
Jacob Neusner
Ernest S. Frerichs, William Scott Green, James Strange

Number 04
The Canonical History of Ideas
The Place of the So-called Tannaite Midrashim:

Mekhilta Attributed to R. Ishmael, Sifra,
Sifré to Numbers, and *Sifré to Deuteronomy*

by
Jacob Neusner

THE CANONICAL HISTORY OF IDEAS
The Place of the So-called Tannaite Midrashim:

Mekhilta Attributed to R. Ishmael, Sifra,
Sifré to Numbers, and Sifré to Deuteronomy

by

Jacob Neusner

Scholars Press
Atlanta, Georgia

THE CANONICAL HISTORY OF IDEAS
The Place of the So-called Tannaite Midrashim:

Mekhilta Attributed to R. Ishmael, Sifra, Sifré to Numbers, and Sifré to Deuteronomy

© 1990
University of South Florida

Publication of this book was made possible by a grant from the Tisch Family Foundation, New York City. The University of South Florida acknowledges with thanks this important support for its scholarly projects.

Library of Congress Cataloging in Publication Data

Neusner, Jacob, 1932-
    The canonical history of ideas : the place of the so-called
Tannaite Midrashim: Mekhilta according to R. Ishmael, Sifra, Sifré
to Numbers, and Sifré to Deuteronomy / by Jacob Neusner.
    p. cm. -- (South Florida studies in the history of Judaism ; no. 04)
    Includes bibliographical references.
    ISBN 1-55540-436-7 (alk. paper)
    1. Halakhic Midrashim--History and criticism. 2. Mishnah-
-Theology. 3. Talmud Yerushalmi--Theology. 4. Judaism--History-
-Talmudic period, 10-425. I. Title.
BM514-N46 1989
296.1'4--dc20   89-48210

Printed in the United States of America
on acid-free paper

Table of Contents

for

Thomas Jonah Tisch

on the occasion of his thirty-fifth birthday

to one-hundred twenty years!

Preface

This book sets forth an account of a method I have devised to study the formation of Judaism in the first seven centuries C.E., a method I call "the canonical history of ideas." The method is defined in Chapter One and explained at greater length in the Appendix.[1] In working out a problem of gaining perspective on the literary situation of certain documents, I further provide the report of an experiment utilizing the method at hand.

The experiment further is built upon the convergence of results of three prior projects of mine. The first was my translations and introductions to the four Tannaite Midrashim, complete for Mekhilta Attributed to R. Ishmael, Sifra, and Sifré to Deuteronomy, and partial for Sifré to Numbers. Second in logical order were my descriptions, analyses, and interpretations of two connected but autonomous Judaisms, the one to which the Mishnah, Tosefta, and tractate Avot attest, the other portrayed by the Yerushalmi (a.k.a. the Talmud of the Land of Israel), Genesis Rabbah, Leviticus Rabbah, and Pesiqta deRab Kahana. Third, I have worked out a long series of studies of the histories of important ideas as a reading of the canonical documents of Judaism in their generally accepted historical sequence. These I call "the canonical history of ideas," an inquiry explained in the appendix.

Now I call upon established results in the description of the documents examined here as to their relationship to the two distinct Judaic systems, the Mishnah's and the Yerushalmi's, in respect to the chapters of the canonical history of ideas that, on other bases altogether, I have already composed. I have differentiated in great

---

[1]The essay in the Appendix originated as The Ben Zion Bokser Lecture at Queens College (1986). I originally printed it in my *Religious Study of Judaism. Description, Analysis, Interpretation. First Series* (Lanham, 1986: University Press of America).

detail the Mishnah's and the Yerushalmi's Judaisms. Among numerous indicators of the points in conflict and in convergence between those two readily distinguished systems, I have selected those I deem representative. I refer, specifically, to seven indicative ideas, words, themes, or concepts. What I want to know, then, is how the four documents commonly called "Tannaite Midrashim," namely, the Mekhilta Attributed to R. Ishmael, Sifra, and the two Sifrés, relate to the Mishnah, at the one side, and the Yerushalmi, at the other.

In this way, treating the results for the two principal documents as fixed and indicative, I can claim to define the intersecting lines of a grid. The grid's horizontals are set by the Judaism defined by the Mishnah and its associated writings, ca. 200, and the verticals, by the one set forth by the Talmud of the Land of Israel and its companion, ca. 450. With a firm description of the points of comparison and contrast of each Judaism well in hand, we may now ask, how do documents position themselves, by appeal to certain known and proved indicative traits of the Mishnah and the Yerushalmi, between those two poles? These indicative traits, then, form the reference points of the grid. Chapters Two through Eight define the Mishnah's and the Yerushalmi's positions on the indicative points and then collect the pertinent information. In Chapter Nine, I set forth the results, which, happily, prove complex and ambiguous. In Chapter Ten I spell out what is at stake in the method as well as in the results at hand.

What makes these seven indicator ideas, concepts, words, and the like, which I have selected, is that through all of them, the Judaism represented by the Mishnah makes its systemic judgment in its distinctive way. The Judaism that animates the Talmud of the Land of Israel does the same in its very particular idiom of thought and expression, and these statements of the two documents and systems they attested do not correspond but in fact conflict. So at each point we shall see how the two documents, and, I maintain, the systems that they adumbrate, intersect and conflict.

What I want to know, then, is, on the range of issues on which the two Judaisms part company, where do the so-called Tannaite Midrashim locate themselves? The first question must be whether they take positions on the indicative points at all. The canonical history of ideas depends upon continuities and intersections among documents. If a document pursues its own program and in no way deals with issues I think indicative elsewhere, then there is no appealing to continuity and change in an ongoing program for situating that document within its larger canonical context. One of the results in this experiment is just that: some of the documents simply ignore issues that prove critical to the Mishnah and the Yerushalmi (and Bavli later on, as a matter of fact). That means there are questions we cannot answer in this context by means of this method, when a document ignores the issues deemed here to be systemically indicative of both the Mishnah and the Yerushalmi.[2]

The second question of course is, on questions important to both the Mishnah and the Yerushalmi, what position does a given document's compilers select for themselves? At the outset I see three logical possibilities: [1] a document in the aggregate stands closer to the Mishnah; [2] a document takes a position, overall, closer to the Yerushalmi. In the concluding chapter we consider the facts and their implications. If the former, then may we situate the document in the period within which the Mishnah was taking shape and among the Mishnah's authorities? Or does the document reach closure after, and in full awareness of the system of, the Mishnah, and simply carry forward the elaboration and extension of the Mishnah's system? The answers to those questions have considerable bearing upon how we work out the history of the formation of the Judaism of the Dual Torah.

In the Introduction I provide a more elaborate account of the nature of the experiment, spelling out the premises defined by now-completed research, the theoretical results we may anticipate, and the method by which I do the work. The work overall draws upon my completed translations of, and introductions to, the four so-called Tannaite Midrashim that are analyzed here. These are as follows:

Sifré to Numbers. An American Translation. I. *1-58.* Atlanta, 1986: Scholars Press for Brown Judaic Studies

Sifré to Numbers. An American Translation. II. *59-115.* Atlanta, 1986: Scholars Press for Brown Judaic Studies. [III. *116-161:* William Scott Green].

Sifré to Deuteronomy. An Analytical Translation. Atlanta, 1987: Scholars Press for Brown Judaic Studies. I. *Pisqaot One through One Hundred Forty-Three. Debarim, Waethanan, Eqeb, Re'eh.*

Sifré to Deuteronomy. An Analytical Translation. Atlanta, 1987: Scholars Press for Brown Judaic Studies. II. *Pisqaot One Hundred Forty-Four through Three Hundred Fifty-Seven. Shofetim, Ki Tese, Ki Tabo, Nesabim, Ha'azinu, Zot Habberakhah.*

---

[2]Then we have to ask whether a document is simply eccentric or merely asymmetrical to the larger canonical context. It appears to me that Sifré to Numbers requires precisely that inquiry. Then the still-unanswered question of how we may define "the Judaism beyond the texts," that is, the system assumed by all documents but fully exposed within, or by, none of them, must be considered again. I plan to do so immediately, through a quite different method from the documentary one.

Sifra. An Analytical Translation. Atlanta, 1988: Scholars Press for Brown Judaic Studies. I. *Introduction and Vayyiqra Dibura Denedabah and Vayiqqra Dibura Dehobah.*

Sifra. An Analytical Translation. Atlanta, 1988: Scholars Press for Brown Judaic Studies. II. *Sav, Shemini, Tazria, Negaim, Mesora, and Zabim.*

Sifra. An Analytical Translation. Atlanta, 1988: Scholars Press for Brown Judaic Studies. III. *Aharé Mot, Qedoshim, Emor, Behar, and Behuqotai.*

Mekhilta Attributed to R. Ishmael. An Analytical Translation. Atlanta, 1988: Scholars Press for Brown Judaic Studies. I. *Pisha, Beshallah, Shirata, and Vayassa.*

Mekhilta Attributed to R. Ishmael. An Analytical Translation. Atlanta, 1988: Scholars Press for Brown Judaic Studies. II. *Amalek, Bahodesh, Neziqin, Kaspa, and Shabbata.*

Sifré to Deuteronomy. An Introduction to the Rhetorical, Logical, and Topical Program. Atlanta, 1987: Scholars Press for Brown Judaic Studies.

Uniting the Dual Torah: Sifra and the Problem of the Mishnah. Cambridge and New York, 1989: Cambridge University Press.

Sifra in Perspective: The Documentary Comparison of the Midrashim of Ancient Judaism. Atlanta, 1988: Scholars Press for Brown Judaic Studies.

Mekhilta Attributed to R. Ishmael. An Introduction to Judaism's First Scriptural Encyclopaedia. Atlanta, 1988: Scholars Press for Brown Judaic Studies.

Further pertinent bibliography is given in the Introduction.

I owe thanks to The Institute for Advanced Study, where I wrote this book, for in its idyllic setting, IAS forms a paradise of learning, but one without a snake. I cannot imagine a more congenial setting for a year of full-time research. At IAS you go into your office, close the door, and think great thoughts. But when you emerge, you always find someone with whom to share them, who is there to tell you things, too (among them: your great thoughts are wrong). I express my genuine appreciation for the Institute's gifts to me: an endowment of peace and cordiality, generosity and collegiality among the Members, and – above all – even respect and appreciation for the shared enterprise of learning. I have learned not to take for granted acts of uncommon grace such as those carried out routinely and in a self-effacing way every day, also, by some of the staff and permanent faculty of The Institute for Advanced Study. But my special thanks go to the Members for 1989-

1990, who in reality formed the community of learning at that brief time, in that enchanted place, of which all of us dream.

During my year as Member of The Institute for Advanced Study, I held a Senior Fellowship of the National Endowment for the Humanities (FA 28396-89), and I take much pride in offering to that agency in the support of humanistic learning my very hearty thanks for the recognition and material support that the Fellowship afforded to me. I found the Endowment, particularly the Division of Fellowships and Seminars, always helpful and courteous in dealing with my application and express my admiration and appreciation to that thoroughly professional staff of public servants.

Brown University complemented that Fellowship with substantial funds to make it possible for me without financial loss to spend the entire academic year, 1989-1990, in full-time research. In my twenty-two years at Brown University, now concluded, I always enjoyed the University's generous support for every research initiative that I undertook, and it was a welcome challenge to be worthy of the unusual opportunities accorded to me from 1968 through 1990 as a research scholar as well as a teacher at that University. I never took for granted the commitment of the University's scarce resources to my work in particular and now that I have taken early retirement in part to pursue my research interests, I express the thanks commensurate to the gift.

I made considerable use of the Firestone Library at Princeton University and the Speare Library at the Princeton Theological Seminary. I am glad to thank the librarians of those two inestimable collections, which turn this small town into as great a center for research in the field of religion as exists anywhere in the world.

This book was just getting underway as my family and I went off to join in celebrating the thirty-fifth birthday of Thomas Jonah Tisch, on October 13, 1989. The model of the man for others, our Tommy gives so much, in so many ways, that those whose lives he illumines were especially grateful for the occasion to say thanks. The dedication is one heart's response to immense and ongoing benefit: friendship and love, counsel and courage, given lavishly and generously and perpetually. I give what I have to give, which is this little book, testament to life as I live it, to someone who has done so much to make that life happy.

Jacob Neusner

The Institute for Advanced Study
Princeton, New Jersey

February 10, 1990.

Introduction

This book presents a working paper that reports on both the method, "the canonical history of ideas," and result of an experiment meant to establish some very simple facts and suggests implications to be drawn from those facts. The method is explained at length in Chapter One and is applied through Chapters Two through Eight, with the results spelled out in Chapter Nine and their implications for contemporary scholarly debate made explicit in Chapter Ten. The method at hand is further tested as to falsification in Appendix I.[1]

That method in studying the history of ideas traces the representation of a given conception from one document to the next, rather than homogenizing what all documents say about that conception into a harmonious account, "the talmudic-midrashic view of...." I have dismissed the received method of studying the history of ideas for two reasons. First, it ignores the distinctive traits, interests, tendencies, and programs of specific documents. Second, it takes at face value all the attributions of sayings to named authorities, therefore assigning to the time in which those authorities lived, rather than the age in which the documents that convey those sayings were redacted,

---

[1]Appendices II and III deal with a different approach to the same problem from the one I have taken in this book. I explain in Appendix II the premises of that other approach, which render all of its results hopelessly uncritical and therefore null. The item noted in Appendix III is of course not to be ignored; only charlatans pretend to ignore books with which they disagree and omit from even their bibliographies all mention of their opposition. It is an easy way, of course, to win an argument among the believers, but it is a mark of scholarly fraud of the most pathetic order: people who cannot find good arguments against viewpoints they reject find it necessary to pretend those positions simply do not exist. The book treated in Appendix II is honest scholarship, which is simply wrong on every point of method, consequently also on all of its proposed results.

the sayings themselves. Either of these flaws would suffice to render null all the results produced on such foundations; together they serve to invalidate all results, as to the history of ideas or mentalités, the characterization of documents, and the representation, in historical context, of Judaism or Judaisms, prior to my own.

My research for a number of years has led me to differentiate among documents and to ask each document to deliver its particular viewpoint to me. That is the foundation for the work of the present volume as well. When, therefore I wish to trace the history of an idea, it produces the representations of that idea as yielded by documents, read singly and one by one, then in the sequence of their closure.[2]

I do not, moreover, appeal to attributions of sayings to named authorities to tell me where and when a given opinion was held because these attributions are not accessible to the normal tests of criticism: falsification or verification. Unless we believe at face value the inerrancy of attributions – and then we cannot claim to conduct scholarship in accord with the established critical norms – we have to find some other medium for historical inquiry. Dismissing as not proved reliable and treating as merely suppositious the entire corpus of attributions represents an innovation and the beginning of critical study, for historical and religions-historical purposes, of the canon of Judaism in its formative age. It reshapes the entire scholarly agenda.

Here, of course, I further innovate by reading documents in relationship to other documents, earlier and later – the set under discussion in relationship to the Mishnah, on the one side, and the Yerushalmi, on the other, for instance. It follows that I do not join together everything I find, without regard to its point of origin in a given compilation of rabbinic sayings. Rather I keep things apart, so that I record what I find in document A, then in document B, and onward through the alphabet. What this yields is a history of the idea at hand as the successive documents, laid out in their sequence, tell me that history.

---

[2]But that approach leaves open the question of the Judaism beyond the texts, before them, and around them: what is everywhere taken for granted and no-where made explicit as the foundation of a document. The problem of the history of religion is not only solved by the evidence of reading what documents say, but also by the testimony given by hearing what documents do not say. However, absent a prior knowledge, gained by us without any evidence at all, we have to frame appropriate methods for describing that nourishing and sustaining corpus of unarticulated attitudes and ideas. As I said in the preface, I am now turning to that problem of method, with an experiment quite different from this one – an experiment that explicitly ignores the limits of documents and asks what travels between and among them.

The experiment, using that method, concerns the intellectual situation of documents that, up to now, have not been examined from the perspectives introduced here. If the design of the experiment is sound, then others should be able to replicate my results, both for my indicators and for others altogether. What I mean to uncover are the facts of the documents studied here – the unknown – as to the relationships to documents that have been fully worked out – the known. These facts will then be established and therefore require explanation. The proposed explanations of those facts will vary, but the facts proved here will stand firm. Chapter Nine is one exercise in explanation, but I do not represent it as the only possible way of explaining the facts I set forth, let alone the best or the sufficient one.

Let us attend first to the experiment, address what is at stake in the results, and then at the end consider the outlines of the method that is utilized in the experiment. What I wish to lay out is the relationship on seven important topics between the so-called Tannaitic Midrashim, on the one side, and the connected but autonomous Judaic systems attested by the Mishnah, on the second side, and the Talmud of the Land of Israel (a.k.a., the Yerushalmi) and related Midrash compilations, on the third. Why does it matter? Because an allegation of received scholarship is that the so-called Tannaitic Midrashim fall within the framework of, and therefore testify to the system presented by, the Mishnah. If we are to affirm that received position, then, if they deal with the topics at hand, some of them, e.g, doctrines concerning Messiah, Israel, the Nations, and the like, absolutely fundamental in the formation of any Judaism, these documents should cohere with the Mishnah on the indicative issues before us. In the aggregate they should not exhibit traits of the Yerushalmi's views of the same subjects. Describing seven positions on which the Mishnah takes a position quite distinctive to itself and different from the position, on the same subjects, put forth by the Talmud of the Land of Israel and associated Midrash compilations, I mean to see whether that received position is valid.

To begin with, let me set forth in their larger literary context the documents under study here. The canon of the Judaism under study consisted of the Hebrew Scriptures of ancient Israel ("the Old Testament"), called in this Judaism the Written Torah, and a set of writings later on accorded the status of Torah as well and assigned origin at Sinai through a process of oral formulation and oral transmission, hence, the Oral Torah. Among those writings, beyond the Hebrew Scriptures, the first of those writings comprising the Oral Torah was the Mishnah, ca. 200; this document carried in its wake two sustained amplifications and extensions called talmuds, the first, the

Talmud produced in the Land of Israel, hence the Talmud of the Land of Israel or Yerushalmi (Jerusalemite Talmud), ca. 400, the other in Babylonia, in the Iranian Empire, hence the Talmud of Babylonia or Bavli, ca. 600.

The other half of the Torah, the written part, served analogously and received a variety of sustained amplifications, called Midrash compilations. These were in three sets. [1] The first, ca. 200-300 (or even 400), addressed the books of Exodus, Leviticus, Numbers, and Deuteronomy, in Mekhilta Attributed to R. Ishmael for Exodus, Sifra, for Leviticus, one Sifré to Numbers, another Sifré, to Deuteronomy. [2] The second, ca. 400-500, took up the books of Genesis and Leviticus, in Genesis Rabbah and Leviticus Rabbah, and the latter begat Pesiqta deRab Kahana in its model. [3] The third, ca. 500-600, addressed a lectionary cycle of the synagogue, dealing with the books of Lamentations (read on the ninth of Ab), Esther (read on Purim), Ruth (read on Pentecost), and Song of Songs (read on Passover), in Lamentations Rabbah, Esther Rabbah I (the first two chapters only), Ruth Rabbah, and Song of Songs Rabbah. The first of the three groups presents marks of transition and mediation from one system to the next; the second, Genesis Rabbah and Leviticus Rabbah, together with Pesiqta deRab Kahana, form a single circle with the Talmud of the Land of Israel, and the third, the final Rabbah compilations, belong together with the Talmud of Babylonia. So much for the literature that attests to the Judaism of the Dual Torah.

Let us now turn to the field of analysis, the compilations of Midrash exegeses called "Tannaitic Midrashim." The authorities of exegesis of the Mishnah gained the title, *Tanna,* or traditions repeater, a person who in the period beyond the closure of the Mishnah mastered Mishnah sayings, memorized them with great precision, and repeated them when called upon. The ungainly adjective, "tannaitic," then was made to stand for a document assigned in the received scholarship to the same period as the Mishnah. Hence assigned to "the tannaitic period," meaning, the age in which the Mishnah was taking shape, because all of the authorities mentioned in those compilations also occur in the Mishnah, these documents provide sustained, verse-by-verse commentaries to parts of Exodus, Leviticus, Numbers, and Deuteronomy. Since the compilations considered here, moreover, are organized by reference to verses of Scripture, they are classified in the category, Midrash, which, it is generally assumed, encompasses Scripture exegesis. Thus Tannaitic Midrash are documents that compile exegeses of Scripture commonly assigned to the same period as the Mishnah, namely, prior to ca. 200 C.E. Among the native categories of later rabbinic study, *halakhah,* law, and *aggadah,* lore, the materials in Mekhilta, Sifré to Numbers, and Sifré to Deuteronomy are mostly devoted to *halakhah,* and everything in Sifra is likewise in that same category. Hence these documents also are called "halakhic Midrashim." But there we find some "aggadic Midrashim" in them, though no *"aggadah"* – narratives – to speak of.

Whether or not the literary classification, Midrash, encompasses these writings or serves for any others, whether or not Midrash forms a viable taxon at all for the canonical writings of the Judaism of the Dual Torah – these questions, while worthy of thought, do not occupy us here. I seek some facts about the *tannaitic* part of the conventional taxon that defines the question to deal with. For by "tannaitic," as I have made clear, people generally mean, "deriving from the period and the authorities who produced the Mishnah."[3] These writings therefore are taken to portray the state of opinion in the first and second centuries C.E.[4] So what I want to know is the relationship between the several Tannaitic Midrashim, respectively, and the Mishnah.

The question, of course, cannot trouble those who take at face value the attributions of sayings, assuming that the named authorities of a determinate age (in this case, mainly the second, but in part the first, centuries) really said what is assigned to them, in the very words before us. As I said at the outset, for those who affirm the inerrancy of

---

[3]In Chapter Ten I cite and discuss at length the position of Hyam Maccoby on this matter, and he expresses the broadly held opinion – generally rejected among informed scholars even now – that the so-called Tannaite Midrashim are to be assigned to the period of the Mishnah and testify to events of that age. The standard encyclopaedia articles on them assign them to much later centuries, e.g., the fourth or the fifth, and the important work of B. Z. Wacholder, "the Date of the Mekilta de-Rabbi Ishmael," *Hebrew Union College Annual* 1968, 39:117-144. Wacholder assigns the document to a period "not much later than the year 800." I am not certain why Maccoby and those he names, such as Sanders, ignore Wacholder's position in assigning Mekhilta to "the tannaitic period." My discussion of Wacholder's thesis is at my *Development of a Legend* (Leiden, 1970: E. J. Brill), pp. xiii-xiv, n. 2. Nothing in my treatment of Mekhilta bears a proposed date, and, as is clear, in these pages I do not propose dates for any of the documents under discussion.

[4]If not much earlier than that period! For an account of the theory that prior to the presentation of laws in a law code, they were assembled as ad hoc exegeses of Scripture, see David Weiss Halivni, *Midrash, Mishnah, and Gemara. The Jewish Predeliction for Justified Law* (Cambridge, 1987: Harvard University Press), and my review in my *Struggle for the Jewish Mind. Debates and Disputes on Judaism Then and Now* (Lanham, 1988: University Press of America), pp. 93-95. These matters are not important here.

attributions in the rabbinic canon,[5] there can be no reason to doubt that the compilations before us derive from the time of the Mishnah, because all those named in them flourished in that same time, and, moreover, most of the names in the Tannaitic Midrash compilations occur also in the Mishnah.

But the true believers are unlikely to open this book in any case, and they do not participate in scholarly discussion, let alone join in scholarly discourse. Therefore they may be ignored, and there is no need to rehearse for everybody else the universally accepted results of critical scholarship of two hundred years standing, in a variety of fields of historical, literary, and religious study of the Greco-Roman and the Near and Middle Eastern worlds of ancient times. It is the simple fact that in no academic study (as distinct from theological or ethnic study) is the inerrancy of attributions (or other holy "traditions") taken for granted, and by no scholar of the Western academy is it conceded, without further inquiry, that if a document assigns a saying to a given authority, then that authority really said what was attributed to him (rarely: her). But if not inerrant attributions, then what will guide us? That simple question explains what precipitates the little experiment set forth in these pages.

For what if we do not know to begin with that the Tannaitic Midrashim contain sayings really said by Mishnah authorities? That is the starting point for this book. What can we know, and how do we know it, about these documents? The answers here consist of facts attained through an entirely inductive inquiry. I ask, how do the several documents supposedly deriving from the same age as the Mishnah position themselves on issues on which the Mishnah exhibits quite indicative traits, and the successor-system through its document, the Yerushalmi (and associated Midrash compilation) for its part exhibits quite different, equally definitive traits? This is a very simple, mechanical exercise, invoking knowns in pursuit of unknown, but accessible facts.

But the ultimate goal – a clear proposal on the temporal relationship between the Tannaitic Midrashim and the Mishnah – will not be reached by the end of these experiments. Nor shall we even come very close to that goal. I end up with no proposals that the so-called Tannaitic Midrashim may be dated within the temporal orbit of the Mishnah, or must be dated only within that of the Yerushalmi. While it is perfectly clear that Sifra and the two Sifrés reached

---

[5]And they are very many. For numerous detailed cases of scholars' credulity, see my *Reading and Believing. Ancient Judaism and Contemporary Gullibility* (Atlanta, 1987: Scholars Press for Brown Judaic Studies).

closure after the Mishnah, since all three documents systematically cite and gloss passages of the Mishnah,[6] that fact by itself only proves that the documents are post-mishnaic,[7] therefore, "amoraic" or "of the talmudic age." But how far past the Mishnah, and – more to the point for the history of ideas, religion, and *mentalités*, how near the Talmud(s)? That we do not know. Rather, let us turn directly to the experiment conducted here.

The experiment that is conducted in these pages joins together the results of three sets of inquiries of mine,[8] [1] on the introduction of the Tannaitic Midrashim; [2] on the treatment of a variety of topics by various documents, read in sequence, yielding what I call the canonical history of ideas (a term explained at the end of this introduction); [3] on the history of the formation of Judaism in two connected, but essentially autonomous stages. Here I combine three sets of results to form a problem for further inquiry.

[1] The first results have accomplished the introduction of the four so-called Tannaitic Midrash dealt with here. Having translated all of Mekhilta Attributed to R. Ishmael, Sifra, and Sifré to Deuteronomy and somewhat over half of Sifré to Numbers,[9] I now have a reliable account of the rhetorical, logical, and topical traits of each of the documents.

[2] The second results have laid out the history of a variety of ideas, as these are treated in one document after another. I have worked out the comparison and contrast of the representation of such topics as purity, history, Messiah, Torah, the people, Israel, such

---

[6]True enough, all three contain important compositions that can have been precipitated only by the questions raised by the Mishnah. I need not rehearse the findings of my introductions to all four documents in order to establish as simple fact that the Tannaitic Midrashim as we now have them are post-mishnaic.

[7]Little of Sifra, and not much more, in proportion, of Sifré to Deuteronomy, can have been framed without the stimulus of the Mishnah and the problems its character and program raised. The criterion for so reading both documents is simple: can the passage at hand have been formulated had the author not known the Mishnah? Has anything other than a passage of the Mishnah precipitated raising the question answered by the author of this composition or compiler of this composite? I cannot find much in Sifra that implicitly ignores the Mishnah's challenge, and a great part of Sifra explicitly cites and responds to the Mishnah. Much in Sifré to Deuteronomy is formulated in response to the Mishnah and can be exhaustively understood only in relationship with the Mishnah.

[8]These translations and introductions are all listed in the preface.

[9]Professor William Scott Green, University of Rochester, is translating the other half; my sample seems to me adequate for the probe at hand.

words as *zekhut*, such themes as the doctrine of virtue, and the like, and have shown that considerable difference marks the treatment of a single theme or word or idea or category as we move from the earlier writings to the later ones.[10]

[3] The third type of work has set the question before us. I have now shown that there are two distinct Judaic systems, each comprising a theory of the social order made up of a worldview, way of life, and doctrine of the social entity ("Israel"); each system, or Judaism, is internally coherent, responding with an answer deemed self-evidently true to a question regarded as urgent and critical. We can easily differentiate one system from the other. And we also know in what ways they are connected, both in form (the later documents present

---

[10]These studies of the canonical history of ideas – a term explained above and further spelled out in Appendix One – encompass these books of mine: *The Idea of Purity in Ancient Judaism. The Haskell Lectures, 1972-1973.* Leiden, 1973: E. J. Brill; *Judaism without Christianity. An Introduction to the Religious System of the Mishnah in Historical Context.* Hoboken, 1989: Ktav Publishing House; *The Foundations of Judaism. Method, Teleology, Doctrine.* Philadelphia, 1983-1985: Fortress Press. I-III. I. *Midrash in Context. Exegesis in Formative Judaism.* Second printing: Atlanta, 1988: Scholars Press for Brown Judaic Studies; *The Foundations of Judaism. Method, Teleology, Doctrine.* Philadelphia, 1983-1985: Fortress Press. I-III. II. *Messiah in Context. Israel's History and Destiny in Formative Judaism.* Second printing: Lanham, 1988: University Press of America. Studies in Judaism Series; *The Foundations of Judaism. Method, Teleology, Doctrine.* Philadelphia, 1983-5: Fortress Press. I-III. III. *Torah: From Scroll to Symbol in Formative Judaism.* Second printing: Atlanta, 1988: Scholars Press for Brown Judaic Studies; *The Foundations of Judaism.* Philadelphia, 1988: Fortress. Abridged edition of the foregoing trilogy; *Vanquished Nation, Broken Spirit. The Virtues of the Heart in Formative Judaism.* New York, 1987: Cambridge University Press. Jewish Book Club selection, 1987; *Judaisms and their Messiahs in the beginning of Christianity.* New York, 1987: Cambridge University Press. [Edited with William Scott Green and Ernest S. Frerichs.]; *Judaism in the Matrix of Christianity.* Philadelphia, 1986: Fortress Press. British edition, Edinburgh, 1988, T. & T. Collins; *Judaism and Christianity in the Age of Constantine. Issues of the Initial Confrontation.* Chicago, 1987: University of Chicago Press; *Judaism and its Social Metaphors. Israel in the History of Jewish Thought.* New York, 1988: Cambridge University Press; *The Incarnation of God: The Character of Divinity in Formative Judaism.* Philadelphia, 1988: Fortress Press; *The Making of the Mind of Judaism.* Atlanta, 1987: Scholars Press for Brown Judaic Studies; *The Formation of the Jewish Intellect. Making Connections and Drawing Conclusions in the Traditional System of Judaism.* Atlanta, 1988: Scholars Press for Brown Judaic Studies; *The Christian and Judaic Invention of History.* [Edited with William Scott Green]. Atlanta, 1989: Scholars Press for American Academy of Religion. Studies in Religion Series; and *From Literature to Theology in Formative Judaism. Three Preliminary Studies.* Atlanta, 1989: Scholars Press for Brown Judaic Studies.

themselves as exegeses of the earlier ones), and in mode of thought or method. The points of connection validate the claim that we deal with a single unfolding Judaism in process. The points of differentiation vindicate the claim that the two systems, though connected, are autonomous of one another, each identifying its urgent question and setting forth its self-evidently true answer.[11]

The former stage sets forth the system set forth by the Mishnah and related documents, particularly the Tosefta and tractate Avot, the latter, the one portrayed by the Talmud of the Land of Israel, Genesis Rabbah, Leviticus Rabbah, and Pesiqta deRab Kahana. The former documents, closed (for the Mishnah) by ca. 200, present a philosophical system, a theory of the social order that concerns the way of life and worldview of a defined social entity, hence, economics, philosophy, and politics. The latter documents, completed (for the Yerushalmi and two Rabbah compilations) by ca. 450, present a religious theory of the social order, in which the received categories are matched by what I call counterpart categories, which transvalue and reverse the received sense of philosophy, politics, and economics and impute to them quite unanticipated meanings.

In the second type of study, producing accounts of how a given topic is treated in successive writings, I have been able to show that some themes are dealt with in pretty much the same way by authorships of documents from the Mishnah through the Yerushalmi, while others are not. Quite to the contrary, the Mishnah handles a given subject in accord with the requirements of its system, while the Yerushalmi and related writings treat that same subject in a very different way.

This book takes as fact the grid defined, as to its vertical lines, by the definition of the two Judaisms, and as to its horizontal lines by certain indicative concepts, seven in all. There are then only two verticals, the Mishnah on the one side, the Yerushalmi and related

---

[11]The third class of prior studies characterizes two systems, or Judaisms, the one adumbrated by the Mishnah, the other attested by the Yerushalmi and associated Midrash compilations. My portrait of the initial system is in a variety of studies, but particularly *Judaism: The Evidence of the Mishnah* (Chicago, 1982: University of Chicago Press); *Philosophy of Judaism: The First Principles* (Baltimore, 1991: The Johns Hopkins University Press); *The Economics of the Mishnah* (Chicago, 1990: The University of Chicago Press); and *The Politics of the Mishnah* (Chicago, 1991: The University of Chicago Press). My portrait of the successor system is in Judaism in Society: The Evidence of the Yerushalmi (Chicago, 1985: The University of Chicago Press) and *The Transformation of Judaism: From Philosophy to Religion* (Princeton, 1992: Princeton University Press). These studies, moreover, rest on detailed literary-critical accounts of the various documents that in my judgment attest the two systems under discussion.

Midrash compilations on the other. The horizontals as is clear comprise [1] the Dual Torah, [2] the gnostic Torah, [3] the Messiah, [4] the Nations, [5] Israel, [6] *Zekhut*, and [7] Woman. In each instance, in Chapters Two through Eight, I set forth the systemic meaning or point(s) of importance assigned to a subject, a conception, or a phrase. In prior works I have already demonstrated that the Mishnah's and the Yerushalmi's treatments of these myths (Dual Torah, Messiah), topics (the Nations, Israel, Woman), words (*Zekhut*), or conceptions (the gnostic Torah, a term defined in context) differ in fundamental ways. In the successive chapters I summarize these results and define the traits that will instruct us to locate a given document's treatment of the subject at hand closer to the Mishnah, closer to the Yerushalmi, or out of phase with both documents' approach to the same matter.

Since, as I shall explain presently, each system mirrors the other on one point after another, at some points, though not all of them, we are able to situate at the interstices between the one and the other the positions of the various compilations. My account of the positions of the two distinct systems on these indicator concepts or words of course is brief, since my extended description, analysis, and interpretation is available. But I do present within the covers of this book all of the information readers require in following my experiments and evaluating them; others may of course formulate their own experiments, or reproduce mine, and I am confident that, in either case, they will produce results congruent with mine. In briefly summarizing other results, I ask that readers simply stipulate as given that when I say, on this subject, the Mishnah says this, the Yerushalmi and associated Midrash compilations say that, I have already demonstrated the facts that form the basis for the statements at hand. That, sum and substance, forms the experiment, the results of which I now set forth.

In a few words, finally, let me differentiate the two systems that define the poles within which, it is generally supposed, the Tannaitic Midrashim took up their positions.

On the one side we find the Mishnah, philosophical in its fundamental modes of thought and media of expression. The Mishnah, set forth in the form of a law code an account of the world ("worldview"), a pattern for everyday and material activities and relationships ("way of life"), and a definition of the social entity ("nation," "people," "us" as against "outsiders," "Israel") that realized that way of life and explained it by appeal to that worldview.

On the other side comes the Yerushalmi and associated Midrash compilations. These successor documents, closed two centuries later, addressed the Mishnah's system and recast its categories into a connected, but also quite revised, one. The result was an essentially fresh system, one that bore its own self-evidently true answer to its own urgent question – a religious answer to a religious question.

But the successor system was also connected to the original one. That is the fact as to form, for these documents attached themselves to the Mishnah, on the one side, and the Hebrew Scriptures, on the other, within the nascent theory that the one stood for the oral, the other, the written, revelation, or Torah, of God to Moses at Mount Sinai. The Talmud of the Land of Israel formed around thirty-nine of the Mishnah's sixty-two tractates, and Genesis Rabbah and Leviticus Rabbah (joined by Pesiqta deRab Kahana), formed around the first and third books of Moses, respectively, along with some other documents, attest to a system that both extended and recast the categorical structure of the system for which the Mishnah stands, and also framed new categories within the same large-scale structure, involving way of life, worldview, and social entity, taken up in the Mishnah's system. The transformation of the one to the other stands for the movement from a philosophical to a religious mode of thinking. For the system to which the Mishnah as a document attests is essentially philosophical in its rhetorical, logical, and topical program; the successor system is fundamentally religious in these same principal and indicative traits of medium of intellect and mentality. It is because of the strikingly distinct traits that characterize the two systems respectively that the present experiment is plausible.

This system of the Mishnah designed the social order by an account of the principal components, a philosophy, an economics, and a politics, corresponding to worldview, way of life, and social entity. The philosophy explained how to think and identified the agenda for sustained thought and learning; the economics set forth a theory of rational action in the face of scarcity and in the increase and disposition of wealth; the politics laid out an account of precisely how power, encompassing legitimate violence, embodied in institutions and their staff, was to realize in everyday social transactions the social entity, "Israel." These categories in the successor documents, the Talmud of the Land of Israel for the Mishnah, the Midrash compilations Genesis Rabbah and Leviticus Rabbah together with Pesiqta deRab Kahana for Scripture, underwent revision, and, alongside, these same documents set forth their own categories for those served, initially, by philosophy, politics, and economics. The successor system united economics and politics in a theory of political economy, and it integrated learning with the godly life in the theory that learning transforms the existential, not merely the intellectual, character of the one who studies the Torah.

These general observations explain the task I propose, which is to draw upon the basic traits of intellect of the system represented by the Mishnah, on the one side, and those of the successor system with the one adumbrated by the Talmud of the Land of Israel, Genesis Rabbah, and Leviticus Rabbah with Pesiqta deRab Kahana, on the other. Our question, specifically, is simple: how shall we classify the Tannaitic Midrash in the context of the documents that frame them, it is generally supposed, temporally? When with reference to the seven indicators used here we compare and contrast the Tannaitic Midrashim with the Mishnah and the successor documents, do we find those intermediate writings like the Mishnah or unlike it, like the Yerushalmi in their convictions on the issues at hand, or unlike it? If like the Mishnah, then of course we classify those documents as within the orbit of that system. But if unlike, then are they like the successor writings? Or do they stand wholly outside the framework of both documents? That is the work of comparison that seems to me to yield very interesting results indeed. These results emerge, to begin with, from that canonical history of ideas that takes at face value only the existence of documents, but nothing in them.[12]

These rather abstract remarks may take on further meaning through a specific example of how a composition may fall wholly within the framework of one system rather than another. For that purpose I cite a passage that invokes four of the conceptions I have shown to be emblematic of the successor system, the Yerushalmi's. The absence of which I have demonstrated shows us we stand within the framework of the Mishnah's system. These indicative matters are as follows: [1] the myth of the Dual Torah; [2] the intransitive Israel or the uniqueness of Israel; [3] the differentiation among the nations; and [4] the systemic centrality of *zekhut avot*, the lien upon Heaven inherited from the ancestors by reason of the ancestors' acts of supererogatory self-abnegation. The following passage joins these themes that are typical of the Yerushalmi's system and the absence of which signify the Mishnah's.

Sifra Parashat Behuqotai Pereq 8
CCLXIX:I
12. A   "[Yet for all that, when they are in the land of their enemies,] I will
              not spurn them, neither will I abhor them so as to destroy them
              utterly:"

---

[12]My explanation of the theory of the method of the canonical history of ideas is given in the Appendix.

B. Now what is left for them, but that they not be spurned nor abhorred? For is it not the fact that all the good gifts that had been given to them were now taken away from them?

C. And were it not for the Scroll of the Torah that was left for them, they were in no way be different from the nations of the world!

D. But "I will not spurn them:" – in the time of Vespasian.

E. "neither will I abhor them:" – in the time of Greece.

F. "So as to destroy them utterly and break my covenant with them:" – in the time of Haman.

G. "For I am the Lord their God:" – in the time of Gog.

13. A. And how do we know that the covenant is made with the tribal fathers?

B. As it is said, "But I will for their sake remember the covenant with their forefathers whom I brought forth out of the land of Egypt:"

C. This teaches that the covenant is made with the tribal fathers.

14. A. "These are the statutes and ordinances and Torahs:"

B. "the statutes:" this refers to the exegeses of Scripture.

C. "and ordinances:" this refers to the laws.

D. "and Torahs:" this teaches that two Torahs were given to Israel, one in writing, the other oral.

E. Said R. Aqiba, "Now did Israel have only two Torahs? And did they not have many Torahs given to them? 'This is the Torah of burnt-offering (Lev. 6:2),' 'This is the Torah of the meal-offering (Lev. 6:27,' 'This is the Torah of the guilt-offering (Lev. 7:1),' 'This is the Torah of the sacrifice of peace-offerings (Lev. 7:11) 'This is the Torah: when a man dies in a tent (Num. 19:1).'"

15. A. "Which the Lord made between him and the people of Israel [on Mount Sinai by Moses]:"

B. Moses had the merit of being made the intermediary between Israel and their father in Heaven.

C. "on Mount Sinai by Moses:"

D. This teaches that the Torah was given, encompassing all its laws, all its details, and all their amplifications, through Moses at Sinai.

It would be difficult to locate a better integration of three emblematic ideas in a single statement than the passage at hand, which has the uniqueness of Israel (by reason of the Torah), the differentiation of the nations, and *zekhut avot*, all explicitly joined together. Not only so, but the same passage identifies the myth of the two Torahs and says it explicitly. The presence of the passage does not prove that the document in which it occurs, Sifra, must fall within the ambience of the Yerushalmi and its associated compilations. In the context of the present argument, it serves, however, to show how emblematic ideas serve as indicators of the place of a document vis-à-vis other documents. The exercise of this book, then, is to inquire into the position of certain indicator words or concepts in documents that are supposed to attest to ideas held by the framers of the Mishnah and in their times.

The so-called Tannaitic Midrash present a more interesting question than has been framed to date, which is, exactly what do these documents tell us about the *mentalité* of exegetes of Scripture[13] supposedly in the age in which the Mishnah took shape? Accordingly, this book means to address in a sustained and encompassing probe: precisely how do these aggadic works that some think are "roughly contemporaneous" with the Mishnah relate to the Mishnah? Answering that question, my descriptions of the seven issues will stress the position of the Mishnah; there we shall concentrate our attention, in the supposition that, if the so-called Tannaitic Midrashim are to tell us about (other) ideas important to the framers of the Judaism attested by the Mishnah, on the ideas on which the Mishnah itself takes a very distinctive and characteristic position, those allegedly tannaitic documents will concur, either at length recapitulating the same points or at least signifying a viewpoint on them similar to that of the Mishnah.

How do I propose to proceed? It is through the method, to which I have now made reference, called the canonical history of ideas. Let me spell out the method here, setting forth in the appendix an argument on why I find this method preferable to the received one.[14] We begin with how the history of ideas has been studied by others until this time. The history of ideas of talmudic or rabbinic Judaism until my *oeuvre* has followed a single method. What scholars have done, when approaching the rabbinic writings of the age, is to collect and organize all the sayings on a given subject and to treat the resulting composite as "the talmudic," or "the rabbinic" view of that subject. The established way in which to investigate the thought of classical Judaism on any given subject was to collect pertinent sayings among the diverse documents and to assemble all these sayings into a composite, a portrait, for example, "*the* rabbinic view of Rome."

---

[13]In the concluding chapter I discuss Hyam Maccoby's position on these same documents. We may charitably ignore Maccoby's rather odd difficulty in keeping straight the categories of Midrash, meaning, scriptural exegesis, and *aggadah*, meaning, narrative or tale. Some Midrash exegesis may contain *aggadot*, that is, tales, and most does not. The volume of *aggadah*-narratives in the so-called Tannaitic Midrashim varies, from practically none, in Sifra, to a fair amount of storytelling, in Mekhilta Attributed to R. Ishmael. I have the impression that Maccoby does not fully realize that fact.

[14]Part of what follows here is repeated in the opening part of Appendix I. It seemed to me worth presenting in general terms my definitions of the method at hand, and then going over the same matter in the context of a specific text of the method in the context of the received method of compiling everything in all documents of the canon, without differentiating the origin of a saying or story by reference to its initial appearance in one or another document.

The composite will divide up the sayings in accord with the logic of the topic at hand. If, for example, we want to know the thought of classical Judaism about God, we collect everything and then divide up the result among such rubrics as God's attributes, God's love, or Providence, or reward and punishment, and the like. Differentiation therefore affects not the documents but the topic. That is to say, whatever we find, without regard to the document in which the saying or story occurs, joins together with whatever else we find, to form an undifferentiated aggregate, thus to illuminate a given aspect of our topic, thus God's love or Providence, as these topics are treated in a diversity of documents. How then do we organize our data? It is by allowing the topic we study to tell us its divisions, that is to say, the logic of differentiation derives from the topic, not the sources from which we draw sayings about the topic at hand.

My research for a number of years has led me to differentiate among documents and to ask each document to deliver its particular viewpoint to me. When, therefore I wish to trace the history of an idea, it produces the representations of that idea as yielded by documents, read singly and one by one, then in the sequence of their closure. I do not join together everything I find, without regard to its point of origin in a given compilation of rabbinic sayings. Rather I keep things apart, so that I record what I find in document A, then in document B, and onward through the alphabet. What this yields is a history of the idea at hand as the documents, laid out in their sequence, tell me that history. That history is what I call "canonical" since it sets forth how documents, read in the received sequence, Mishnah first, Bavli last, portray a given idea or theme. What we know is not how in the social world of Jews people were thinking about that idea or theme, only what is the literary evidence deriving from a particular textual community that idea or theme was represented.

Let me begin by asking, how shall we know which approach is better, or even right? The answer to the question derives from a test of falsification: how can we show, therefore how do we know, whether we are right or wrong? One way of testing the viability of a method is to ask whether it facilitates or impedes the accurate description and analysis of data. Let me spell out this criterion.

My test of the proposed approach of differentiating among documents consists in trying one approach and then its opposite to see the result: a perfectly simple experiment. Our criterion for evaluating results is simple: if we do things in two different ways, in the results of which of the two ways do we see the evidence with greater, in which lesser, perspicacity? That criterion will rapidly prove its entirely objective value. So these are the questions to be raised. If we do not differentiate among documents, then we ask what happens if we do differentiate. If we do differentiate, we ask what happens if we do not. These are simple research experiments, which anyone can replicate.

To spell them out also poses no great difficulty.[15] If differentiating yields results we should have missed had we not read the documents one by one, then our category has obscured important points of difference. If *not* differentiating yields a unity that differentiating has obscured, so that the parts appear, seen all together, to cohere, then the category that has required differentiation has obscured important points in common. How shall we know one way or the other? Do we not invoke a subjective opinion when we conclude that there is, or is not, a unity that differentiation has obscured? I think not. In fact the operative criterion is a matter of fact and does not require subjective judgment. How so? Let me state the objective criterion with emphasis:

[1] *If we find that each one of the documents says on its own essentially what all of the documents say together, so that the parts do turn out to be interchangeable, then imposing distinctions suggests differences where there is none. The parts not only add up to the sum of the whole, as in the case of a homogenizing category. Each of the parts replicates the fundamental structure of the whole. In that case, differentiation proves misleading.*

[2] *If, by contrast, when viewed one by one, our documents in fact do not say the same thing by themselves that all of them say when read together, our category, failing to recognize differences, suggests a unity and a cogency where there is none. The parts may well add up to the sum of the whole, but each of the parts appears to stand by itself and does not replicate the statement to which, as part of a larger whole, it contributes. In that case, not effecting a considerable labor of description of the documents one by one will obscure the very center and heart of matters: that the documents, components of the whole, are themselves autonomous, though connected (if that can be shown) and also continuous (if that can be shown).*

What we see in the experiment at hand – with numerous points at which the results are null – is that the documents, read separately, do differ from one another. Were we to read them all together and continuously, we should miss the differences.

Accordingly, the results of an experiment of differentiation where, up to now, everything has been read as a single harmonious statement, will prove suggestive – an interesting indicator of the effect and

---

[15]In Appendix I, I go over this ground again in the context of other research altogether.

usefulness of the category at hand. At the end we shall return to these questions and answer them. We ask what each source produced by Jews in late antiquity, read by itself, has to say about the subject at hand. How shall we differentiate among the available writings? The simplest route is to follow the lines of distinction imposed by the writings themselves, that is, simply, to read one book at a time, and in the order in which the several books are generally held to have reached closure.

The limns of documents then generate, form, and define our initial system of categories. That is, the document to begin with is what demands description, then analysis by comparison and contrast to other documents, then interpretation as part of the whole canon of which it forms a part.[16] Each document, it is clear, demands description, analysis, and interpretation, all by itself. Each must be viewed as autonomous of all others. At a later stage, each document also is to be examined for its relationships with other documents that fall into the same classification (whether that classification is simply "Jewish" or still more narrowly and hence usefully defined). Then, at the end, each document is to be allowed to take its place as part of the undifferentiated aggregation of documents that, all together, constitute the evidence of a Judaism, in the case of the rabbinic kind, the canon of the Torah.

If a document reaches us within its own framework as a complete book with a beginning, a middle, and an end, we do not commit an error in simple logic by reading that document as it has reached us, that is, as a book by itself. If, further, a document contains materials shared verbatim or in substantial content with other documents of its classification, or if a document explicitly refers to some other writings and their contents, then we have to ask the question of connection. We have to seek the facts of connectedness and ask for the meaning of those connections. In the description of a Judaism, we have to take as our further task the description of the whole out of the undifferentiated testimony of all of its parts. For a Judaism does put together a set of once discrete documents and treat them as its canon.

So in our setting we do want to know how a number of writings fit together into a single continuous and harmonious statement. In the present context, only the part of the work is required, the analytical part – hence, the canonical history of ideas. So much for the context in

---

[16]I hasten to add, I do not take the canon to be a timeless category, as my analysis of the Mishnah and its associates indicates. Quite to the contrary, the canon itself takes shape in stages, and these form interesting categories for study.

scholarly debate in general terms. In Chapter Ten I shall frame the issues of scholarly debate in light of the experiment undertaken here. Now to the experiments themselves: what the Mishnah says, what the Yerushalmi and associated Midrash compilations say, and the pertinent materials in the four documents under study here, concerning seven indicative topics.

I

Defining and Explaining the Canonical History of Ideas

To define and explain the experiment at hand, let me first place into context the method I have titled, "the canonical history of ideas." Since this new method means to solve problems neglected (or precipitated) by existing approaches, I have, to begin with, to state what I conceive to be the condition of academic scholarship[1] in the study of ancient Judaism prior to my own work.[2] Then, having identified the operative methods and conceptions, I shall specify the problems that precipitated my rethinking what we know concerning the history and context of ideas in the formation of Judaism and how we

---

[1]I do not engage in discourse shared with the nonacademic setting of study of the same documents treated here, that is, in the world of the yeshivas. Premises of learning and teaching in those institutions bear no points in common whatseover with the premises of academic study, so no dialogue is possible. Whether or not the other institutional setting – Israeli universities, rabbinical seminaries, and other schools under the auspices of the Jewish community, and even Jewish studies professorships, programs, and departments, within the academy but paid for by the Jewish community – can be classified as academic in any material sense is not at issue here. For the purposes of discussion, I stipulate that all institutions not within the orbit of the yeshiva world are academic, and all scholarship conducted in those institutions is guided by the principles of academic learning in the West. While, as a matter of fact, what I ask readers to stipulate is manifestly a dubious proposition, for the present discussion it makes possible an exchange of ideas, by which I mean, criticism of one position by another position formed within the same premises.

[2]In the introduction I have already pointed to the specific question deriving from a polemic against my work (and against me personally) that attracted my interest in the question of how the documents treated in the shank of the book relate to the Mishnah.

know it. The results of that judgment and method then encompass and explain the question that I ask and the experiment in response to that question that I set forth in these pages.

When we investigate the history of the formative stage of the Judaism of the Dual Torah, what can we now learn from the generations of academic scholarship in Hebrew and in English[3] that began with Solomon Schechter and concluded with Ephraim E. Urbach?[4] For, during that long period, the premises of learning in the rabbinic literature of late antiquity joined new historical interest with a received theological conviction. The former wished to describe in context ideas that had formerly been assigned no context at all: they were "Torah," and now were to be the history of ideas. The latter maintained that the documents of the rabbinic corpus were essentially seamless and formed one vast Dual Torah, oral and written; and that all attributions were valid, so that if a given authority was supposed to have made a statement, he really made it. On the basis of that received conviction, imputing inerrancy to the attributions (as well as to the storytellers) just as had many generations of the faithful, but asking questions of context and development that were supposed to add up to history, Schechter, Moore, Kadushin, Urbach, and all the other great figures of the first three quarters of the twentieth century set forth their accounts.

But what if we recognize that documentary formulations play a role in the representation of compositions, so that the compositors' formulation of matters takes a critical place in the making of the

---

[3]I ignore scholarship in German because the premises were the same as those characteristic of English- and Hebrew-language scholarship: [1] all documents testify to the same uniform and essentially a-historical system; [2] all attributions are sound and tell us what a given authority really said, in the age in which he is assumed to have lived. Of course German-language scholarship is to be divided between that done by Jews, which in general was informed and responsible, and that done by non-Jews, which was anti-Semitic, not terribly competent in the reading of the Hebrew and Aramaic sources, and irresponsible by the canons of academic scholarship. But for the purposes of this discussion, attention to German-language scholarship would produce simply more cases in which the premises and methods characteristic of the English- and Hebrew-language books predominate, so a single argument suffices to cover all work, surveyed and not, prior to mine.

[4]If I ignore lesser figures, such as Shmuel Safrai, Abraham Goldberg, Y. Gafni, Daniel R. Schwartz, Albert Baumgarten, and the like, it is because, while they have published some valuable papers here and there, they have made no important contribution to historical scholarship and are not to be taken seriously in the way in which Schechter, Moore, and Urbach are. That seems to me to constitute a judgment that is no more than a common consensus among nearly all scholars in the field outside of Jerusalem.

documentary evidence? And what if, further, we no longer assume the inerrancy of the Oral Torah's writings, so that attributions are no longer taken at face value, stories no longer believed unless there are grounds for disbelief (as the Jerusalem canard has it)? Then the fundamental presuppositions of the writing of Schechter, Moore, Kadushin, Urbach, and lesser figures prove null.

And that fact bears in its wake the further problem: since we cannot take their answers at face value, can we pursue their questions any more? In my judgment, the answer is negative. The only reason nowadays to read Schechter, Moore, Kadushin, Urbach and others is to see what they have to say about specific passages upon which, episodically and unsystematically, they have comments to make. All work in the history of the formative age of the Judaism of the Dual Torah that treats documentary lines as null and attributions as invariably valid must be dismissed as a mere curiosity, a collection and arrangement of this and that, bearing no compelling argument or proposition to be dealt with by the new generation.[5]

---

[5]William Horbury, reviewing my *Vanquished Nation, Broken Spirit* (*Epworth Review*, May, 1989), correctly observes: "Emotional attitudes form a traditional moral topic, and the recommendations on them in rabbinic ethics have often been considered, for example, in the *Rabbinic Anthology* of C. G. Montefiore and H. Loewe....This historical inquiry is closely related to the author's other work, and it is written on his own terms; he does not mention other writers on rabbinic ethics, and he gives no explicit criticism or development of modern study by others of the rabbinic passages and ideas with which he deals. He cannot be said to have fulfilled his obligation to his readers." Horbury does not seem to know my extensive writings on others who have worked on the formative history of Judaism, even though these have been collected and set forth in a systematic way, both as book reviews and as methodological essays, time and again. My *Ancient Judaism: Disputes and Debates* (Chico, 1986: Scholars Press for Brown Judaic Studies) is only one place in which I have indeed done just what Horbury asks, addressing Urbach and Moore and some of their most recent continuators in a systematic and thorough way. I am amazed that he can imagine I have not read the literature of my field; I not only have read and repeatedly criticized it, but I have done so in every accessible medium. His reviews of my work are simply uninformed and captious. His treatment of my *Incarnation of God* in *Expository Times*, which makes the same point in a more savage manner, shows the real problem; he does not find it possible to state more than the topic (the title!) of the book and cannot tell his readers what thesis or proposition is set forth in the book. Given those limitations of intellect, one can hardly find surprising his inability to grasp why Urbach, Schechter, Moore, Kadushin, and others by contemporary standards simply have nothing to teach us about the formative history of Judaism. Horbury wants us to do chemistry by appeal to not the oxygen but the phlogiston theory, and he wants geography to be carried out in accord with the convictions of the flat-earthers. But the latter have a better sense of humor

Let me now reframe the question in a manner which will make clear the right way in which to work. For when we grasp how we must now investigate the formative history of Judaism, we shall also see why Schechter, Moore, and Urbach no longer compel attention for any serious and important purpose.

The question that demands a response before any historical issues can be formulated is this: How are we to determine the particular time and circumstance in which a writing took shape, and how shall we identify the generative problems, the urgent and critical questions, that informed the intellect of an authorship and framed the social world that nurtured that same authorship? Lacking answers to these questions, we find our work partial, and, if truth be told, stained by sterile academicism. Accordingly, the documentary method requires us to situate the contents of writings into particular circumstances, so that we may read the contents in the context of a real time and place. How to do so? I maintain that it is by reference to the time and circumstance of the closure of a document, that is to say, the conventional assignment of a piece of writing to a particular time and place, that we proceed outward from context to matrix.

Everyone down to Urbach, including Montefiore and Loewe, Schechter, Moore, and the rest, simply take at face value attributions of sayings to particular authorities and interpret what is said as evidence of the time and place in which the cited authorities flourished. When studying topics in the Judaism of the sages of the rabbinic writings from the first through the seventh centuries, people routinely cite sayings categorized by attribution rather than by document. That is to say, they treat as one group of sayings whatever is assigned to Rabbi X. This is without regard to the time of redaction of the documents in which those sayings occur or to similar considerations of literary context and documentary circumstance. The category defined by attributions to a given authority furthermore rests on the premise that the things given in the name of Rabbi X really were said by him. No other premise would justify resort to the category deriving from use of a name, that alone. The history of ideas, then, comprised sayings, collected from all documents of every period, assigned to a given authority; ideas held by him, representative then of the time in which he lived, would be adduced in evidence of a given stage in the unfolding of Judaism.

---

about themselves. They are happy being fools – and bear no grudge for the round-worlders, who, as in the present range of learning, do have a certain amount of probative evidence in support of their views.

Commonly, the next step is to treat those sayings as evidence of ideas held, if not by that particular person, then by people in the age in which the cited authority lived.   Once more the premise that the sayings go back to the age of the authority to whom they are attributed underpins inquiry. Accordingly, scholars cite sayings in the name of given authorities and take for granted that those sayings were said by the authority to whom they were attributed and, of course, in the time in which that authority flourished. By contrast, in my method of the documentary study of Judaism, I treat the historical sequence of sayings only in accord with the order of the documents in which they first occur. Let me expand on why I have taken the approach that I have, explain the way the method works, and then, as before, set forth an example of the method in action.[6]

Since many sayings are attributed to specific authorities, why not lay out the sayings in the order of the authorities to whom they are attributed, rather than in the order of the books in which these sayings occur, which forms the documentary method for the description of the matrix of texts in context?   It is because the attributions cannot be validated, but the books can. The first of the two principles by which I describe the matrix that defines the context in which texts are framed is that we compose histories of ideas of the Judaism of the Dual Torah in accord with the sequence of documents that, in the aggregate, constitute the corpus and canon of the Judaism of the Dual Torah. And those histories set forth dimensions of the matrix in which that Judaism, through its writings, is to be situated for broader purposes of interpretation.   Documents reveal the system and structure of their authorships, and, in the case of religious writing, out of a document without named authors we may compose an account of the authorship's religion: a way of life, a worldview, a social entity meant to realize both. Read one by one, documents reveal the interiority of intellect of an authorship, and that inner-facing quality of mind inheres even when an authorship imagines it speaks outward, toward and about the world beyond. Even when set side by side, moreover, documents illuminate the minds of intersecting authorships, nothing more.

Then why not simply take at face value a document's *own* claims concerning the determinate situation of its authorship? Readers have already noted innumerable attributions to specific authorities. One obvious mode of determining the matrix of a text, the presently

---

[6]My example is drawn from a whole series of books in which I worked on the histories of specific conceptions or problems, formulated as I think correct, out of the sequence of documents. These works of mine have been listed in the Introduction.

paramount way, as I said, is simply to take at face value the allegation that a given authority, whose time and place we may identify, really said what is attributed to him, and that if a writing says something happened, what it tells us is not what its authorship thought happened, but what really happened. That reading of writing for purposes of not only history, but also religious study, is in fact commonplace. It characterizes all accounts of the religion, Judaism, prior to mine, and it remains a serious option for all those outside of my school and circle.[7] Proof of that fact is to be shown, lest readers who find accommodation in more contemporary intellectual worlds, where criticism and the active intellect reign, doubt my judgment of competing methods and differing accounts. Accordingly, let me characterize the prevailing way of determining the historical and religious matrix of texts, and then proceed to explain my alternate mode for answering the question of what is to be learned, from within a piece of writing, about the religious world beyond.

In historical study, we gain access to no knowledge a priori. All facts derive from sources that have been correctly situated, for example, classified, comprehensively and completely described, dispassionately analyzed, and evaluated. Nothing can be taken for granted. What we cannot show, we do not know. These simple dogmas of all historical learning derive not from this writer but go back to the very beginnings of Western critical historical scholarship, to the age of the Renaissance. But all historical and religions-historical scholarship on the documents of the Judaism of the Dual Torah in its formative age, except for mine and for that of a very few others, ignores the canons of criticism that govern academic scholarship. Everyone in the past and many even now take for granted that pretty much everything they read is true – except what they decide is not true.

They cannot and do not raise the question of whether an authorship knows what it is talking about, and they do not address the issue of the purpose of a text: historical or imaginative, for example. For them the issue always is history, namely, what really happened, and that issue was settled, so to speak, at Sinai: it is all true (except, on an episodic basis, what is not true, which the scholars somehow know

---

[7]That is why people can still read Urbach or Moore as though we learned anything of historical and not merely ad hoc exegetical interest from their compilations of sayings under their various rubrics. In this regard Urbach's various asides are quite interesting, even though not a single account of the history and context of an idea can stand; and the straight historical chapters – e.g., on the social role of sages, on the life of Hillel, on the history of the time – are not only intellectually vulgar, they are a travesty of scholarship, even for the time and within the premises in which they were written.

instinctively). They exhibit the credulity characteristic of the believers, which in the circle of piety is called faith, and rightly so, but in the center of academic learning is mere gullibility. The fundamentalists in the talmudic academies and rabbinical seminaries and Israeli universities take not only as fact but at face value everything in the holy books. "Judaism" is special and need not undergo description, analysis, and interpretation in accord with a shared and public canon of rules of criticism. "We all know" how to do the work, and "we" do not have to explain to "outsiders" either what the work is or why it is important. It is a self-evidently important enterprise in the rehearsal of information. Knowing these things the way "we" know them explains the value of knowing these things.

Scholarship formed on the premise that the sources' stories are to be believed at face value does not say so. Rather, it frames questions that implicitly affirm the accuracy of the holy books, asking questions, for example, that can only be answered in the assumption that the inerrant Scriptures contain the answers – therefore, as a matter of process, do not err. By extension holy books that tell stories produce history through the paraphrase of stories into historical language: this is what happened, this is how it happened, and here are the reasons why it happened. If the Talmud says someone said something, he really said it, then and there. That premise moreover dictates their scholarly program, for it permits these faithful scholars to describe, analyze and interpret events or ideas held in the time in which that person lived. Some of these would deny the charge, and all of them would surely point, in their writing, to evidence of a critical approach. But the premise remains the old gullibility. Specifically, the questions they frame to begin with rest on the assumption that the sources respond. The assumption that, if a story refers to a second century rabbi, then the story tells us about the second century, proves routine. And that complete reliance merely on the allegations of sayings and stories constitutes perfect faith in the facticity of fairy tales.

The operative question facing anyone who proposes to translate writing into religion – that is, accounts of "Judaism," as Moore claims to give, or "The Sages," that Urbach imagines he has made for us, is the historical one: How do you know exactly what was said and done, that is, the history that you claim to report about what happened long ago? Specifically, how do you know he really said it? And if you do not know that he really said it, how can you ask the questions that you ask, which has as its premise the claim that you can say what happened or did not happen?

The wrong, but commonplace, method is to assume that if a given document ascribes an opinion to a named authority the opinion actually was stated in that language by that sage. On this assumption a much richer history of an idea, not merely of the literary evidences of that idea, may be worked out without regard only to the date of the document at hand. Within this theory of evidence, we have the history of what individuals thought on a common topic. I have already set forth the reason that we cannot proceed to outline the sequence of ideas solely on the basis of the sequence of the sages to whom ideas are attributed. We simply cannot demonstrate that a given authority really said what a document assigns to him. Let me list the range of uncertainty that necessitates this fresh approach, which I have invented.

First, if the order of the documents were fully sound and the contents representative of rabbinical opinion, then the result would be a history of the advent of the idea at hand and the development and articulation of that idea in formative Judaism. We should then have a fairly reliable picture of ideas at hand as these unfolded in orderly sequence. But we do not know that the canonical history corresponds to the actual history of ideas. Furthermore, we cannot even be sure that the order of documents presently assumed in scholarly convention is correct. Second, if a rabbi really spoke the words attributed to him, then a given idea would have reached expression within Judaism *prior* to the redaction of the document. Dividing things up by documents will tend to give a later date and thus a different context for interpretation to opinions held earlier than we can presently demonstrate. Third, although we are focusing upon the literature produced by a particular group, again we have no clear notion of what people were thinking outside of that group. We therefore do not know how opinions held by other groups or by the Jewish people in general came to shape the vision of rabbis. When, for example, we note that there also existed poetic literature and translations of Scriptures characteristic of the synagogue worship, we cannot determine whether the poetry and most translations spoke for rabbis or for some quite different group.

For these reasons I have chosen to address the contextual question within the narrow limits of the canon. That accounts for my formulation of the episteme as "the canonical history of ideas" and explains, also, why I have carefully avoided claiming that a given idea was broadly held only at a given time and place. All I allege is that a given document underscores the presence of an idea for that authorship – that alone. Obviously, if I could in a given formulation relate the appearance of a given idea to events affecting rabbis in particular or to the life of Israel in general, the results would be exceedingly suggestive. But since we do not know for whom the documents speak, how broadly representative they are, or even how comprehensive is their evidence about rabbis' views, we must carefully define what we do and do not know. So for this early stage in research the context in which a given idea is described, analyzed, and interpreted is the canon. But this first step alone carries us to new territory. I hope that in due course others will move beyond the limits which, at the moment, seem to me to mark the farthest possible advance. Now let us turn to the specific case meant to illustrate the method.

Let me now explain in some greater detail the alternative, which I call the documentary history of ideas. It is a mode of relating writing to religion through history through close attention to the circumstance in which writing reached closure. It is accomplished, specifically, by assessing shifts exhibited by a sequence of documents and appealing to the generally accepted dates assigned to writings in explaining those shifts. In this way I propose to confront questions of cultural order, social system and political structure, to which the texts respond explicitly and constantly. Confronting writings of a religious character, we err by asking questions of a narrowly historical character: what did X really say on a particular occasion, and why. These questions not only are not answerable on the basis of the evidence in hand. They also are trivial, irrelevant to the character of the evidence. What strikes me as I review the writings just now cited is how little of real interest and worth we should know, even if we were to concede the historical accuracy and veracity of all the many allegations of the scholars we have surveyed. How little we should know – but how much we should have *missed* if that set of questions and answers were to encompass the whole of our inquiry.

If we are to trace the unfolding, in the sources of formative Judaism, of a given theme or ideas on a given problem, the order in which we approach the several books, that is, components of the entire canon, gives us the sole guidance on sequence, order, and context, that we are apt to find. As is clear, we have no way of demonstrating that authorities to whom, in a given composition, ideas are attributed really said what is assigned to them. The sole fact in hand therefore is that the framers of a given document included in their book sayings imputed to named authorities. Are these dependable? Unlikely on the face of it. Why not? Since the same sayings will be imputed to diverse authorities by different groups of editors, of different books, we stand on shaky ground indeed if we rely for chronology upon the framers' claims of who said what. More important, attributions by themselves cannot be shown to be reliable.

What we cannot show we do not know.[8] Lacking firm evidence, for
example, in a sage's own clearly assigned writings, or even in writings
redacted by a sage's own disciples and handed on among them in the
discipline of their own community, we have for chronology only a single
fact. It is that a document, reaching closure at a given time, contains
the allegation that Rabbi X said statement Y. So we know that people
at the time of the document reached closure took the view that Rabbi X
said statement Y. We may then assign to statement Y a position, in the
order of the sequence of sayings, defined by the location of the document
in the order of the sequence of documents. The several documents' dates,
as is clear, all constitute guesses. But the sequence explained in the
prologue – Mishnah, Tosefta, Yerushalmi, Bavli – for the exegetical
writings on the Mishnah is absolutely firm and beyond doubt. The
sequence for the exegetical collections on Scripture Sifra, the Sifrés,
Genesis Rabbah, Leviticus Rabbah, the Pesiqtas and beyond is not
entirely sure. Still the position of the Sifra and the two Sifrés at the
head, followed by Genesis Rabbah, then Leviticus Rabbah, then
Pesiqta deR. Kahana and Lamentations Rabbati and some related
collections, seems likely.

What are the canonical mainbeams that sustain the history of
ideas as I propose to trace that history? Three principal periods
presently delineate the canonical sequence, the Mishnah's, in the first
two centuries; the Yerushalmi's, in the next, ca. 200-400; and the
Bavli's, in the third, ca. 400-600. The formative age of Judaism is the
period marked at the outset by the Mishnah, taking shape from
sometime before the Common Era and reaching closure at ca. 200 C.E.,
and at the end by the Talmud of Babylonia, ca. 600 C.E. In between

---

[8]It should be underlined that a British scholar, Hyam Maccoby, maintains
exactly the opposite, alleging in a letter to the editor of *Commentary* and in
various other writings that there is historical knowledge that we possess a priori.
We must be thankful to him for making explicit the position of the other side.
No historical scholarship known to me concurs with his position on a priori
historical knowledge; all modern learning in history begins with sources, read
de novo. But Maccoby has learned remarkably little from contemporary
critical scholarship, which he declines to read or dismisses in a half sentence;
his work on problems in New Testament studies has been universally rejected
by specialists in that field, as reviews of his writings on Paul and Jesus
demonstrate. I have dealt with Maccoby in my "Hermeneutics and the
Judaism beyond the Text," *Conservative Judaism*, 1989, 41:35-43. His mode of
argument and ad hominem rhetoric should not deny him a hearing for his
position, which surely deserves a hearing. Maccoby is not an academic scholar
and does not respect the norms of civility of the academy, but that should not
serve as an excuse merely to ignore him as a crank or a crackpot, though many
would like to do so.

these dates, two streams of writings developed, one legal, explaining the meaning of the Mishnah, the other theological and exegetical, interpreting the sense of Scripture. The high points of the former come with tractate Abot which is the Mishnah's first apologetic, the Tosefta, a collection of supplements ca. 300 C.E., the Talmud of the Land of Israel ca. 400 C.E., followed by the Babylonian Talmud. The latter set of writings comprise compositions on Exodus, in Mekhilta attributed to R. Ishmael and of indeterminate date, Sifra on Leviticus, Sifré on Numbers, and another Sifré, on Deuteronomy at a guess to be dated at ca. 300 C.E., then Genesis Rabbah ca. 400 C.E., Leviticus Rabbah ca. 425 C.E., and at the end, Pesiqta deRab Kahana, Lamentations Rabbati, and some other treatments of biblical books, all of them in the fifth or sixth centuries. The so-called Tannaitic Midrashim, Mekhilta, Sifra, the two Sifrés, dealt with in these pages, in general appear to form transitional documents, between the Mishnah and the Yerushalmi and its Midrash companions, Genesis Rabbah, Leviticus Rabbah, and Pesiqta deRab Kahana. Alongside the Bavli are its Midrash associates, Lamentations Rabbah, Song of Songs Rabbah, Esther Rabbah I, and Ruth Rabbah. These books and some minor related items together form the canon of Judaism as it had reached its definitive shape by the end of late antiquity.

If we lay out these writings in the approximate sequence in which – according to the prevailing consensus, within which I do my work – they reached closure beginning with the Mishnah, the Tosefta, then Sifra and its associated compositions, followed by the Talmud of the Land of Israel, and alongside Genesis Rabbah and Leviticus Rabbah, then Pesiqta deRab Kahana and its companions, and finally the Talmud of Babylonia, we gain what I call "canonical history." This is, specifically, the order of the appearance of ideas when the documents, read in the outlined sequence, address a given idea or topic. The consequent history consists of the sequence in which a given statement on the topic at hand was made (early, middle, or late) in the unfolding of the canonical writings. To illustrate the process, what does the authorship of the Mishnah have to say on the theme? Then how does the compositor of Abot deal with it? Then the Tosefta's compositor's record comes into view, followed by the materials assembled in the Talmud of the Land of Israel, alongside those now found in the earlier and middle ranges of compilations of scriptural exegeses, and as always, the Talmud of Babylonia at the end. In the illustrative exercise that follows we shall read the sources in exactly the order outlined here. I produce a picture of how these sources treat an important principle of the Judaism of the Dual Torah. We shall see important shifts and changes in the unfolding of ideas on the symbol under study.

So, in sum, this story of continuity and change rests upon the notion that we can present the history of the treatment of a topical program in the canonical writings of that Judaism. I do not claim that the documents represent the state of popular or synagogue opinion. I do not know whether the history of the idea in the unfolding official texts corresponds to the history of the idea among the people who stand behind those documents. Even less do I claim to speak about the history of the topic or idea at hand outside of rabbinical circles, among the Jewish nation at large. All these larger dimensions of the matter lie wholly beyond the perspective of this book. The reason is that the evidence at hand is of a particular sort and hence permits us to investigate one category of questions and not another. The category is denied by established and universally held conventions about the order in which the canonical writings reached completion. Therefore we trace the way in which matters emerge in the sequence of writings followed here.

We trace the way in which ideas were taken up and spelled out in these successive stages in the formation of the canon. Let the purpose of the exercise be emphasized.

When we follow this procedure, we discover how, within the formation of the rabbinical canon of writings, the idea at hand came to literary expression and how it was then shaped to serve the larger purposes of the nascent canonical system as a whole.

By knowing the place and uses of the topic under study within the literary evidences of the rabbinical system, we gain a better understanding of the formative history of that system. What do we not learn? Neither the condition of the people at large nor the full range and power of the rabbinical thinkers' imagination comes to the fore. About other larger historical and intellectual matters we have no direct knowledge at all. Consequently we claim to report only what we learn about the canonical literature of a system evidenced by a limited factual base. No one who wants to know the history of a given idea in all the diverse Judaisms of late antiquity, or the role of that idea in the history of all the Jews in all parts of the world in the first seven centuries of the Common Era, will find it here.

In order to understand the documentary method we must again underline the social and political character of the documentary evidence presented. These are public statements, preserved and handed on because people have adopted them as authoritative. The sources constitute a collective, and therefore official, literature. All of the documents took shape and attained a place in the canon of the rabbinical movement as a whole. None was written by an individual in such a way as to testify to personal choice or decision. Accordingly, we cannot provide an account of the theory of a given individual at a particular time and place. We have numerous references to what a given individual said about the topic at hand. But these references do not reach us in the authorship of that person, or even in his language. They come to us only in the setting of a *collection* of sayings and statements, some associated with names, other unattributed and anonymous. The collections by definition were composed under the auspices of rabbinical authority – a school or a circle. They tell us what a group of people wished to preserve and hand on as authoritative doctrine about the meaning of the Mishnah and Scripture. The compositions reach us because the larger rabbinical estate chose to copy and hand them on. Accordingly, we know the state of doctrine at the stages marked by the formation and closure of the several documents.

We follow what references we find to a topic in accord with the order of documents just now spelled out. In this study we learn the order in which ideas came to expression in the canon. We begin any survey with the Mishnah, the starting point of the canon. We proceed systematically to work our way through tractate Abot, the Mishnah's first apologetic, then the Tosefta, the Yerushalmi, and the Bavli at the end. In a single encompassing sweep, we finally deal with the entirety of the compilations of the exegeses of Scripture, arranged, to be sure, in that order that I have now explained. Let me expand on the matter of my heavy emphasis on the order of the components of the canon. The reason for that stress is simple. We have to ask not only what documents viewed whole and all at once ("Judaism") tell us about our theme. In tracing the order in which ideas make their appearance, we ask about the components in sequence ("history of Judaism") so far as we can trace the sequence. Then and only then shall we have access to issues of *history*, that is, of change and development. If our theme makes its appearance early on in one form, so one set of ideas predominate in a document that reached closure in the beginnings of the cannon and then that theme drops out of public discourse or undergoes radical revision in writings in later stages of the canon, that fact may make considerable difference. Specifically, we may find it possible to speculate on where and why a given approach proved urgent and also on the reasons that that same approach receded from the center of interest.

In knowing the approximate sequence of documents and therefore the ideas in them (at least so far as the final point at which those ideas reached formal expression in the canon), a second possibility emerges. What if – as is the case – we find pretty much the same views, treated in the same proportion and for the same purpose, yielding the same message, early, middle, and late in the development of the canon? Then we shall have to ask why the literature remains so remarkably constant. Given the considerable shifts in the social and political condition of Israel in the land of Israel as well as in Babylonia over a period of more than four hundred years, that evident stability in the teachings for the affective life will constitute a considerable fact for analysis and interpretation.

History, including the history of religion, done rightly thus produces two possibilities, both of them demanding sustained attention. Things change. Why? Things do not change. Why not? We may well trace the relationship between the history of ideas and the history of the society that holds those same ideas. We follow the interplay between society and system – worldview, way of life, addressed to a particular social group – by developing a theory of the relationship between contents and context, between the world in which people live and the world which people create in their shared social and imaginative life. When we can frame a theory of how a system in substance relates to its setting, of the interplay between the social matrix and the mode and manner of a society's worldview and way of life, then we may develop theses of general intelligibility, theories of why this, not that, of why, and why not and how come.

The story of continuity and change rests upon the notion that we can present the history of the treatment of a topical program in the canonical writings of that Judaism. I do not claim that the documents represent the state of popular or synagogue opinion. I do not know whether the history of the idea in the unfolding official texts corresponds to the history of the idea among the people who stand behind those documents. Even less do I claim to speak about the history of the topic or idea at hand outside of rabbinical circles, among the Jewish nation at large. All these larger dimensions of the matter lie wholly beyond the perspective of this method. The reason is that the evidence at hand is of a particular sort and hence permits us to investigate one category of questions and not another. The category is defined by established and universally held conventions about the order in which the canonical writings reached completion. Therefore we trace the way in which matters emerge in the sequence of writings followed here. We trace the way in which ideas were taken up and spelled out in these successive stages in the formation of the canon. When we follow this procedure, we discover how, within the formation of the rabbinical canon of writings, the idea at hand came to literary expression and how it was then shaped to serve the larger purposes of the nascent canonical system as a whole.

What do I conceive to be at stake in the documentary history of Judaism? It is to set forth the history of the formation of Judaism, as the canonical writings of late antiquity allow us to trace that history. Let me explain. Between 200 and 400, Judaism changed from a philosophy to a religion. In current work I explain the meaning of that simple sentence, starting with the subject, Judaism.[9] Defining the word

---

[9]Everything I say here concerning the movement from philosophy to religion to theology in the formation of the Judaic system of the Dual Torah, so far as it speaks of theology, is based on preliminary impressions and is purely speculative. By contrast, the monographic foundations for this account of the transformation of the Judaic system from philosophy to religion are nearly complete and certainly adequate to this task. The principal works are as follows:

> *A History of the Mishnaic Law of Purities.* Leiden, 1977: Brill. XXI. *The Redaction and Formulation of the Order of Purities in the Mishnah and Tosefta.*
> *A History of the Mishnaic Law of Purities.* Leiden, 1977: Brill. XXII. *The Mishnaic System of Uncleanness. Its Context and History.*
> *The Mishnah before 70.* Atlanta, 1987: Scholars Press for Brown Judaic Studies. [Reprise of pertinent results of *A History of the Mishnah Law of Purities* Vols. III, V, VIII, X, XII, XIV, XVI, XVII, and XVIII.]
> *A History of the Mishnaic Law of Holy Things.* Leiden, 1979: Brill. VI. *The Mishnaic System of Sacrifice and Sanctuary.*
> *A History of the Mishnaic Law of Women.* Leiden, 1980: Brill. V. *The Mishnaic System of Women.*
> *A History of the Mishnaic Law of Appointed Times.* Leiden, 1981: Brill. V. *The Mishnaic System of Appointed Times.*
> *A History of the Mishnaic Law of Damages.* Leiden, 1985: Brill. V. *The Mishnaic System of Damages.*
> *Uniting the Dual Torah: Sifra and the Problem of the Mishnah.* Cambridge and New York, 1989: Cambridge University Press.
> *Judaism. The Evidence of the Mishnah.* Chicago, 1981: University of Chicago Press.
> *The Making of the Mind of Judaism.* Atlanta, 1987: Scholars Press for Brown Judaic Studies.
> *The Economics of the Mishnah.* Chicago, 1989: The University of Chicago Press.
> *The Formation of the Jewish Intellect. Making Connections and Drawing Conclusions in the Traditional System of Judaism.* Atlanta, 1988: Scholars Press for Brown Judaic Studies.
> *The Mishnah. An Introduction.* Northvale, New Jersey, 1989: Jason Aronson Inc.

Judaism in this context involves the understanding of a religion as an account of a system of the social order formed (whether in fact or in imagination) by the believers, an account portrayed in writing. The problem I address concerns the transformation by continuator documents of a Judaic system of the social order, fully set forth in its initial document. That problem, therefore, directs attention to systemic description, analysis, and interpretation of documentary evidence, for by comparing one set of writings with another I compare one system to another. This work is carried out in my *Transformation of Judaism. From Philosophy to Religion.*

Since the word "system" occurs throughout my account of the formation of Judaism, let me define it. Writings that are read all together, such as those of the unfolding canon of Judaism in late antiquity, are deemed to make a cogent and important statement. I call that encompassing, canonical picture a "system" when it is composed of three necessary components: an account of a worldview, a prescription of a corresponding way of life, and a definition of the social entity that finds definition in the one and description in the other. When those three fundamental components fit together, they sustain one another in explaining the whole of a social order, hence constituting the theoretical account of a system.

Systems defined in this way work out a cogent picture, for those who make them up, of *how* things are correctly to be sorted out and fitted together, of *why* things are done in one way, rather than in some other, and of *who* they are that do and understand matters in this particular way. When, as is commonly the case, people invoke God as

---

The Politics of the Mishnah. The Initial Structure and System. Submitted to University of Chicago Press. Sixth draft to be filed: 7/1/89.

The Philosophical Mishnah. Volume I. *The Initial Probe.* Atlanta, 1989: Scholars Press for Brown Judaic Studies.

The Philosophical Mishnah. Volume II. *The Tractates' Agenda. From Abodah Zarah to Moed Qatan.* Atlanta, 1989: Scholars Press for Brown Judaic Studies.

The Philosophical Mishnah. Volume III. *The Tractates' Agenda. From Nazir to Zebahim.* Atlanta, 1989: Scholars Press for Brown Judaic Studies.

The Philosophical Mishnah. Volume IV. *The Repertoire.* Atlanta, 1989: Scholars Press for Brown Judaic Studies.

The Philosophy of Judaism. The First Principles. Under consideration by Johns Hopkins University Press.

From Literature to Theology in Formative Judaism. Three Preliminary Studies. Atlanta, 1989: Scholars Press for Brown Judaic Studies.

the foundation for their worldview, maintaining that their way of life corresponds to what God wants of them, projecting their social entity in a particular relationship to God, then we have a religious system. When, finally, a religious system appeals as an important part of its authoritative literature or canon to the Hebrew Scriptures of ancient Israel or "Old Testament," we have a Judaism.

Let me specify what I conceive to be at stake in this approach to the reading of the formation of the Judaism of the Dual Torah. I am trying to find out how to describe that "Judaism" beyond the specific texts, moving beyond the text and the context and toward the matrix of all of the canonical texts. What is it that each document takes for granted but no document spells out? To answer that question I have to describe the processes of category formation, to specify the categorical imperative in the description of a Judaism. That accounts for the focus on the re-formation of received categories and the formation of new ones, wholly congruent to the received ones but also entirely fresh, as well.

The categories that I bring to the study are those of the social order: philosophy or science, politics, and economics. These correspond to worldview, theory of the social entity, and way of life, or ethos, ethnos, and ethics. The reason it is legitimate to describe the categorical unfolding of Judaism within the categories of political economy is simple. The Mishnah, the foundation document, after Scripture, of the canonical corpus we study here, in point of fact sets forth a full account of the social order, to which philosophy, politics, and economics are integral, just as philosophy, politics, and economics are integral to the social order conceived by Greco-Roman philosophy in the tradition of Aristotle. These deal with the worldview (in philosophy), the way of life (in economics), and the definition of the social entity (in politics) of the (imagined, or real) social order portrayed in documents identified as canonical.

Then at stake in systemic description is the reading of written evidence as the evidence has been combined to form an authoritative statement. Then I ask, in the analysis at hand, what happened, in the unfolding of the canon, to these categories of description of the social order, the issues of the way of life, worldview, and definition of the social entity, that altogether form the social system imagined by the authors or authorships of authoritative writings? I know how to answer that question.

These three inquiries of Greco-Roman political economy, philosophy, politics, and economics, set forth only the initial system of Judaism, the one to which the Mishnah attests. But that Judaism in many important ways hardly turned out wholly symmetrical with the final system of Judaism that emerged from the formative age and defined matters to the present day. The economics, politics, and philosophy of the initial formation of Judaism set the agenda and formed the court of appeal. But successors and continuators picked and chose, and, it follows, they framed a fresh definition for the social foundations of the world they proposed to invent. The philosophy, politics, and economics of the next phase in the formation of Judaism, seen on their own but also in relationship with the initial theories, will therefore demand sustained description, analysis, and interpretation. That explains why I know how the initial system was revised and adapted by later system makers. What is at stake, in all, is how intellectuals defined the rationalities of Judaism as a social composition: a theory of the society of Israel, the holy people of God.

Now to return to the definition of Judaism. By Judaism I mean a Judaic system, which is a cogent account of the social order, comprising a worldview, way of life, and theory of the social entity, "Israel," all together setting forth a response to a question deemed urgent and encompassing providing an answer found self-evidently valid. The Jews' long history has witnessed the formation of a variety of such Judaic systems. In the first seven centuries of the Common Era (=A.D.) one such system, the one that has predominated since that time, took shape. That is the Judaic system the transformation of which is under discussion here. I describe that system through the canonical writings produced by sages bearing the title "rabbis."

The ultimate system of Judaism itself formed during those seven centuries in three distinct stages, marked in each case by the distinctive traits of the literature that reached closure at the end of each successive stage.[10] More to the point, each stage produced a Judaic system. Formed in the first two hundred years and represented by the Mishnah and its associated writings, the first is utterly free standing. The second, taking shape from 200 to 400 and represented by the Talmud of the Land of Israel and its compansions, is connected to the first but essentially distinct from it. The third, expressed in documents that reached closure between 400 and 600 within and around the Talmud of Babylonia, is connected to the second but in important traits distinct from it as well. These three systems, autonomous when viewed synchronically but connected when seen diachronically, ultimately, at the end of their formative age, formed a single, wholly and utterly continuous structure, that one we call Judaism. But in their successive stages of autonomy, then autonomy and connection, the three distinct systems may be classified, respectively, as philosophical, religious,

---

[10]These are set forth presently.

and theological. Judaism then took shape in a passage from a philosophical, to a religious, and finally to a theological system, each one taking over and revising the definitive categories of the former and framing its own fresh, generative categories as well. The formative history of Judaism then is the story of the presentations and re-presentations of categorical structures. In method it is the exegesis of taxonomy and taxic systems.

To begin with, then, the classification of types of systems – philosophical, religious, theological – requires explanation. A philosophical system forms its learning inductively and syllogistically by appeal to the neutral evidence of the rules shown by the observation of the order of universally accessible nature and society. A religious system frames its propositions deductively and exegetically by appeal to the privileged evidence of a corpus of writing deemed revealed by God.

A theological system imposes upon a religious one systematic modes of thought of philosophy, so in its message regularizing and ordering in a cogent and intellectually rigorous way the materials received from a religious system. The movement from the religious to the theological will involve the systematization and harmonization of the religious categories, their re-formation into a single tight and cogent statement. It is an initiative as radical, in its way, as the passage from the philosophical to religious formation is in its way. For the modes of thought, media of expression, and, as a matter of fact, categorical structure and system are reworked in the enterprise of turning a merely imputed order, imputed within the single heart of the faith, into a wholly public order, subject to sustained and cogent representation and expression, each component in its place and proper sequence, beginning, middle, and end. Religious conviction differs from theological proposition as do bricks and mortar from a building.

Religious and the theological systems of course work over the same issues in ways that are common to themselves and that also distinguish them jointly from philosophical ones. But the rigorous task of forming of religious attitudes and convictions a cogent composition, a system and not merely a structure of beliefs, imposes on systems of the theological sort disciplines of mind and perception, modes of thought and media of expression, quite different from those that characterize the work of making a religious system. The connection is of course intimate, for a theological system succeeding and reshaping a religious one appeals to the same sources of truth in setting forth (often identical) answers to (ordinarily) the same urgent questions. But the theological type of system is different from the religious type in fundamental ways as well, for while there can be a religious system without theological order, there can be no theological system without a religious core. So much for the distinctions among types of systems.

In the transformation of the Judaic system from philosophical to religion in its basic character, the very raw materials, the categories themselves, undergo transformation. When a philosophical becomes a religious system, the categorical change yields not the reframing or re-formation or re-presentation. What happens is rather the fundamental revaluation of categories, which I call "counterpart categories," transvaluation and transformation – these comprise the history of religion, so far as history records connections, comparisons, and contrasts, between one thing and something else.

How do I know that these categorical transformations and reconsiderations have taken place in the systems in transition? The answer requires us to read literary evidence as testament to systemic formation. The evidence for systems of world-construction, such as those with which we deal in the history of Judaism, derives from the correct description and analysis of the surviving writings of the formative age. These provide our evidence of how system builders chose to express their ideas (rhetoric), conceived that their ideas expressed cogent thought and formed intelligible statements to be shared by others (logic of cogent discourse), and formed the categories through which the facts attained sense and constituted orderly and systematic accounts of the world (topical, propositional program). All three together – the mode of discourse, the media of thought and expression, the message brought to representation through the particular rhetoric and logic at hand – prove accessible when we ask the documentary heritage of the system builders to point us toward the system expressed therein in detail. In the Introduction I have defined the documentary evidence to which the method of the canonical history of ideas applies.

The documentary evidence set forth a system of a very particular kind. The evidence is canonical, because the canon recapitulates the system that animates the mentality of the framers of canonical writers and the authorities that adopted those writings for a single canonical composite. Cogent accounts of the social order, from beginning to end, the Judaic systems defined as their problem the construction of a social world. Each, in succession, framed its categories for intelligible thought by appeal to the issues of the world framed by a particular ethnos, the social entity (the most neutral language I can find), which was called (an) "Israel," and every Judaic system would take as its task the definition of the social world of an Israel: the way of life or (broadly speaking) ethics, the worldview or ethos, and the account of the social entity or the "Israel" that realized in its shared and corporate being the ethics (again, broadly construed), and explained that ethos by appeal to the ethos. So, as a matter of definition, a Judaic system is a system that derives its generative categories from the (theoretical) requirements of framing a social order: who are "we," what do we do together, and why are we the corporate body that we are, thus, ethnos, ethics, ethos.

The canonical history of ideas serves for systemic description, encompassing not only phenomenology but history. It shows us the sequential development, attested by documents that came to closure one after another, of a set of religious theories of the social order, the first autonomous, the second connected to the first, the third wholly continuous with the received theories. The stakes are therefore very high. The possibility of constructing such an experiment as has been carried out in these pages demonstrate the promise of the method – and also, of course, its limitations. What we get is not dates for documents but perspective upon documents, not the history of ideas as these circulated in the streets and marketplaces of the villages and towns where Jews lived in the Land of Israel and in Babylonia, but only the formation and development of ideas from book to book. But that story, too, bears its illumination, if only of the works of intellectuals: holy men who thought that, in living the life of mind, they served and worshiped and with all their heart and soul and might loved God.

II

The Dual Torah

1. The Mishnah as against the Yerushalmi

The Mishnah's use of the word *Torah* carried forward a long tradition, in which Torah bore a definite article, *the Torah*. *The Torah* referred to a particular corpus of writings, a set of scrolls, accorded the status of divine revelation to Moses at Sinai, and to the act of study and knowledge of the contents of those scrolls. But Judaism as we know it at the end of late antiquity reached its now familiar definition when "the Torah" lost its capital letter and definite article and ultimately became "torah." And a principal indicator of the shift is the conception of the Dual Torah, one in writing, contained within the scrolls, the other oral, preserved in memory of sages. The first indicator of what is distinctive to the successor system is the conception of the Dual Torah, which, as a matter of fact, the Mishnah does not know, but which the Yerushalmi knows full well. This Dual Torah – written and oral, that is, formulated and transmitted in writing, formulated and transmitted orally, then forms the first of our indicators. What we shall now ask is whether documents know about the myth, or at least, the symbol, of the Dual Torah, whether they even acknowledge a canon that encompasses writings other than the Written Torah, or whether, like the Mishnah, they know as *torah* only The Torah.

The process of redefinition of the Torah into the Dual Torah formed part of a larger expansion of the meaning of the word *Torah*. Only when the word *Torah* could encompass more than a particular book or set of books and knowledge thereof could the myth of the Dual Torah make its way – by definition, as a matter of fact. That process was fully exposed in the Yerushalmi and related writings, for there, what for nearly a millennium had been a particular scroll or book thus came to serve as a symbol of an entire system. When a rabbi spoke of torah, he no longer meant only a particular object, a scroll and its contents.

Now he used the word to encompass a distinctive and well-defined worldview and way of life. Torah had come to stand for something one does. Knowledge of the Torah promised not merely information about what people were supposed to do but ultimate redemption or salvation. The scrolls of the Torah thus developed into an abstract and encompassing symbol, so that everything was contained in that one thing. How so? When we speak of torah, in rabbinical literature of late antiquity, we no longer denote a particular book, on the one side, or the contents of such a book, on the other. Instead, we connote a broad range of clearly distinct categories of noun and verb, concrete fact and abstract relationship alike. When, therefore, we wish to describe the unfolding of the definitive doctrine of Judaism in its formative period, the first exercise consists in paying close attention to the meanings imputed to a single word.

The meaning of the several meanings of the Torah should require only brief explanation. When the Torah refers to a particular thing, it is to a scroll containing divinely revealed words. The Torah may further refer to revelation, not as an object but as a corpus of doctrine. When one "does Torah" the disciple "studies" or "learns," and the master "teaches," Torah. Hence while the word *Torah* never appears as a verb, it does refer to an act. The word also bears a quite separate sense, torah as category or classification or corpus of rules, for example, "the torah of driving a car" is a usage entirely acceptable to some documents. This generic usage of the word does occur. The word *Torah* very commonly refers to a status, distinct from and above another status, as "teachings of Torah" as against "teachings of scribes." For the two Talmuds that distinction is absolutely critical to the entire hermeneutic enterprise. But it is important even in the Mishnah. Obviously, no account of the meaning of the word *Torah* can ignore the distinction between the two Torahs, written and oral. It is important only in the secondary stages of the formation of the literature. Finally, as we shall see in Chapter Three, the word *Torah* further refers to a source of salvation, often fully worked out in stories about how the individual and the nation will be saved through Torah. In general, the sense of the word "salvation" is not complicated. It is simply salvation in the way in which Deuteronomy and the deuteronomic historians understand it: kings who do what God wants win battles, those who do not, lose. So too here, people who study and do Torah are saved from sickness and death, and the way Israel can save itself from its condition of degradation also is through Torah.

In focusing for the purpose of this experiment upon the myth of the Dual Torah, we ask first of all, what accounts for the indicative value of the word *Torah* when it refers to the Dual Torah? The reason is that the conception of the Dual Torah responded to the formidable authority conferred upon the Mishnah when it emerged, at the end of the second century, as a principal law code for the community of Judaism. Upon its closure, the Mishnah gained an exalted political status as the constitution of Jewish government of the Land of Israel. Accordingly, the clerks who knew and applied its law had to explain the standing of that law, meaning its relationship to the law of the Torah. But the Mishnah provided no account of itself. Unlike biblical law codes, the Mishnah begins with no myth of its own origin. It ends with no doxology. Discourse commences in the middle of things and ends abruptly. What follows from such laconic mumbling is that the exact status of the document required definition entirely outside the framework of the document itself. The framers of the Mishnah gave no hint of the nature of their book, so the Mishnah reached the political world of Israel without a trace of self-conscious explanation or any theory of validation.

The one thing that is clear, alas, is negative. The framers of the Mishnah nowhere claim, implicitly or explicitly, that what they have written forms part of the Torah, enjoys the status of God's revelation to Moses at Sinai, or even systematically carries forward secondary exposition and application of what Moses wrote down in the wilderness. Later on, two hundred years beyond the closure of the Mishnah, the need to explain the standing and origin of the Mishnah led some, whose views are represented in the Talmud of the Land of Israel and related writings, to posit two things. First, God's revelation of the Torah at Sinai encompassed the Mishnah as much as Scripture. Second, the Mishnah was handed on through oral formulation and oral transmission from Sinai to the framers of the document as we have it. These two convictions, fully exposed in the ninth-century letter of Sherira, in fact emerge from the references of both Talmuds to the Dual Torah. One part is in writing. The other was oral and now is in the Mishnah.

As for the Mishnah itself, however, it contains not a hint that anyone has heard any such tale. The earliest apologists for the Mishnah, represented in Abot and the Tosefta alike, know nothing of the fully realized myth of the Dual Torah of Sinai. It may be that the authors of those documents stood too close to the Mishnah to see the Mishnah's standing as a problem or to recognize the task of accounting for its origins. Certainly they never refer to the Mishnah as something out there, nor speak of the document as autonomous and complete. Only the two Talmuds reveal that conception – alongside their mythic explanation of where the document came from and why it should be obeyed. So the Yerushalmi marks the change. In any event, the absence of explicit expression of such a claim in behalf of the Mishnah requires little specification. It is just not there.[1]

It follows that we do not know whether the Mishnah was supposed to be part of the Torah or to enjoy a clearly defined relationship to the existing Torah. We also do not know what else, if not the Torah, was meant to endow the Mishnah's laws with heavenly sanction. To state matters simply, we do not know what the framers of the Mishnah said they had made, nor do we know what the people who received and were supposed to obey the Mishnah thought they possessed.

A survey of the uses of the word *Torah* in the Mishnah, to be sure, provides us with an account of what the framers of the Mishnah, founders of what would emerge as rabbinic Judaism, understood by that term. But it will not tell us how they related their own ideas to the Torah, nor shall we find a trace of evidence of that fully articulated way of life – the use of the word *Torah* to categorize and classify persons, places, things, relationships, all manner of abstractions – that we find fully exposed in some later redacted writings.

True, the Mishnah places a high value upon studying the Torah and upon the status of the sage. A "*mamzer*-disciple of a sage takes priority over a high-priest *am-haares*," as at M. Hor. 3:8. But that judgment, distinctive though it is, cannot settle the question. All it shows is that the Mishnah pays due honor to the sage. But if the Mishnah does not claim to constitute part of the Torah, then what

---

[1]But the absence of an implicit claim demands explanation. When ancient Jews wanted to gain for their writings the status of revelation, of torah, or at least to link what they thought to what the Torah had said, they could do one of four things. They could sign the name of a holy man of old, for instance, Adam, Enoch, Ezra. They could imitate the Hebrew style of Scripture. They could claim that God had spoken to them. They could, at the very least, cite a verse of Scripture and impute to the cited passage their own opinion. These four methods – pseudepigraphy, stylistic imitation (hence, forgery), claim of direct revelation from God, and eisegesis – found no favor with the Mishnah's framers. to the contrary, they signed no name to their book. Their Hebrew was new in its syntax and morphology, completely unlike that of the Mosaic writings of the Pentateuch. They never claimed that God had anything to do with their opinions. They rarely cited a verse of Scripture as authority. It follows that, whatever the authors of the Mishnah said about their document, the implicit character of the book tells us that they did not claim God had dictated or even approved what they had to say. Why not? The framers simply ignored all the validating conventions of the world in which they lived. And, as I said, they failed to make explicit use of any others.

makes a sage a sage is not mastery of the Mishnah in particular. What we have in hand merely continues the established and familiar position of the wisdom writers of old. Wisdom is important. Knowledge of the Torah is definitive. But to maintain that position, one need hardly profess the fully articulated Torah myth of rabbinic Judaism. Proof of that fact, after all, is the character of the entire wisdom literature prior to the Mishnah itself.

So the issue is clearly drawn. It is not whether we find in the Mishnah exaggerated claims about the priority of the disciple of a sage. We do find such claims. The issue is whether we find in the Mishnah the assertion that whatever the sage has on the authority of his master goes back to Sinai. We seek a definitive view that what the sage says falls into the classification of Torah, just as what Scripture says constitutes Torah from God to Moses. That is what distinguishes wisdom from the Torah as it emerges in the context of rabbinic Judaism. To state the outcome in advance: we do not find the Torah in the Mishnah, and the Mishnah is not part of the Torah.

When the authors of the Mishnah surveyed the landscape of Israelite writings down to their own time, they saw only Sinai, that is, what we now know as Scripture. Based on the documents they cite or mention, we can say with certainty that they knew the pentateuchal law. We may take for granted that they accepted as divine revelation also the Prophets and the Writings, to which they occasionally make reference. That they regarded as a single composition, that is, as revelation, the Torah, Prophets, and Writings appears from their references to the Torah, as a specific "book", and to a Torah scroll. Accordingly, one important meaning associated with the word *Torah*, was concrete in the extreme. The Torah was a particular book or sets of books, regarded as holy, revealed to Moses at Sinai. That fact presents no surprise, since the Torah scroll(s) had existed, it is generally assumed, for many centuries before the closure of the Mishnah in 200.

What is surprising is that everything from the formation of the canon of the Torah to their own day seems to have proved null in their eyes. Between the Mishnah and Mount Sinai lay a vast, empty plain. From the perspective of the Torah myth as they must have known it, from Moses and the prophets, to before Judah the Patriarch, lay a great wasteland. So the concrete and physical meaning attaching to the word *Torah*, that is the Torah, the Torah revealed by God to Moses at Mount Sinai (including the books of the Prophets and the Writings), bore a contrary implication. Beyond The Torah there was no torah. Besides the Pentateuch, Prophets, and Writings, not only did no physical scroll deserve veneration, but no corpus of writings demanded obedience. So the very limited sense in which the words the Torah were used passed a stern judgment upon everything else, all the other writings that we know circulated widely, in which other Jews alleged that God had spoken and said "these things."

Abot draws into the orbit of Torah-talk the names of authorities of the Mishnah. But Abot does not claim that the Mishnah forms part of the Torah. Nor, obviously, does the tractate know the doctrine of the two Torahs. Only in the Talmuds do we begin to find clear and ample evidence of that doctrine. Abot, moreover, does not understand by the word *Torah* much more than the framers of the Mishnah do. Not only does the established classification scheme remain intact, but the sense essentially replicates already familiar usages, producing no innovation. On the contrary, I find a diminution in the range of meanings.

Yet Abot in the aggregate does differ from the Mishnah. The difference has to do with the topic at hand. The other sixty-two tractates of the Mishnah contain Torah sayings here and there. But they do not fall within the framework of Torah discourse. They speak about other matters entirely. The consideration of the status of Torah rarely pertains to that speech. Abot, by contrast, says a great deal about Torah study. The claim that Torah study produces direct encounter with God forms part of Abot's thesis about the Torah. That claim, by itself, will hardly have surprised Israelite writers of wisdom books over a span of many centuries, whether those assembled in the Essene commune at Qumran, on the one side, or those represented in the pages of Proverbs and in many of the Psalms, or even the deuteronomistic circle, on the other.

A second glance at tractate Abot, however, produces a surprising fact. In Abot, Torah is instrumental. The figure of the sage, his ideals and conduct, forms the goal, focus, and center. To state matters simply: Abot regards study of Torah as what a sage does. The substance of Torah is what a sage says. That is so whether or not the saying relates to scriptural revelation. The content of the sayings attributed to sages endows those sayings with self-validating status. The sages usually do not quote verses of Scripture and explain them, nor do they speak in God's name. Yet, it is clear, sages talk Torah. What follows? It is this: if a sage says something, what he says is Torah. More accurately, what he says falls into the classification of Torah. Accordingly, as I said, Abot treats Torah learning as symptomatic, an indicator of the status of the sage, hence, as I said, as merely instrumental.

The simplest proof of that proposition lies in the recurrent formal structure of the document, the one thing the framers of the document never omit and always emphasize: (1) the name of the authority behind a saying, from Simeon the Righteous on downward, and (2) the connective-attributive "says." So what is important to the redactors is what they never have to tell us. Because a recognized sage makes a statement, what he says constitutes, in and of itself, a statement in the status of Torah.

To spell out what this means, let us look at the opening sentences. "Moses received Torah," and it reached "the Men of the Great Assembly." "The three things" those men said bear no resemblance to anything we find in written Scripture. They focus upon the life of sagacity – prudence, discipleship, a fence around the Torah. And, as we proceed, we find time and again that, while the word *Torah* stands for two things, divine revelation and the act of study of divine revelation, it produces a single effect, the transformation of unformed man into sage. One climax comes in Yohanan ben Zakkai's assertion that the purpose for which a man (an Israelite) was created was to study Torah, followed by his disciples' specifications of the most important things to be learned in the Torah. All of these pertain to the conduct of the wise man, the sage.

We have to locate the document's focus not on Torah but on the life of sagacity (including, to be sure, Torah study). But what defines and delimits Torah? It is the sage himself. So we may simply state the tractate's definition of Torah: Torah is what a sage learns. Accordingly, the Mishnah contains Torah. It may well be thought to fall into the classification of Torah. But the reason, we recognize, is that authorities whose sayings are found in the Mishnah possess Torah from Sinai. What they say, we cannot overemphasize, is Torah. How do we know it? It is a fact validated by the association of what they say with their own names.

So we miss the real issue when we ask Abot to explain for us the status of the Mishnah, or to provide a theory of a Dual Torah. The principal point of insistence – the generative question – before the framers of Abot does not address the status of the Mishnah. And the instrumental status of the Torah, as well as of the Mishnah, lies in the net effect of their composition: the claim that through study of the Torah sages enter God's presence. So study of Torah serves a further goal, that of forming sages. The theory of Abot pertains to the religious standing and consequence of the learning of the sages. To be sure, a secondary effect of that theory endows with the status of revealed truth things sages say. But then, as I have stressed, it is because they say them, not because they have heard them in an endless chain back to Sinai. The fundament of truth is passed on through sagacity, not through already formulated and carefully memorized truths. That is why the single most important word in Abot also is the most common, the word *says*.

At issue in Abot is not the Torah, but the authority of the sage. It is that standing that transforms a saying into a Torah saying, or to state matters more appropriately, that places a saying into the classification of the Torah. Abot then stands as the first document of the doctrine that the sage embodies the Torah and is a holy man, like Moses "our rabbi," in the likeness and image of God. The beginning is to claim that a saying falls into the category of Torah if a sage says it as Torah. The end will be to view the sage himself as Torah incarnate.

The Mishnah is held in the Talmud of the Land of Israel to be equivalent to Scripture (Y. Hor. 3:5). But the Mishnah is not called Torah. Still, once the Mishnah entered the status of Scripture, it would take but a short step to a theory of the Mishnah as part of the revelation at Sinai – hence, Oral Torah. In the first Talmud we find the first glimmerings of an effort to theorize in general, not merely in detail, about how specific teachings of Mishnah relate to specific teachings of Scripture. The citing of scriptural prooftexts for Mishnah propositions, after all, would not have caused much surprise to the framers of the Mishnah; they themselves included such passages, though not often. But what conception of the Torah underlies such initiatives, and how do Yerushalmi sages propose to explain the phenomenon of the Mishnah as a whole? The following passage gives us one statement. It refers to the assertion at M. Hag. 1:8D that the laws on cultic cleanness presented in the Mishnah rest on deep and solid foundations in the Scripture.

Y. Hagigah 1:7
V
A.   The laws of the Sabbath [M. 1:8B]: R. Jonah said R. Hama bar Uqba raised the question [in reference to M. Hag. 1:8D's view that there are many verses of Scripture on cleanness], "And lo, it is written only, 'Nevertheless a spring or a cistern holding water shall be clean; but whatever touches their carcass shall be unclean (Lev. 11:36). And from this verse you derive many laws. [So how can M. 8:8D say what it does about many verses for laws of cultic cleanness?]"
B.   R. Zeirah in the name of R. Yohanan: "If a law comes to hand and you do not know its nature, do not discard it for another one, for lo, many laws were stated to Moses at Sinai, and all of them have been embedded in the Mishnah."

The truly striking assertion appears at B. The Mishnah now is claimed to contain statements made by God to Moses. Just how these statements found their way into the Mishnah, and which passages of the Mishnah contain them, we do not know. That is hardly important, given the fundamental assertion at hand. The passage proceeds to a further, and far more consequential, proposition. It asserts that part of the Torah was written down, and part was preserved in memory and transmitted orally. In context, moreover, that distinction must encompass the Mishnah, thus explaining its origin as part of the Torah. Here is a clear and unmistakable expression of the distinction between two forms in which a single Torah was revealed and handed on at Mount Sinai, part in writing, part orally.

While the passage below does not make use of the language, Torah-in-writing and Torah-by-memory, it does refer to "the written" and "the oral." I believe myself fully justified in supplying the word *Torah* in square brackets. The reader will note, however, that the word *Torah* likewise does not occur at K, L. Only when the passage reaches its climax, at M, does it break down into a number of categories – Scripture, Mishnah, Talmud, laws, lore. It there makes the additional point that everything comes from Moses at Sinai. So the fully articulated theory of two Torahs (not merely one Torah in two forms) does not reach final expression in this passage. But short of explicit allusion to Torah-in-writing and Torah-by-memory, which (so far as I am able to discern) we find mainly in the Talmud of Babylonia, the ultimate theory of Torah of formative Judaism is at hand in what follows.

Y. Hagigah 1:7

V

D. R. Zeirah in the name of R. Eleazar: "'Were I to write for him my laws by ten thousands, they would be regarded as a strange thing' (Hos. 8:12). Now is the greater part of the Torah written down? [Surely not. The oral part is much greater.] But more abundant are the matters which are derived by exegesis from the written [Torah] than those derived by exegesis from the oral [Torah]."

E. And is that so?

F. But more cherished are those matters which rest upon the written [Torah] than those which rest upon the oral [Torah].

J. R. Haggai in the name of R. Samuel bar Nahman, "Some teachings were handed on orally, and some things were handed on in writing, and we do not know which of them is the more precious. But on the basis of that which is written, "And the Lord said to Moses, Write these words; in accordance with these words I have made a covenant with you and with Israel' (Ex. 34:27), [we conclude] that the ones which are handed on orally are the more precious."

K. R. Yohanan and R. Yudan b. R. Simeon – One said, "If you have kept what is preserved orally and also kept what is in writing, I shall make a covenant with you, and if not, I shall not make a covenant with you."

L. The other said, "If you have kept what is preserved orally and you have kept what is preserved in writing, you shall receive a reward, and if not, you shall not receive a reward."

M.   [With reference to Deut. 9:10: "And on them was written according to all the words which the Lord spoke with you in the mount,"] said R. Joshua b. Levi, "He could have written, 'On them,' but wrote, 'And on them.' He could have written, 'All,' but wrote, 'According to all.' He could have written, 'Words,' but wrote 'The words.' [These, then, serve as three encompassing clauses, serving to include] Scripture, Mishnah, Talmud, laws, and lore. Even what an experienced student in the future is going to teach before his master already has been stated to Moses at Sinai."

N.   What is the scriptural basis for this view?

O.   "There is no remembrance of former things, nor will there be any remembrance of later things yet to happen among those who come after" (Qoh. 1:11).

P.   If someone says, "See, this is a new thing," his fellow will answer him, saying to him, "This has been around before us for a long time."

Here we have absolutely explicit evidence that people believed part of the Torah had been preserved not in writing but orally. Linking that part to the Mishnah remains a matter of implication. But it surely comes fairly close to the surface, when we are told that the Mishnah contains Torah traditions revealed at Sinai. From that view it requires only a small step to the allegation that the Mishnah is part of the Torah, the oral part.

The history of the symbolization of the Torah and formation of the myth of the Dual Torah responds to the promulgation of the Mishnah and the requirement to explain the authority and standing of that document. The broader process, involving the conception of the Torah and studying the Torah as source of supernatural power now and salvation after death, will demand attention in Chapter Three. But the two sides to the matter have to be seen together. The transformation of the Torah, a scroll, to *torah*, which covers a variety of matters, proceeds from its removal from the framework of material objects, even from the limitations of its own contents, to its transformation into something quite different and abstract, quite distinct from the document and its teachings. The Torah stands for this something more, specifically, when it comes to be identified with a living person, the sage, and endowed with those particular traits that the sage claimed for himself. While we cannot say that the process of symbolization leading to the pure abstraction at hand moved in easy stages, we may still point to the stations that had to be passed in sequence.

The word *Torah* reached the apologists for the Mishnah in its long-established meanings: Torah scroll, contents of the Torah scroll. But even in the Mishnah itself, these meanings provoked a secondary development, status of Torah as distinct from other (lower) status, hence, Torah teaching in contradistinction to scribal teaching. With that small and simple step, the Torah ceased to denote only a concrete and material thing – a scroll and its contents. It now connoted an abstract matter of status. And once made abstract, the symbol entered a secondary history beyond all limits imposed by the concrete object, including its specific teachings, the Torah scroll.

I believe that Abot stands at the beginning of this process. In the history of the word *Torah* as abstract symbol, a metaphor serving to sort out one abstract status from another regained concrete and material reality of a new order entirely. For the message of Abot, as we saw, was that the Torah served the sage. How so? The Torah indicated who was a sage and who was not. Accordingly, the apology of Abot for the Mishnah was that the Mishnah contained things sages had said. What sages said formed a chain of tradition extending back to Sinai. Hence it was equivalent to the Torah. The upshot is that words of sages enjoyed the status of the Torah.

The small step beyond, I think, was to claim that what sages said was Torah, as much as what Scripture said was Torah. And, a further small step (and the steps need not have been taken separately or in the order here suggested) moved matters to the position that there were two forms in which the Torah reached Israel: one [Torah] in writing, the other [Torah] handed on orally, that is, in memory. The final step, fully revealed in the Talmud at hand, brought the conception of Torah to its logical conclusion: what the sage said was in the status of the Torah, was Torah, because the sage was Torah incarnate. So the abstract symbol now became concrete and material once more. We recognize the many diverse ways in which the Talmud stated that conviction. Every passage in which knowledge of the Torah yields power over this world and the next, capacity to coerce to the sage's will the natural and supernatural worlds alike, rests upon the same viewpoint.

The first Talmud's theory of the Torah carries us through several stages in the processes of the symbolization of the word *Torah*. First transformed from something material and concrete into something abstract and beyond all metaphor, the word *Torah* finally emerged once more in a concrete aspect, now as the encompassing and universal mode of stating the whole doctrine, all at once, of Judaism in its formative age.

The evidence we seek in the present experiment is verbal – reference to "Oral Torah" or "Dual Torah." Do we find in the so-called Tannaitic Midrashim references to Moses' having given to Israel Torah in two media, oral and written?

2. Mekhilta Attributed to R. Ishmael

I find no sustained interest in the myth of the Dual Torah, for example, in the representation of the giving of the Torah, or of the Ten Commandments, no effort goes into insisting that there were two Torahs, oral and written. This result is confirmed in Kosovsky's *Osar leshon Hattanaim* for Mekhilta, which contains no reference to either *Torah shebikhtab* or *Torah shebeal peh.*

3. Sifra

The following passage, already cited in the Introduction, and to be cited again when we come to the conception of *zekhut avot*, joins the themes of the uniqueness of Israel and the differentiation of the nations, typical then of the Yerushalmi's system's treatment of both matters. It further introduces the conception of *zekhut* inherited from the tribal progenitors and the myth of the Dual Torah. I could not imagine a more complete statement of the successor system at its principal emblematic components.

Sifra Parashat Behuqotai Pereq 8

CCLXIX:I

12. A. "[Yet for all that, when they are in the land of their enemies,] I will not spurn them, neither will I abhor them so as to destroy them utterly:"

    B. Now what is left for them, but that they not be spurned nor abhorred? For is it not the fact that all the good gifts that had been given to them were now taken away from them?

    C. And were it not for the Scroll of the Torah that was left for them, they were in no way be different from the nations of the world!

    D. But "I will not spurn them:" – in the time of Vespasian.

    E. "neither will I abhor them:" – in the time of Greece.

    F. "So as to destroy them utterly and break my covenant with them:" – in the time of Haman.

    G. "For I am the Lord their God:" – in the time of Gog.

13. A. And how do we know that the covenant is made with the tribal fathers?

    B. As it is said, "But I will for their sake remember the covenant with their forefathers whom I brought forth out of the land of Egypt:"

    C. This teaches that the covenant is made with the tribal fathers.

14. A. "These are the statutes and ordinances and Torahs:"

    B. "the statutes:" this refers to the exegeses of Scripture.

    C. "and ordinances:" this refers to the laws.

    D. "and Torahs:" this teaches that two Torahs were given to Israel, one in writing, the other oral.

    E. Said R. Aqiba, "Now did Israel have only two Torahs? And did they not have many Torahs given to them? 'This is the Torah of burnt-offering (Lev. 6:2),' 'This is the Torah of the meal-offering

(Lev. 6:27),' 'This is the Torah of the guilt-offering (Lev. 7:1),' 'This is the Torah of the sacrifice of peace-offerings (Lev. 7:11) 'This is the Torah: when a man dies in a tent (Num. 19:1).'"

15. A. "Which the Lord made between him and the people of Israel [on Mount Sinai by Moses]:"

B. Moses had the merit of being made the intermediary between Israel and their father in Heaven.

C. "on Mount Sinai by Moses:"

D. This teaches that the Torah was given, encompassing all its laws, all its details, and all their amplifications, through Moses at Sinai.

The passage at hand has the myth of the two Torahs, the uniqueness of Israel (by reason of the Torah), the differentiation of the nations, and *zekhut avot*, all explicitly joined together. While a singleton in its document, it attests on its own to the situation of Sifra: not only post-mishnaic, but, in indicative traits, talmudic.

4. Sifré to Numbers 1-115

I identified not a single line relevant to this topic. This result is confirmed in Kosovsky's *Osar leshon Hattanaim* for the two Sifrés, which contains no reference to either *Torah shebikhtab* or *Torah shebeal peh*.

5. Sifré to Deuteronomy

The following passages are pertinent to the Torah theme and suggest an answer to the problem of situating this Sifré. We shall see that, as to the indicative evidence before us, we stand closer to the Yerushalmi than to the Mishnah. That fact adumbrates the conclusion we shall reach in Chapter Nine, which is that, in the aggregate, the evidence places Sifra and Sifré to Deuteronomy within the circle of the Yerushalmi.

Sifré to Deuteronomy Pisqa
CCCXVII:III

1. A. Another teaching concerning the verse, "He set him atop the highlands:"

B. This refers to the Torah, as it is said, "The Lord acquired me at the beginning of his way" (Prov. 8:22).

2. A. "...to feast on the yield of the earth:"

B. This refers to Scripture.

3. A. "...he fed him honey from the crag:"

B. This refers to the Mishnah.

4. A. "...and oil from the flinty rock:"

B. This refers to the Talmud.

5. A. "...curd of kine and milk of flocks; with the best of lambs and rams and he-goats:"

    B.   This refers to arguments a fortiori, analogies, laws, and responses
             to queries.
6.   A.   "... with the very finest wheat:"
     B.   This refers to those laws that form the essentials of the Torah.
7.   A.   "...and foaming grape-blood was your drink:"
     B.   This refers to lore, which entices the heart of a person as does
             wine.

The exposition of the base verse has gone from the sacred service of
the cult; now we turn to the Torah and its components, and here too the
blessings have been realized. The entire corporate life of Israel, in
concrete, material terms, in terms of relationship to Heaven, and in
terms of the life of the people with the Torah, fulfills the promise.
What is important from our perspective is not what the passage says,
but what it does not say. The conception that only Israel has the Oral
Torah, the stress on Torah as the heart and center of Israel's life – these
play no role. There is an altogether different focus, and the Torah
theme is contingent, not central, to the point the passage wishes to
make. In fact, the passage is eschatological.

Sifré to Deuteronomy Pisqa
CCCXLIII:IV
1.   A.   Another teaching concerning the phrase, "He said, 'The Lord
             came from Sinai:"
     B.   When the Omnipresent appeared to give the Torah to Israel, it
             was not to Israel alone that he revealed himself but to every
             nation.
     C.   First of all he came to the children of Esau. He said to them, "Will
             you accept the Torah?"
     D.   They said to him, "What is written in it?"
     E.   He said to them, "'You shall not murder' (Ex. 20:13)."
     F.   They said to him, "The very being of 'those men' [namely, us] and
             of their father is to murder, for it is said, 'But the hands are the
             hands of Esau'"(Gen. 27:22). 'By your sword you shall live' (Gen.
             27:40)."
     G.   So he went to the children of Ammon and Moab and said to them,
             "Will you accept the Torah?"
     H.   They said to him, "What is written in it?"
     I.   He said to them, "'You shall not commit adultery' (Ex. 20:13)."
     J.   They said to him, "The very essence of fornication belongs to
             them [us], for it is said, 'Thus were both the daughters of Lot with
             child by their fathers' (Gen. 19:36)."
     K.   So he went to the children of Ishmael and said to them, "Will you
             accept the Torah?"
     L.   They said to him, "What is written in it?"
     M.   He said to them, "'You shall not steal' (Ex. 20:13)."
     N.   They said to him, "The very essence of their [our] father is
             thievery, as it is said, 'And he shall be a wild ass of a man' (Gen.
             16:12)."

O.   And so it went. He went to every nation, asking them, "Will you accept the Torah?"

P.   For so it is said, "All the kings of the earth shall give you thanks, O Lord, for they have heard the words of your mouth" (Ps. 138:4).

Q.   Might one suppose that they listened and accepted the Torah?

R.   Scripture says, "And I will execute vengeance in anger and fury upon the nations, because they did not listen" (Mic. 5:14).

S.   And it is not enough for them that they did not listen, but even the seven religious duties that the children of Noah indeed accepted upon themselves they could not uphold before breaking them.

T.   When the Holy One, blessed be He, saw that that is how things were, he gave them to Israel.

The amplification of the cited verse reaches a climax in its praising Israel for accepting the Torah after all the other nations declined it or proved incapable. No myth of the Dual Torah intervenes, for example, to show the uniqueness of Israel. The following passages provide other occasions for the appearance of the myth, for example, when God spoke to Moses, part of what he said was written down, part not; or he spoke in such a way that interpretation was invited. We find nothing of such conceptions, which are indicative of the presence of the myth of the Dual Torah. But the Torah marks Israel as unique among the nations, and that is a conception critical to the theory of Israel in the Yerushalmi.

Sifré to Deuteronomy Pisqa
CCCXLIII:X

1.   A.   "...lightning flashing at them from his right, [lover, indeed, of the people, their hallowed are all in your hand]:"

        B.   When the act of speech went forth from the mouth of the Holy One, blessed be He, it went out by the right of the Holy One, blessed be He, at the left of the Israelites, circumambulating the camp of Israel twelve *mils* by twelve *mils* and then returned along the right hand of Israel, at the left of the Holy One, blessed be He.

        C.   The Holy One, blessed be He, would then receive it by his right hand and incise it upon a tablet.

        D.   And its voice would go forth from one end of the earth to the other,

        E.   As it is said, "The voice of the Lord hews out flames of fire" (Ps. 29:7).

Sifré to Deuteronomy Pisqa
CCCXLIII:XI

1.   A.   "Lightning flashing at them from his right, [lover, indeed, of the people, their hallowed are all in your hand]:"

        B.   This tells us that the words of the Torah are compared to fire.

        C.   Just as fire is given from Heaven, so words of the Torah were given from Heaven, as it is said, "You yourselves have seen that I have talked with you from Heaven" Ex. 20:19).

D.   Just as fire lives forever, so words of the Torah live forever.

E.   Just as if a man comes close to fire, he is burned, but if he stands far from it, he is cold, so in the case of words of the Torah, so long as a person labors in them, they live for him. When he leaves off from them, they kill him.

F.   Just as people make use of fire in this world and in the world to come, so people make use of words of the Torah in this world and in the world to come.

G.   Just as whoever makes use of fire leaves a mark on his body, so whoever makes use of words of the Torah makes a mark on his body.

H.   Just as whoever works in fire is readily distinguished among people, so disciples of sages are readily distinguished in the market by the way they walk, by the way they talk, and by the way they cloak themselves.

The upshot is simple. Where we speak of the Torah and of the giving of the Torah, we hear nothing at all about the dual medium of revelation. This result is confirmed in Kosovsky's *Osar leshon Hattanaim* for the two Sifrés, which contains no reference to either *Torah shebikhtab* or *Torah shebeal peh*. But the sense of Torah here vastly transcends the rather limited meaning accorded to the word by the Mishnah and related writings (Avot, Tosefta). And, as we shall now see, Sifré to Deuteronomy represents the Torah as a source of salvific truth, as a gnostic Torah, and the materials before us are entirely congruent to that theory of the Torah. So while the evidence of Sifré to Deuteronomy as to the myth of the Dual Torah is to be judged as negative, the materials on the Torah as a source of salvific knowledge, even the ones before us now, place the document well within the orbit of the Yerushalmi.

III

The Gnostic Torah

1. The Mishnah as against the Yerushalmi

This leads us to a second aspect of the doctrine of the Torah in the Yerushalmi and related writings, in addition to the myth of the Dual Torah, derived from the effects of learning, the view of knowing the Torah as a gnostic experience. In the expansion of the sense of the Torah, "Torah" came to stand for not only the dual media of revelation but also a kind of regenerated human being. If people wanted to explain how they would be saved, they would use the word *Torah*. If they wished to sort out their parlous relationships with gentiles, they would use the word *Torah*. Torah stood for salvation and accounted for Israel's this-worldly condition and the hope, for both individual and nation alike, of life in the world to come. Hence knowing the Torah changed the individual and reformed Israel, and that kind of knowledge we call gnostic.

What I mean by "the gnostic Torah" – gnostic with a small g – and why whether or not the knowledge of the Torah is deemed gnostic may be explained in a very simple way. The word *gnostic* refers to knowledge that bears meaning beyond (mere) information or even illumination; gnostic learning transforms the knower. The concept of the Torah as gnostic means, therefore, that by studying the Torah a person is changed from what he or she had been into something else, and that change does not derive merely from knowledge, but from the impact of knowing upon the being of the person. Gnosis is knowledge that saves, transforms the one who knows, and what is changed in the one who knows is not mind alone but heart, soul, virtue, and character. In the context of the Dual Torah, study of Torah endows the disciple of the sage with supernatural power, and that has nothing to do with mere acquisition of information.

To make this more graphic and accessible, let me explain in personal terms. What happens to me in Torah study in the theory of the Yerushalmi and related compilations that does not happen to me in Torah study in the theory of the Mishnah is that I am changed in my very being, not alone as to knowledge or even as to virtue and taxic status, but as to what I am. I become something different from, better and more holy than, what I was. In this context, Torah and the study thereof transform and save the disciple of the sage.

To define the category of the Torah as a source of salvation, as the Yerushalmi states matters, I point to a story that explicitly states the proposition that the Torah constitutes a source of salvation. In this story we shall see that because people observed the rules of the Torah, they expected to be saved. And if they did not observe, they accepted their punishment. So the Torah now stands for something more than revelation and life of study, and (it goes without saying) the sage now appears as a holy, not merely a learned, man. This is because his knowledge of the Torah has transformed him. Accordingly, we deal with a category of stories and sayings about the Torah entirely different from what has gone before.

Y. Taanit 3:8

II.   A.   As to Levi ben Sisi: troops came to his town. He took a scroll of the Torah and went up to the roof and said, "Lord of the ages! If a single word of this scroll of the Torah has been nullified [in our town], let them come up against us, and if not, let them go their way."

B.   Forthwith people went looking for the troops but did not find them [because they had gone their way].

C.   A disciple of his did the same thing, and his hand withered, but the troops went their way.

D.   A disciple of his disciple did the same thing. His hand did not wither, but they also did not go their way.

E.   This illustrates the following apophthegm: You can't insult an idiot, and dead skin does not feel the scalpel.

What is interesting here is how taxa into which the word *Torah* previously fell have been absorbed and superseded in a new taxon. The Torah is an object: "He took a scroll...." It also constitutes God's revelation to Israel: "If a single word...." The outcome of the revelation is to form an ongoing way of life, embodied in the sage himself: "A disciple of his did the same thing...." The sage plays an intimate part in the supernatural event: "His hand withered...." Now can we categorize this story as a statement that the Torah constitutes a particular object, or a source of divine revelation, or a way of life? Yes and no. The Torah represents one more thing which takes in all the others. Torah is a source of salvation. How so? The Torah stands for, or constitutes, the way in which the people Israel saves itself from marauders. This straightforward sense of salvation will not have surprised the author of Deuteronomy.

In the canonical documents up to the Yerushalmi, we look in vain for sayings or stories that fall into such a category. True, we may take for granted that everyone always believed that, in general, Israel would be saved by obedience to the Torah. That claim would not have surprised any Israelite writers from the first prophets down through the final redactors of the Pentateuch in the time of Ezra and onward through the next seven hundred years. But, in the rabbinical corpus from the Mishnah forward, the specific and concrete assertion that by taking up the scroll of the Torah and standing on the roof of one's house, confronting God in Heaven, a sage in particular could take action against the expected invasion – that kind of claim is not located, so far as I know, in any composition surveyed so far.

Still, we cannot claim that the belief that the Torah in the hands of the sage constituted a source of magical, supernatural, and hence salvific power, simply did not flourish prior, let us say, to ca. 400 C.E. All we can say with assurance is that no stories containing such a viewpoint appear in any rabbinical document associated with the Mishnah. So what is critical here is not the generalized category – the genus – of conviction that the Torah serves as the source of Israel's salvation. It is the concrete assertion – the speciation of the genus – that in the hands of the sage and under conditions specified, the Torah may be utilized in pressing circumstances as Levi, his disciple, and the disciple of his disciple, used it. That is what is new.

This stunningly new usage of Torah found in the Talmud of the Land of Israel emerges from a group of stories not readily classified in our established categories. All of these stories treat the word *Torah* (whether scroll, contents, or act of study) as source and guarantor of salvation. Accordingly, evoking the word *Torah* forms the centerpiece of a theory of Israel's history, on the one side, and an account of the teleology of the entire system, on the other. Torah indeed has ceased to constitute a specific thing or even a category or classification when stories about studying the Torah yield not a judgment as to status (i.e., praise for the learned man) but promise for supernatural blessing now and salvation in time to come.

To the rabbis the principal salvific deed was to "study Torah," by which they meant memorizing Torah sayings by constant repetition, and, as the Talmud itself amply testifies (for some sages) profound analytic inquiry into the meaning of those sayings. The innovation now is that this act of "study of Torah" imparts supernatural power of a material character. For example, by repeating words of Torah, the sage could ward off the angel of death and accomplish other kinds of miracles as well. So Torah formulas served as incantations. Mastery of Torah transformed the man engaged in Torah learning into a supernatural figure, who could do things ordinary folk could not do. The category of "Torah" had already vastly expanded so that through transformation of the Torah from a concrete thing to a symbol, a Torah scroll could be compared to a man of Torah, namely, a rabbi. Now, once the principle had been established, that salvation would come from keeping God's will in general, as Israelite holy men had insisted for so many centuries, it was a small step for rabbis to identify their particular corpus of learning, namely, the Mishnah and associated sayings, with God's will expressed in Scripture, the universally acknowledged medium of revelation.

The key to the first Talmud's theory of the Torah lies in its conception of the sage, to which that theory is subordinate. Once the sage reaches his full apotheosis as Torah incarnate, then, but only then, the Torah becomes (also) a source of salvation in the present concrete formulation of the matter. That is why we traced the doctrine of the Torah in the salvific process by elaborate citation of stories about sages, living Torahs, exercising the supernatural power of the Torah, and serving, like the Torah itself, to reveal God's will. Since the sage embodied the Torah and gave the Torah, the Torah naturally came to stand for the principal source of Israel's salvation, not merely a scroll, on the one side, or a source of revelation, on the other.

The marks of the transformation emerge in the supernatural power that I have by reason of my (new) knowledge, learning in the Torah. That is what I mean by the new learning and what justifies the classification of Torah learning as *gnostic*. For when (mere) knowledge so transforms the knower that he or she is deemed "saved," or otherwise transformed into something utterly different from the condition characteristic of the prior one marked by ignorance and by unredemption, then that knowledge may be called gnostic. For in general, by *gnostic*, with a small g, people mean salvific knowledge, transitive, transformative learning, joining the two quite distinct categories of intellect and personal salvation or regeneration.[1]

That jarring juxtaposition, identifying ignorance (not knowing a given fact) with one's personal condition – that of unregeneracy –

---

[1] I of course bypass the word *Gnostic* with a capital G, bearing quite specific meanings in the study of late antiquity. A variety of meanings circulate, attached to various writings. What the common adjective, *gnostic*, with the denotative adjective, *Gnostic*, have in common is that the latter falls into the class of the former: saving knowledge.

relates what need not, and commonly is not, correlated. The moral or existential condition of the person hardly is to be routinely treated as an indicator of the level of intellectual enlightenment of that same person. Certainly the framers of the Mishnah did not imagine that such a correlation could be made, nor did their heirs for quite some time. But in the Yerushalmi and related compilations of Midrash exegeses, a principal point of integration of what the Mishnah's philosophy had deemed distinct was between knowledge and one's condition or classification as to supernatural things. Knowledge of the Torah, quite specifically, changed a person and made him (never her) simply different from what he had been before or without that same knowledge: physically weaker, but also strengthened by power that we might call magical, but that they called supernatural. A principal indicator of the Yerushalmi's position, then, is the transformative and salvific power imputed to knowledge of the Torah, and an equally indicative trait of the Mishnah's view is the position that knowledge of the Torah forms a taxic indicator as to status, but not a medium for the transformation of the one who knows from one thing to something else.

The single example of the gnostic theory of Torah learning given above suffices. The story explicitly states the proposition that obeying the Torah, with obedience founded on one's own knowledge thereof, constitutes the source of salvation. In this story we noted that because people observed the rules of the Torah, they expected to be saved. And if they did not observe, they accepted their punishment. So the Torah now stands for something more than revelation and life of study, and (it goes without saying) the sage now appears as a holy, not merely a learned, man. This is because his knowledge of the Torah has transformed him. Accordingly, we deal with a category of stories and sayings about the Torah entirely different from what has gone before.

In the Talmud of the Land of Israel, therefore, we discern an approach to the mere learning of the Torah – as distinct from obedience to its rules – that promises not merely intellectual enlightenment but personal renewal or transfiguration or some other far-reaching change. And since that view presents a gnostic[2] reading of learning, in the Yerushalmi and related compilations of Midrash exegeses we confront a Torah (the Dual Torah of the preceding chapter), knowledge of which not merely informs or presents right rules of conduct, but which transforms, regenerates, saves.[3] In that context and by these

---

[2]Resorting to the adjective *faustian*, while defensible, seems to me less exact.
[3]Obviously, this *gnostic* is with a small g; I in no way mean to identify the Torah of the successor-Judaism with the Gnostic systems, Christian, Judaic, and

definitions, the theory of the Torah and of Torah study set forth in the
the Yerushalmi and associated Midrash compilations promises a fully
realized transformation to those who study and therefore know the
Torah. They gained not merely intellectual enlightenment but
supernatural power and standing. In this context, that encompassed
such salvation as would take place prior to the end of time. The new
learning defined as the consequence of Torah study imputed by the
Talmud of the Land of Israel, Genesis Rabbah, Leviticus Rabbah, and
Pesiqta deRab Kahana – but not by the Mishnah and its companions,
tractate Avot and the Tosefta – changes not merely the mind but the
moral and salvific condition of the one who engages in that learning.

Since the indicative category defined here defies a generally held,
but false, conception of the meaning of Torah learning in the Mishnah,
Tosefta, and Avot, a somewhat protracted survey of the effects of
Torah learning, their effects upon the one who studies, is required. The
conception of the gnostic Torah, as just now defined, will have surprised
the philosophers represented by the Mishnah.[4] For if we ask

---

pagan, of which we have knowledge in the same time and place, as well as
earlier and later. My supposition is that, in any religious system, the
intellectual component by the nature of the systemic setting is going to bear
the same transformative and salvific valence as I show here pertained to the
Torah. The counterparts in other religions, which impute to knowledge of the
correct sort in the proper manner salvific power, are numerous. That seems to
me to justify treating *gnostic* as a generic classification for religious knowledge.
But is there religious knowledge that is not gnostic, but merely (for one
example) validating or qualifying? Indeed, there is a great deal of such
knowledge, and the Mishnah's conception of knowing, as set forth in the
apologetic of tractate Avot, is exactly of that kind. There, as we shall see,
studying the Torah brings God's presence to join those who repeat Torah
words, whether one or many. But there is no consequent claim that the Torah
words' repetition has changed those who have said them, only that God has
joined their study circle. And that claim is of a considerably different kind from
the one we shall see in numerous stories of the correlation between knowing
the Torah and supernatural power.

[4]And hardly them alone. For the prevailing philosophical traditions the
consequence of enlightenment in intellect cannot be said to have
encompassed personal salvation (let alone national salvation, such as, in the
Yerushalmi, was covered as well). Virtue depended upon right thinking, e.g.,
knowing what is the good, the true, and the beautiful. But the consequence of
that knowledge did not commonly yield supernatural power in the
philosophical systems of Greco-Roman antiquity. And, along these same lines,
knowledge of the Torah served, e.g., the Israelite priesthood as a medium of
validation, in that through knowledge they knew how to do their job, but it was a
job that they got by reason of genealogy, not knowledge, as Mishnah-tractate
Yoma 1:3 has already reminded us. So too, the Israelite scribal profession

ourselves, where, in the Mishnah, do we find promises of transformation of the person effected through study of the Torah? these concern only the issue of one's status in the hierarchical order of being, but not one's very character and essence. Quite to the contrary, as to the Mishnah's generative concerns on taxonomy, knowledge of the Torah changed nothing; the *mamzer* who mastered the Torah remained in the caste of the *mamzer*, so that, while if he lost his ass along with others, his would be returned first, still, he could not marry the daughter of a priest or even an Israelite. That means the transformation in no way affected the being of the man, but only his virtue.

True, we find at M. Hagigah 2:1 statements that have suggested to some[5] knowledge possessed traits of an other-than-wholly secular character, in that correct knowledge required attention to status (sage) and also the source and character of learning ("understands of his own knowledge," whatever that means):

Mishnah-tractate Hagigah 2:1

A. They do not expound upon the laws of prohibited relationships [Lev. 18] before three persons, the works of creation [Gen. 13] before two, or the Chariot [Ezek. 1] before one,

B. unless he was a sage and understands of his own knowledge.

C. Whoever reflects upon four things would have been better off had he not been born:

D. what is above, what is below, what is before, and what is beyond.

E. And whoever has no concern for the glory of his Maker would have been better off had he not been born.

These sentences have been quite plausibly interpreted to refer to personal, not merely intellectual, change effected by knowledge, hence to a gnostic reading of learning.

But they then do not impute to Torah study as such, that is, as a general classification of intellectual activity, the potentiality of (dangerous) change in one's own being. They speak of only specific topics and texts. The statements before us identify a very few specific

---

identified knowledge of the Torah as the foundation of their professional qualification.

[5]It is conventional to read the following as *Gnostic,* for instance, note Gershom G. Scholem, *Jewish Gnosticism, Merkabah Mysticism, and Talmudic Tradition* (New York, 1960: Jewish Theological Seminary of America). Taking the attributions at face value, moreover, various scholars, typified by Scholem, have forthwith assigned to "Judaism," or to "the rabbis" a fully realized Gnostic experience. But if they had not decided in advance that these sayings had to mean what they suppose they mean, the proponents of such views about the condition of "Judaism" in the first century will have had to consider a variety of meanings and alternatives, including the one that we simply do not know what is going on in these statements.

passages and do not contain the conception that studying the Torah in general constitutes a transformative and salvific action. Their specificity may justify spelling the adjective *Gnostic,* but not *gnostic.*[6] At best, therefore, we may say that, within the compilation of the authorship of the Mishnah, we find *in nuce* the possibility of a gnostic approach to knowledge; but that very representation, unrealized in context, hardly extends to the entirety of learning in the Torah and indeed by its formulation precludes such a general approach to the act of intellect performed upon the Torah.

A survey of the Mishnah's and tractate Avot's theory of what happens to me because I study the Torah that will not happen to me if I do not readies us to see what is fresh and unprecedented in the representation of the same matter in the Yerushalmi and associated Midrash compilations.[7] When we come to tractate Avot, a generation beyond the Mishnah, we find heavy emphasis upon the importance of correlating one's actions with one's knowledge. A variety of sayings insist that if one knows the Torah but does not act in accord with its teachings, one gains nothing. One must change one's life to conform with one's knowledge of the Torah. That point of insistence, of course, invites as its next, small step, the doctrine that knowing the Torah changes one in being and essence, not only intellectually, by reason of illumination, but taxically, by reason of transformation. But the gnostic Torah, which would treat knowing the Torah on its own as a medium for one's transformation from merely natural to supernatural character,[8]

---

[6]And here, in the received scholarly tradition in all languages, Gnostic with a capital G is routinely given. But that seems to me to read into the passage much that is not explicit and need not be present at all; still, I admit, I do not claim to understand the passage at all, nor those in proximity in the Tosefta.

[7]Without a full review of the sayings on the relationship of learning to one's personal condition as to salvation, what is fully new in the later documents will not be discerned. The nuances of language here do matter, especially since the received reading of the sayings surveyed in the following paragraphs imposes upon them the supernatural valence accorded only in the later writings to Torah knowledge or Torah study. Here the master of Torah learning is saved only by what he does in consequence of what he knows, or by matching what he knows with what he does. Knowing by itself does not save, though it can affect attitudes that will affect one's actions in one way rather than in some other, and right action will then yield salvation. Not only so, but Torah study will draw God's presence among those who study, but that does not yield the claim either that the sages are changed or that they thereby gain supernatural power. None of the indicators of the gnostic Torah occur, but only by the following survey will readers appreciate how much has been read into the sayings adduced in behalf of the contrary view.

[8]Indeed, the emphasis on the importance of correlating learning and deed and on the priority of deed seems to me to deny that very correlation of learning

would be some time in coming and would make its appearance only in the Yerushalmi and related compilations of Midrash exegeses.

A survey of tractate Avot yields no such conception, but only the point that knowledge must be confirmed in deeds, a conception of moral but not existential weight, as in the following saying in Avot:

Tractate Avot 1:17
> A.   Simeon his son says, "Not the learning is the main thing but the doing. And whoever talks too much causes sin."

True, the statement that if one keeps his eye on three things, he will not sin, can yield the conception that knowledge bears salvific consequence. But that does not speak of a personal transformation in one's status and condition. The knowledge that saves me from sin is instrumental, not transformative:

> "Know what is above you: (1) An eye which sees, and (2) an ear which hears, and (3) all your actions are written down in a book."

The same conception, that knowledge is essential to attitudes that bring salvation, is stated in the following:

Tractate Avot 3:1
> A.   Aqabiah b. Mehallalel says, "Reflect upon three things and you will not fall into the clutches of transgression:
> B.   "Know (1) from whence you come, (2) whither you are going, and (3) before whom you are going to have to give a full account [of yourself].
> C.   "From whence do you come? From a putrid drop.
> D.   "Whither are you going? To a place of dust, worms, and maggots.
> E.   "And before whom are you going to give a full account of Yourself? Before the King of kings of kings, the Holy One, blessed be He."

We have not strayed far from the notion that knowledge of the Torah promises a good reward here and after death because it keeps me from sin, that is to say, the position, vis-à-vis studying a trade, of Nehorai. Here again, what I get for knowing treats knowledge as necessary in an instrumental sense; it yields a given goal, it does not effect a desired transformation. A promise that in context is quite consistent is that, if I study the Torah, I encounter God:

---

with transformation. Merely knowing is insufficient. But to a gnostic theory of knowledge, merely knowing itself saves. So I suppose proponents of the theory of a Gnostic Judaism of the first and second centuries will adduce these statements as evidence of not Gnostic Judaism but a reaction against Gnostic Judaism. But the evidence once more would then be asked to bear too heavy a burden of interpretation.

Tractate Avot 3:2

C.   R. Hananiah b. Teradion says, "[If] two sit together and between them do not pass teachings of Torah, lo, this is a seat of the scornful....

E.   "Two who are sitting, and words of Torah do pass between them – the Presence is with them, as it is said, 'Then they that feared the Lord spoke with one another, and the Lord hearkened and heard, and a book of remembrance was written before him, for them that feared the Lord and gave thought to His name' (Mal. 3:16)...."

G.   I know that this applies to two.

H.   How do I know that even if a single person sits and works on Torah, the Holy One, blessed be He, sets aside a reward for him? As it is said, 'Let him sit alone and keep silent, because he has laid it upon him' (Lam. 3:28)."

Tractate Avot 3:6

A.   R. Halafta of Kefar Hananiah says, "Among ten who sit and work hard on Torah the Presence comes to rest,

B.   "As it is said, 'God stands in the congregation of God' (Ps. 82:1).

C.   "And how do we know that the same is so even of five? For it is said, 'And he has founded his group upon the earth' (Amos. 9:6).

D.   "And how do we know that this is so even of three? Since it is said, 'And he judges among the judges' (Ps. 82:1).

E.   "And how do we know that this is so even of two? Because it is said, 'Then they that feared the Lord spoke with one another, and the Lord hearkened and heard' (Mal. 3:16).

F.   "And how do we know that this is so even of one? Since it is said, 'In every place where I record my name I will come to you and I will bless you' (Ex. 20:24)."

"Knowing God" or bringing God into one's study circle certainly represent desirable goals of illumination. But these do not encompass the transformative experience promised the one who knows – as we shall see – by the gnostic theory of the Torah. Why not? Because even though God has joined my study circle and brought the divine presence to rest among the disciples, we still do not then claim supernatural powers as the consequence; in neither the Mishnah nor the Tosefta nor Avot do we find the claim that the disciple of the sage by reason of his learning does miracles.[9]

---

[9]The contrary view, that the one who does miracles is not necessarily a disciple of a sage, though he may be a holy man, is presented at Mishnah-tractate Taanit 3:8 with reference to Honi, for one instance. What is important to my argument is simply that no one correlates Torah learning with wonder-working. Whether or not the component of the canon represented by the Mishnah and its associated writings favors wonder-working or opposes it, fears it, or admires it, is not at stake here. What concerns me is the working of the categories, and the process of category formation adumbrated by the correlation of distinct

The contrast between getting a good name for oneself and getting the world to come, in the following saying, also is not quite to the point:

> "[If] one has gotten a good name, he has gotten it for himself. [If] he has gotten teachings of Torah, he has gotten himself life eternal."

Here we speak of repute, a form of virtue, but not wonder-working. The same point as Simeon's, above, moreover comes to the fore in the following:

Tractate Avot 3:9

A. R. Haninah b. Dosa says, "For anyone whose fear of sin takes precedence over his wisdom, his wisdom will endure,

B. "And for anyone whose wisdom takes precedence over his fear of sin, his wisdom will not endure."

C. He would say, "Anyone whose deeds are more than his wisdom – his wisdom will endure.

D. "And anyone whose wisdom is more than his deeds – his wisdom will not endure."

Tractate Avot 3:17

I. He would say, "Anyone whose wisdom is greater than his deeds – to what is he to be likened? To a tree with abundant foliage, but few roots.

J. "When the winds come, they will uproot it and blow it down,

K. "As it is said, 'He shall be like a tamarisk in the desert and shall not see when good comes but shall inhabit the parched places in the wilderness' (Jer. 17:6).

L. "But anyone whose deeds are greater than his wisdom – to what is he to be likened? To a tree with little foliage but abundant roots.

M. "For even if all the winds in the world were to come and blast at it, they will not move it from its place,

N. "As it is said, 'He shall be as a tree planted by the waters, and that spreads out its roots by the river, and shall not fear when heat comes, and his leaf shall be green, and shall not be careful in the year of drought, neither shall cease from yielding fruit' (Jer. 17:8)."

Tractate Avot 4:5

A. R. Ishmael, his son, says, "He who learns so as to teach – they give him a chance to learn and to teach.

B. "He who learns so as to carry out his teachings – they give him a chance to learn, to teach, to keep, and to do."

A variety of sayings, indeed, explicitly identify not Torah learning but other virtues as primary, and furthermore scarcely concede to Torah learning transformative, let alone salvific, power:

---

categories simply has not taken place by the end of the formation of the Mishnah's component of the canon of the Dual Torah.

Tractate Avot 4:13
  C.   R. Simeon says, "There are three crowns: the crown of Torah, the
          crown of priesthood, and the crown of sovereignty.
  D.   "But the crown of a good name is best of them all."

Tractate Avot 4:17
  A.   He would say, "Better is a single moment spent in penitence and
          good deeds in this world than the whole of the world to come.
  B.   "And better is a single moment of inner peace in the world to
          come than the whole of a lifetime spent in this world."

These and similar sayings attest to a variety of modes of human
regeneration, none of them connected with Torah learning in particular.

Now, as a matter of fact, in the Yerushalmi and associated
Midrash compilations, a quite different theory of Torah learning
predominates. It is the simple fact that knowledge of the Torah
changes the one who knows. He becomes physically weaker,[10] but
gains, in compensation, supernatural powers. The legitimating power of
the Torah and study thereof imputed in the pages of the Talmud of the
Land of Israel is explicit: knowledge of the Torah changes a man into a
sage and also saves Israel. The Torah then involves not mere
knowledge, for example, correct information, valid generalization, but
gnosis: saving knowledge.[11]

To the rabbis the principal salvific deed was to "study Torah," by
which they meant memorizing Torah sayings by constant repetition,
and, as the Talmud itself amply testifies, (for some sages) profound
analytic inquiry into the meaning of those sayings. This act of "study of
Torah" imparted supernatural power. For example, by repeating words
of Torah, the sage could ward off the angel of death and accomplish
other kinds of miracles as well. So Torah formulas served as
incantations. Mastery of Torah transformed the man who engaged in
Torah learning into a supernatural figure, able to do things ordinary
folk could not do. In the nature of things, the category of Torah was
vastly expanded so that the symbol of Torah, a Torah scroll, could be
compared to a man of Torah, namely, a rabbi. Since what made a man
into a sage or a disciple of a sage or a rabbi was studying the Torah

---

[10]As we noted in Chapter Two.

[11]One important qualification is required. Knowledge is not the only medium
of salvation. Salvation, as before, derives from keeping the law of the Torah.
Keeping the law in the right way is the way to bring the Messiah, the son of
David. This is stated by Levi, as follows."If Israel would keep a single Sabbath
in the proper way, forthwith the son of David would come" (Y. Taanit 1:1.IX.X,
cited above). But the issue of not doing but (mere) knowing, of salvation
through study of the Torah, is distinct.

through discipleship, what is at stake in the symbolic transfer is quite obvious. A very brief repertoire on this matter suffices, since it is a very familiar conception.

Knowledge of the Torah itself changed the sage in such a way that he not only could manipulate the supernatural power inhering in the Torah but also could himself join in the processes of forming the Torah. For the man himself was transformed through Torah study. Specifically, if I know the Torah, I can join in the making of the Torah, and that claim in my behalf as a sage forms solid evidence of the allegation that studying the Torah not only endows one with power but actually changes the man from what he had been into something else. He had been ordinary, now he is not merely powerful but holy. And his holiness is shown by the fact that, just as we study the Torah in its written and oral forms, so we may study the Torah in its quotidian form: the sage himself, his gestures, his actions then forming precedents valid within the practice of the Torah itself. And when I allege that because I have studied the Torah, I am changed so that I can now join in the process of revealing the Torah, studying the Torah provides a gnostic experience of transformation, regeneration, and salvation. Accordingly, I have now to demonstrate that the supernatural status accorded to the person of the sage endowed his deeds with normative, therefore revelatory power.

What the sage did had the status of law; the sage was the model of the law, thus having been changed, transformed, regenerated, saved, turned by studying the Torah into the human embodiment of the Torah. That gnostic view of Torah study as transformative and salvific – now without explicit appeal to deeds in conformity to the law, though surely that is taken for granted – accounts for the position that the sage was a holy man. For what made the sage distinctive was his combination of this-worldly authority and power and otherworldly influence. The clerk in the court and the holy man on the rooftop praying for rain or calling Heaven to defend the city against marauders, in the Yerushalmi's view were one and the same. The tight union between salvation and law, the magical power of the sage and his lawgiving authority, was effected through the integrative act of studying the Torah. And that power of integration accounts for the Yerushalmi and related compilations of Midrash exegeses's insistence that if the sage exercised supernatural power as a kind of living Torah, his very deeds served to reveal law, as much as his word expressed revelation.

The correlation between learning and teaching, on the one side, and supernatural power or recognition, on the other, is explicit in the following.

Y. *Ketubot* 12:3.

VII A.   R. Yosa fasted eighty fasts in order to see R. Hiyya the Elder [in a
          dream]. He finally saw him, and his hands trembled and his eyes
          grew dim.

    B.   Now if you say that R. Yosa was an unimportant man, [and so was
          unworthy of such a vision, that is not the case]. For a weaver came
          before R. Yohanan. He said to him, "I saw in my dream that the
          heaven fell, and one of your disciples was holding it up."

    C.   He said to him, "Will you know him [when you see him]?"

    D.   He said to him, "When I see him, I shall know him." Than all of
          his disciples passed before him, and he recognized R. Yosa.

    E.   R. Simeon b. Laqish fasted three hundred fasts in order to have a
          vision of R. Hiyya the Elder, but he did not see him.

    F.   Finally he began to be distressed about the matter. He said, "Did
          he labor in learning of Torah more than I?"

    G.   They said to him, "He brought Torah to the people of Israel to a
          greater extent than you have, and not only so, but he even went
          into exile [to teach on a wider front]."

    H.   He said to them, "And did I not go into exile too?"

    I.   They said to him, "You went into exile only to learn, but he went
          into exile to teach others."

This story shows that the storyteller regarded as a fact of life the
correlation between mastery of Torah sayings and supernatural power –
visions of the deceased, in this case. That is why Simeon b. Laqish
complained, E-F, that he had learned as much Torah as the other, and
so had every right to be able to conjure the dead. The greater
supernatural power of the other then was explained in terms of the
latter's superior service to "Torah." The upshot is that the sage was
changed by Torah learning and could save Israel through Torah.
Enough has been set forth to suggest that I mean to represent the gnostic
Torah as the centerpiece of the Yerushalmi and related compilations of
Midrash exegeses.

In unifying the distinct categories of learning and not deeds or
virtue but one's personal condition in the supernatural world, the
recasting of the category of the worldview from an intellectual and
even a moral to a salvific and a supernatural indicator, the Yerushalmi
and related compilations of Midrash exegeses integrate what the
Mishnah had kept distinct. If Torah study changes me not only in my
knowledge or status or even virtue but in my relationship to Heaven,
therefore endowing me with the supernatural power, then the system
as a whole signals a union of Heaven and earth that was formerly
unimagined. What I know concerns not only earth but Heaven, the
power that knowledge brings governs in both realms. Study of the
Torah changed the one who studied because through it he entered into
the mind of God, learning how God's mind worked when God formed the

Torah, written and oral alike and (in the explicit view of Genesis Rabbah 1:1) consulted the Torah in created the world. And there, in the intellect of God, in their judgment humanity gained access to the only means of uniting intellect with existential condition as to salvation.

The Mishnah had set forth the rules that governed the natural world in relationship to Heaven. But knowledge of the Torah now joined the one world, known through nature, with the other world, the world of supernature, where, in the end, intellect merely served in the quest for salvation. Through Torah study sages claimed for themselves a place in that very process of thought that had given birth to nature; but it was a supernatural process, and knowledge of that process on its own terms would transform and, in the nature of things, save. That explains the integrative power of imputing supernatural power to learning. And, now that we realize what was at stake in the gnostic Torah, we see why the presence of the conception of the gnostic Torah, as much as of the Dual Torah, indicates we stand close to the Yerushalmi and related writings, the absence of that theory of the Torah correlates with a situation close to the Mishnah.

The evidence we seek is not verbal but narrative or exhortatory. Do we find in the so-called Tannaitic Midrashim stories[12] about how because the sage masters the Torah, he possesses supernatural powers? Such stories would signify the presence of a conception of the Torah congenial to the Yerushalmi and alien to the Mishnah. Do we find exhortations to study the Torah as a medium of attaining salvation? Is study of the Torah represented as bearing implications for one's supernatural capacities? Then we stand close to the position of the Yerushalmi and distant from that of the Mishnah, inclusive of Avot.

2. Mekhilta Attributed to R. Ishmael

I find nothing relevant to the conception of the sage as supernatural or of knowledge of the Torah as a source of transformative power.

3. Sifra

The following exposition of Lev. 26:3-13 seems to me to signal the presence of a conception of Torah knowledge and Torah study nearer to that of the Yerushalmi than to that of the Mishnah. I cite only bits and pieces of the whole.

---

[12]Since Maccoby refers to "the *aggadah*," it is legitimate to ask for stories or the absence of stories to serve as a principal indicator of the systemic position of a document. We shall make this point again where it is pertinent.

Sifra 260. Parashat Behuqotai Parashah 1
CCLX:I
1. B.   "If you walk in my statutes":
    C.   This teaches that the Omnipresent desires the Israelites to work in the Torah.
    D.   And so Scripture says, "O that my people would listen to me, that Israel would walk in my ways! I would soon subdue their enemies and turn my hand against their foes" (Ps. 81:13-14).
    E.   O that you had hearkened to my commandments! Then your peace would have been like a river, and your righteousness like the waves of the sea; your offspring would have been like the sand, and your descendants like its grains; their name would never be cut off or destroyed from before me" (Isa. 48:18).
    F.   And so Scripture says, "Oh that they had such a mind as this always, to fear me and to keep all my commandments, that it might go well with them and with their children for ever" (Dt. 5:29).
    G.   This teaches that the Omnipresent desires the Israelites to work in the Torah.
2. A.   "If you walk in my statutes":
    B.   Might this refer to the religious duties?
    C.   When Scripture says, "and observe my commandments and do them,"
    D.   Lo, the religious duties are covered. Then how shall I interpret, "If you walk in my statutes"?
    E.   It is that they should work in the Torah.
    F.   And so it is said, "But if you will not hearken to me."
    G.   Might that refer to the religious duties?
    H.   When Scripture says, "and will not do all these commandments,"
    I.   Lo, the religious duties are covered.
    J.   If so, why is it said, "But if you will not hearken to me"?
    K.   It is that they should be working in the Torah.

Studying the Torah is valued as what God wants Israelites to do, and in the context of Lev. 26, we do not vastly exaggerate if we suppose that knowledge of the Torah serves not only to inform but also to transform. True, the matter is not explicit in the way in which, as I have shown, it is expressed in the Talmud and related writings. But Torah study in a supernatural context seems to me at least suggested here.

4. Sifré to Numbers 1-115

I found nothing pertinent.

5. Sifré to Deuteronomy

We have already noted, in Chapter Two, passages that seem to me to fall well within the framework of Torah study as a salvific or gnostic experience. Still more to the point are the discussions that follow.

Sifré to Deuteronomy Pisqa Forty-One

XLI:II

1. A. "That you may learn them and observe to do them" (Dt. 5:1):
    B. The phrasing of this clause indicates that deed depends on learning, and learning does not depend on deed.
    C. And so we find that a more severe penalty pertains to [neglect of] learning more than to [neglect of doing required] deeds.
    D. For it is said, "Hear the word of the Lord, you children of Israel. For the Lord has a controversy with the inhabitants of the land, because there is no truth nor mercy nor knowledge of God in the land" (Hos. 4:1).
    E. "...there is no truth": truthful words are not said: "Buy the truth and do not sell it [also wisdom, instruction, and understanding]" (Prov. 23:23).
    F. "...nor mercy": merciful words are not said: "The earth, O Lord, is full of your mercy" (Ps. 119:64).
    G. "...nor knowledge of God in the land": knowledgeable words are not said: "My people are destroyed for lack of knowledge [because you have rejected knowledge, I will also reject you, that you shall not be a priest of mine, seeing that you have forgotten the law of your God, I also will forget your children]" (Hos. 4:6).
6. A. And just as a more severe penalty pertains to [neglect of] learning more than to [neglect of doing required] deeds,
    B. so a more abundant reward pertains to learning than to the doing of required deeds,
    C. for it is said, "You shall teach them to your children, speaking of them" (Dt. 11:19).
    D. What is then said? "That your days may be multiplied and the days of your children" (Dt. 11:21).
    E. And further: "And he gave them the lands of the nations, and they took the labor of the peoples in possession; that they might keep his statutes and observe his laws" (Ps. 105:44-45).

Not only is the syllogism, 1.B, amply instantiated. It also predominates in the formation of this cogent statement, which time and again makes the point that study of the Torah is the more important category. No. 6 picks up the discourse of No. 1, as though nothing else had been inserted, yet further evidence to the imperfection of the whole. The paramount importance accorded to learning seems to me to invite the conception of learning as salvific.

Sifré to Deuteronomy Pisqa

XLI:III

1. A. "...that I enjoin upon you this day":
    B. How on the basis of Scripture may one show that if one has heard a teaching from the most unimportant person in Israel, it should

		be regarded by him as though he had heard it on the authority of a great sage?
	C.	Scripture says, "...that I enjoin upon you."
	D.	And it is not as if one has heard it only from a single sage, but as if one has heard it on the authority of the collegium of sages:
	E.	"The words of the sages are as goads" (Qoh. 12:11).
2.	A.	["The words of the sages are as goads" (Qoh. 12:11):] just as a goad guides an ox in its furrow to produce life-sustaining crops for its master,
	B.	so teachings of Torah guide a person's intellect to know the Omnipresent.
3.	A.	And it is not as if one has heard it merely on the authority of the collegium of sages, but as if one has heard it from a formally constituted sanhedrin:
	B.	"...Masters of assemblies" (Qoh. 12:11),
	C.	and "assemblies" refers only to the sanhedrin,
	D.	as it is said, "Assemble to me seventy men of the elders of Israel" (Num. 11:16).
	E.	And it is not as if one has heard it merely from a formally constituted sanhedrin, but as if one has heard it from the mouth of Moses:
	F.	"Then his people remembered the days of old, the days of Moses" (Isa. 63:11).
	G.	And it is not as if one has heard it from Moses, but as if one has heard it from the mouth of the Omnipotent God:
	H.	"They are given from one shepherd," "Give ear, shepherd of Israel, thou who leads Joseph like a flock" (Ps. 80:2), "Hear O Israel, the Lord our God, the Lord is one" (Ps. 6:4).

The basic proposition, B and its secondary expansion, yields the point that whatever Torah teaching one hears comes from God, without regard to the standing and authority of the person who repeats it. There is only one interruption in the smooth exposition from one stage to the next, and that is at No. 2. Beyond that point the flow is uninterrupted and compelling. The main point bears repeating: so teachings of Torah guide a person's intellect to know the Omnipresent.

Sifré to Deuteronomy

XLI:VI

1.	A.	"...and serving him [with all your heart and soul]":
	B.	This refers to study [of the Torah].
	C.	You say that it refers to study. But perhaps it refers only to actual service?
	D.	Lo, Scripture says, "And the Lord God took the man and put him into the Garden of Eden to work it and to guard it" (Gen. 2:15).
	E.	Now in the past what sort of work was there to do, and what sort of guarding was there to do?
	F.	But you learn from that statement that "to work it" refers to study of the Torah, and "to guard it" refers to keeping the religious duties.

G.   And just as the service at the altar is called work, so study of the Torah is called work.

The point is that studying the Torah is comparable to making a sacrifice on the altar. That then has nothing to do with mere acquisition of information. The act of learning bears supernatural weight.

Sifré to Deuteronomy

XLVIII:I

1.   A.   "If then you faithfully keep all this instruction [that I command you, loving the Lord your God, walking in all his ways, and holding fast to him, the Lord will dislodge before you all these nations; you will dispossess nations greater and more numerous than you. Every spot on which your foot treads shall be yours; your territory shall extend from the wilderness to the Lebanon, and from the River, the Euphrates, to the Western Sea. No man shall stand up to you: the Lord your God will put the dread and the fear of you over the whole land in which you set foot, as he promised you]" (Dt. 11:22-25):

   B.   Why is this said?

   C.   Since it is said, "And it shall come to pass, if you will certainly listen to my commandments," (Dt. 11:13), might I draw the inference that if someone has heard teachings of the Torah and rested on his laurels and not repeated [and so reviewed] them, [that suffices]?

   D.   Scripture says, "If then you faithfully keep...,"

   E.   which indicates that just as one has to take care of his coin, that it not get lost, so he has to take care of his learning, that it not get lost.

2.   A.   And so Scripture says, "If you seek her as silver" (Prov. 2:45) –

   B.   just as silver is hard to come by, so teachings of the Torah are hard to come by.

   C.   Might one then say, just as silver is hard to lose, so teachings of Torah are hard to lose?

   D.   Scripture says, "Gold and glass cannot equal it" (Prov. 2:4).

   E.   [Teachings of the Torah] are as hard to come by as gold and as easy to lose as glass.

   F.   "...neither shall the exchange thereof be vessels of fine gold" (Job 28:17).

3.   A.   R. Ishmael says, "'Only watch out and keep your soul diligently' (Dt. 4:9) –

   B.   "The matter may be compared to a mortal king who caught a bird and handed it over to his servant, saying to him, 'Keep this bird for my son. If you lose it, do not think that you lost a bird worth a penny, but it is tantamount to your life that you will have lost.'

   C.   "So Scripture says, "For it is no vain thing for you, because of it is your very life' (Dt. 32:47).

   D.   "Something that you say is vain in fact is your very life."

4.   A.   R. Simeon b. Yohai says, "The matter may be compared to the case of two brothers who inherited money from their father.

B.   "One of them converted it into ready cash and consumed it, and the other converted it into ready cash and put it aside.

C.   "As to the one of them who converted it into ready cash and consumed it, he turned out to have nothing in hand.

D.   "But the one who converted it into ready cash and put it aside got rich after a while.

E.   So disciples of sages learn two or three things in a day, two or three chapters in a week, two or three lections in a month. Such a one turns out to get rich after a while.

F.   "That is in line with the following verse of Scripture: "He who gathers little by little shall increase' (Prov. 13:11).

G.   "But the one who says, 'Today I shall learn [what I need], tomorrow I shall learn [what I need], today I shall review [what I need], tomorrow I shall review [what I need], turns out to have nothing in hand. And concerning him Scripture says, "A wise son gathers in summer, but a son who does shamefully sleeps in harvest' (Prov. 10:5).

H.   "And further: 'The sluggard will not plow when winter comes, therefore he shall beg in harvest and have nothing' (Prov. 20:4).

I.   "And further: 'He who observes the wind shall not sow' (Qoh. 11:4).

J.   "'I went by the field of the slothful man and by the vineyard of the man void of understanding, and lo, it was all grown over with thistles; the face of it was covered with nettles, and the stone wall was broken down' (Prov. 24:30-31)."

5. A.   ["I went by the field of the slothful man and by the vineyard of the man void of understanding, and lo, it was all grown over with thistles; the face of it was covered with nettles, and the stone wall was broken down" (Prov. 24:30-31):]

B.   "I went by the field of the slothful man": this refers to one who had already acquired a field.

C.   "...and by the vineyard of the man void of understanding": this refers to one who had already acquired a vineyard.

D.   Now since such a one had already acquired a field and already acquired a vineyard and is called a man, why is he then called slothful and void of understanding?

E.   It is because he acquired a field and a vineyard but did not work them.

F.   How do we know on the basis of Scripture that such a one in the end will leave two or three things in a lection [unlearned]?

G.   It is said, "...lo, it was all grown over with thistles; [the face of it was covered with nettles, and the stone wall was broken down]."

H.   And how do we know that he will seek the sense of the passage but not find it?

I.   "...the face of it was covered with nettles...."

J.   And concerning him Scripture says, "...and the stone wall was broken down...."

K.   Though such a person sees that nothing stayed with him, he nonetheless goes into session, declaring what is clean to be unclean and what is unclean to be clean and breaking down the walls constructed by sages.

L.   What punishment is inflicted on this? Solomon came and made
       it explicit in tradition: "Who breaks through a fence a serpent
       shall bite" (Qoh. 10:8).

M.   Whoever breaks through fences made by sages in the end will
       suffer punishments.

What is relevant to our problem is how high are the stakes of
Torah study. The desired theme is the importance of Torah study, and
this is introduced at No. 1. What the compositor wishes to say is that
someone must not only listen to Torah teachings but repeat them and
learn them faithfully. No. 2 then underlines the proposition
introduced at No. 1. No. 3 repeats the same matter, this time in a
parable of some immediacy. No. 4 then underlines the same conception,
but in a quite different way. No. 5 then repeats the same point, now in
an exegetical form. Forgetting one's learning bears consequences for the
person, not merely for knowledge. The opposite proposition then is the
one we seek: knowing has consequences for the person, not merely for the
intellect.

Sifré to Deuteronomy Pisqa

XLVIII:II

7. A.   And so Scripture says, "[Drink waters out of your own cistern, and
          running waters out of your own well.] Let your springs be
          dispersed abroad [and courses of water in the streets' (Prov. 5:15-
          16):

    B.   Teachings of the Torah are compared to water.

    C.   Just as water goes on forever, so teachings of the Torah are
          compared to water, as it is said, "For they are life to those who find
          them" (Prov. 4:22).

    D.   Just as water raises up out of their uncleanness things that have
          been made unclean, so teachings of the Torah raise up out of
          their uncleanness things that have been made unclean, as it is
          said, "Your word is tried to the utmost and your servant loves it"
          (Ps. 119:140).

    E.   Just as water restores the soul of a person, as it is said, "As cold
          waters to a faint soul" (Prov. 25:25), so teachings of the Torah
          restore the soul of a person, as it is said, "The Torah of the Lord is
          perfect, restoring the soul" (Ps. 19:8).

    F.   Just as water is free to all the world, so teachings of the Torah are
          there for the taking, as it is said, "Ho, everyone who is thirsty,
          come for water, and he who has no money, come and buy and eat
          without money" (Isa. 55:1).

    G.   Just as water is not subject to price, so teachings of the Torah are
          beyond all price, as it is said, "It is more precious than rubies"
          (Prov. 3:15).

    H.   Might one say, just as water does not make the heart happy [as
          wine does], so teachings of the Torah do not make the heart
          happy?

    I.   Scripture says, "For your love is better than wine" (Song 1:23).

J.   Just as wine makes the heart happy, so teachings of the Torah make the heart happy, as it is said, "The precepts of the Lord are right, rejoicing the heart" (Ps. 19:9).

K.   Just as in the case of wine, you cannot taste a good flavor in it at the outset, and the longer it ages in the bottle, the more it improves, so teachings of the Torah, as they age in the body, they continually improve, as it is said, "Wisdom is with aged men" (Job 12:12).

L.   Just as wine cannot be stored in silver or gold utensils, but only in the humbled of all utensils, one made of clay, so teachings of the Torah cannot endure in someone who in his own eyes is like a silver or a gold utensil, but only in someone who in his own eyes is like the humblest of vessels, in a clay utensil.

M.   Might one say, just as wine sometimes is bad for the head or bad for the body, so also teachings of the Torah are the same way?

N.   Scripture states, "Your ointments have a nice smell" (Song 1:3): just as oil is good for the head and good for the body, so teachings of the Torah are good for the head and good for the body,

O.   as it is said, "For they shall be a chaplet of grace for your head and chains around your neck" (Prov. 1:9).

P.   And so too: "She will give your head a chaplet of grace" (Prov. 4:9).

Q.   Teachings of Torah are compared to oil and honey, as it is said, "Sweeter also than honey and the honeycomb" (Ps. 19:11).

The theme of Torah study carries us to this vast composition in praises of teachings of the Torah. The pertinent verses bring us to two subthemes, first, the condition of the disciple, second, the worth of what the disciple studies, Torah teachings. The exegesis of Prov. 5:15-16 at Nos. 4-7 leads us to the secondary expansion that brings us to the end of this sustained paen. Once more, knowledge of the Torah transforms the disciple, not only as to status, which the Mishnah knows, but as to his standing in the supernatural world.

Sifré to Deuteronomy
CCCVI:XVI
1.   A.   "[May my discourse come down] as the rain,":
        B.   Just as the rain is life for the world, so words of Torah are life for the world.
        C.   Might one argue, in the case of rain, part of the world is happy with it and part is distressed by it.
        D.   Specifically, one whose well is full of wine and whose threshing floor is awaiting will be distressed by it.
        E.   Might one then maintain that the same is so of words of Torah?
        F.   Scripture says, "my speech distill as the dew,"
        G.   [bearing this implication:] just as the whole world is happy to have dew, so the whole world is happy with words of Torah.

The theme of rain comparable to teachings of Torah is developed in the proposition at hand, differentiating, in accord with Scripture's metaphor, between rain and words of Torah. We now find ourselves in a context in which "words of Torah" bear salvific weight and supernatural consequence.

Sifré to Deuteronomy Pisqa
CCCVI:XX
1. A. Another teaching concerning the phrase, "May my discourse come down as the rain, [my speech distill as the dew, like showers on young growths, like droplets on the grass]":
   B. R. Eliezer, son of R. Yosé the Galilean, says, "The word 'come down' bears the sense of 'slaughtering,'
   C. "for so it is said, 'Break the neck of the heifer in the valley [by throwing it down].' (Dt. 21:4).
   D. "For what sin does the heifer atone? It is for the sin of bloodshed.
   E. "So words of Torah atone for all transgressions."
2. A. "like showers on young growths":
   B. For what sin do goats [which word uses the same letters as the word for 'showers'] atone?
   C. It is for sins [done inadvertently].
   D. So words of Torah atone for all inadvertent sins.
3. A. "like droplets on the grass":
   B. Just as droplets come down whole and atone, so words of Torah effect atonement for all manner of sins and transgressions.

Study of the Torah is once more compared to sacrifices of the Temple cult. The new proposition relies on a somewhat forced reading of the pertinent verses, but the important point comes through with great power and clarity. It is now that through studying Torah Israel atones for sin. In my judgment, the gnostic character of Torah learning is fully exposed in that proposition.

Sifré to Deuteronomy Pisqa
CCCVI:XXVIII
2. A. And so did R. Simai say, "All creatures that are formed from the Heaven – their soul and body derives from Heaven, and all creatures that are formed from the earth – their soul and their body derive from the earth,
   B. "except for the human being, whose soul is from Heaven and whose body is from earth.
   C. "Therefore if a man has worked [in] the Torah and done the will of his Father in Heaven, lo, he is like the creatures of the upper world, as it is said, "I said, "You are godlike beings, and all of you are sons of the Most High"' (Ps. 82:6).
   D. "But if one has not worked [in] the Torah and done the will of his Father in Heaven, lo, he is like the creatures of the lower world, as it is said, 'Nevertheless you shall die like Adam' (Ps. 82:7)."

Once more, "labor in the Torah" yields something much more transcendent than mere information. The person becomes like the creatures of the upper world. Further evidence seems to me not required to demonstrate the proposition at hand. Here it is fully exposed.

IV

The Messiah

1. The Mishnah as against the Yerushalmi

In the Talmud of the Land of Israel, not only the Torah, but also the Messiah theme, bears salvific burden. The matter is entirely specific and indicative. The Mishnah expresses its teleology without recourse to an eschatological theory of any kind. As we shall see, moreover, eschatological teleologies can, and do, come to full exposure without resort to the Messiah theme at all. So the Messiah theme proves emblematic of the Yerushalmi and related writings (though in markedly diminished degree, as a matter of fact), by contrast to the Mishnah, on the one side, and the so-called Tannaite Midrashim, on the other.

The Messiah as a salvific figure coming at the end of time to mark the beginning of the last days, serving as the goal and purpose of the system throughout time, plays no role in the Mishnah. In that document the Messiah theme forms a taxic indicator, pertaining to various types of high priest. The few references to the eschatological Messiah prove systemically inert. The Messiah theme in the Yerushalmi defines the eschatological teleology of that document's system. The Messiah as person comes at the end of time to save Israel and bring history to a close; he will come as soon as Israel fully conforms to the Torah. There is no more striking indicator of the distinctive conceptions of the two systems, the Mishnah's and the Yerushalmi's, than the systemic irrelevance of the Messiah in the first system, and the critical importance of the Messiah in the successor system. Not only so, but once systemic teleology is framed around other than historical events – history as progression, with beginning, middle, and end – then the definition and use of events shift radically.

To state the matter simply, the Mishnah's system absorbs one-time events into a rule-seeking system, which classifies events and so deprives them of their one-time and unique character. The Yerushalmi's system, by contrast, dwells on distinct events and treats them as particular and instructive on their own; there is no classification of diverse events within a single rule, but rather the specification of the conclusion to be drawn from a unique event. The Mishnah's ahistorical system finds its counterpart and opposite in the Yerushalmi's profoundly historical reading of human, and Israel's, existence. For the purpose of this chapter in our experiment, however, we concentrate on the simple indicator of the role and uses of the Messiah theme in the mediating documents under study here.

The Mishnah's systemic teleology took a form other than the familiar eschatological one; historical events were absorbed, through their trivialization in taxonomic structures, into an ahistorical system. Messiahs in the Mishnah were merely a species of priest, falling into one classification rather than another. The teleology of the Yerushalmi and related writings, by contrast, appealed to the Messiah theme in setting forth an eschatological formulation of the theory of the purpose and end of the systemic construction. We see that fact in a very simple way. If we ask the Mishnah to answer the questions, What of the Messiah? When will he come? To whom, in Israel, will he come? and, What must, or can, we do while we wait to hasten his coming? we find no answers. To state the simple fact as baldly as I can, answering these questions out of the resources of the Mishnah is not possible. The Mishnah's teleology is not eschatological, and the Messiah theme simply plays no role in the expression, or the composition, of that teleology.

Negative facts provide one kind of evidence. The Mishnah presents no large view of history. It contains no reflection whatever on the nature and meaning of the destruction of the Temple in A.D. 70, an event which surfaces only in connection with some changes in the law explained as resulting from the end of the cult. The Mishnah pays no attention to the matter of the end time. The word *salvation* is rare, *sanctification* commonplace. More striking, the framers of the Mishnah are virtually silent on the teleology of the system; they never tell us why we should do what the Mishnah tells us, let alone explain what will happen if we do. Incidents in the Mishnah are preserved either as narrative settings for the statement of the law, or, occasionally, as precedents. Historical events are classified and turned into entries on lists. But incidents in any case come few and far between. True, events do make an impact. But it always is for the Mishnah's own purpose and within its own taxonomic system and rule-seeking mode of thought. To be sure, the framers of the Mishnah may also have had a theory of the Messiah and of the meaning of Israel's history and destiny. But they kept it hidden, and their document manages to provide an immense account of Israel's life without explicitly telling us about such matters.

Negative evidence bearing positive verification concerns the Messiah. The negative side is that the Messiah in the Mishnah does not stand at the forefront of the framers' consciousness. The issues encapsulated in the myth and person of the Messiah are scarcely addressed. The framers of the Mishnah do not resort to speculation about the Messiah as a historical-supernatural figure. When the Mishnah does refer to Messiah, it concerns a kind of high priest.

So far as a historical kind of speculation provides the vehicle for reflection on salvific issues, or in mythic terms, narratives on the meaning of history and the destiny of Israel, we cannot say that the Mishnah's philosophers take up those encompassing categories of being: Where are we heading? What can we do about it? That does not mean questions found urgent in the aftermath of the destruction of the Temple and the disaster of Bar Kokhba failed to attract the attention of the Mishnah's sages. But they treated history in a different way, offering their own answers to its questions. To these we now turn.

By *history* I mean not merely events, but how events serve to teach lessons, reveal patterns, tell us what we must do and what will happen to us tomorrow. In that context, some events contain richer lessons than others; the destruction of the Temple of Jerusalem teaches more than a crop failure, being kidnapped into slavery more than stubbing one's toe. Furthermore, lessons taught by events – *history* in the didactic sense – follow a progression from trivial and private to consequential and public. The framers of the Mishnah explicitly refer to very few events, treating those they do mention with a focus quite separate from the unfolding events themselves. They rarely create narratives; historical events do not supply organizing categories or taxonomic classifications. We find no tractate devoted to the destruction of the Temple, no complete chapter detailing the events of Bar Kokhba nor even a sustained celebration of the events of the sages' own historical lives. When things that have happened are mentioned, it is neither to narrate nor to interpret and draw lessons from the events. It is either to illustrate a point of law or to pose a problem of the law – always *en passant*, never in a pointed way.

The Mishnah absorbs into its encompassing system all events, small and large. With them the sages accomplish what they accomplish in everything else: a vast labor of taxonomy, an immense construction of the order and rules governing the classification of everything on earth and in Heaven. The disruptive character of history – one-time events of ineluctable significance – scarcely impresses the philosophers. They find no difficulty in showing that what appears unique and beyond classification has in fact happened before and so falls within the range of trustworthy rules and known procedures. Once history's components, one-time events, lose their distinctiveness, then history as a didactic intellectual construct, as a source of lessons and rules, also loses all pertinence.

So lessons and rules come from sorting things out and classifying them from the procedures and modes of thought of the philosopher seeking regularity. To this labor of taxonomy, the historian's way of selecting data and arranging them into patterns of meaning to teach lessons proves inconsequential. One-time events are not important. The world is composed of nature and supernature. The laws that count are those to be discovered in Heaven and, in Heaven's creation and counterpart, on earth. Keep those laws and things will work out. Break them, and the result is predictable: calamity of whatever sort will supervene in accordance with the rules. But just because it is predictable, a catastrophic happening testifies to what has always been and must always be, in accordance with reliable rules and within categories already discovered and well explained. That is why the lawyer-philosophers of the mid-second century produced the Mishnah – to explain how things are. Within the framework of well-classified rules, there could be messiahs, but no single Messiah.

If the end of time and the coming of the Messiah do not serve to explain, for the Mishnah's system, why people should do what the Mishnah says, then what alternative teleology does the Mishnah's first apologetic, Abot, provide? Only when we appreciate the clear answers given in that document, brought to closure at ca. 250, shall we grasp how remarkable is the shift, which took place in later documents of the rabbinic canon, to a messianic framing of the issues of the Torah's ultimate purpose and value. Let us see how the framers of Abot, in the aftermath of the creation of the Mishnah, explain the purpose and goal of the Mishnah: an ahistorical, nonmessianic teleology.

The first document generated by the Mishnah's heirs took up the work of completing the Mishnah's system by answering questions of purpose and meaning. Whatever teleology the Mishnah as such would ever acquire would derive from Abot, a collection of sayings by authorities who flourished in the generation after Judah the Patriarch; in all likelihood the document is of the mid-third-century rabbinic estate of the Land of Israel. Abot presents statements to express the ethos and ethic of the Mishnah, and so provides a kind of theory. Abot agreed with the other sixty-two tractates: history proved no more important here than it had been before. With scarcely a word about history and no account of events at all, Abot manages to provide an ample account of how the Torah – written and oral, thus in later eyes, Scripture and Mishnah – came down to its own day. Accordingly, the passage of time as such plays no role in the explanation of the origins of the document, nor is the Mishnah presented as eschatological. Occurrences of great weight (history) are never invoked. How then does the tractate tell the story of Torah, narrate the history of God's revelation to Israel, encompassing both Scripture and Mishnah? The answer is that Abot's framers manage to do their work of explanation without telling a story or invoking history at all. They pursue a different way of answering the same question, by exploiting a nonhistorical mode of thought and method of legitimation. And that is the main point: teleology serves the purpose of legitimation, and hence is accomplished in ways other than explaining how things originated or assuming that historical fact explains anything.

Disorderly historical events entered the system of the Mishnah and found their place within the larger framework of the Mishnah's orderly world. But to claim that the Mishnah's framers merely ignored what was happening would be incorrect. They worked out their own way of dealing with historical events, the disruptive power of which they not only conceded but freely recognized. Further, the Mishnah's authors did not intend to compose a history book or a work of prophecy or apocalypse. Even if they had wanted to narrate the course of events, they could hardly have done so through the medium of the Mishnah. Yet the Mishnah presents its philosophy in full awareness of the issues of historical calamity confronting the Jewish nation. So far as the philosophy of the document confronts the totality of Israel's existence, the Mishnah by definition also presents a philosophy of history.

The Talmud of the Land of Israel defines a position on both the Messiah specifically, and history in general, quite opposed to that of the Mishnah inclusive of Avot. The Messiah appears as a named, salvific figure, and the coming of the Messiah defines the systemic teleology. That of course is a teleology that speaks of the purpose of the system in its realization at the end of time, hence an eschatological teleology. It goes without saying, therefore, that narratives of history form an end in themselves, that is, a portrait of events that are unique and that (therefore) bear consequences, meanings particular to themselves.

The most important change is the shift in historical thinking adumbrated in the pages of the Talmud of the Land of Israel, a shift from focus upon the Temple and its supernatural history to close attention to the people Israel and its natural, this-worldly history.

Once Israel, holy Israel, had come to form the counterpart to the Temple and its supernatural life, that other history – Israel's – would stand at the center of things. Accordingly, a new sort of memorable event came to the fore in the Talmud of the Land of Israel. Let me give this new history appropriate emphasis: it was the story of Israel's suffering, remembrance of that suffering, on the one side, and an effort to explain events of such tragedy, on the other. So a composite "history" constructed out of the Yerushalmi's units of discourse which were pertinent to consequential events would contain long chapters on what happened to Israel, the Jewish people, and not only, or mainly, what had earlier occurred in the Temple.

The components of the historical theory of Israel's sufferings were manifold. First and foremost, history taught moral lessons. Historical events entered into the construction of a teleology for the Yerushalmi's system of Judaism as a whole. What the law demanded reflected the consequences of wrongful action on the part of Israel. So, again, Israel's own deeds defined the events of history. Rome's role, like Assyria's and Babylonia's, depended upon Israel's provoking divine wrath as it was executed by the great empire. This mode of thought comes to simple expression in what follows.

Y. Erubin 3:9

IV   B.   R. Ba, R. Hiyya in the name of R. Yohanan: "'Do not gaze at me because I am swarthy, because the sun has scorched me. My mother's sons were angry with me, they made me keeper of the vineyards; but, my own vineyard, I have not kept!' [Song 1:6]. What made me guard the vineyards? It is because of not keeping my own vineyard.

    C.   What made me keep two festival days in Syria? It is because I did not keep the proper festival day in the Holy Land.

    D.   "I imagined that I would receive a reward for the two days, but I received a reward only for one of them.

    E.   "Who made it necessary that I should have to separate two pieces of dough-offering from grain grown in Syria? It is because I did not separate a single piece of dough-offering in the Land of Israel."

Israel had to learn the lesson of its history also to take command of its own destiny.

But this notion of determining one's own destiny should not be misunderstood. The framers of the Talmud of the Land of Israel were not telling the Jews to please God by doing commandments in order that they should thereby gain control of their own destiny. To the contrary, the paradox of the Yerushalmi's system lies in the fact that Israel can free itself of control by other nations only by humbly agreeing to accept God's rule. The nations – Rome, in the present instance – rest on one side of the balance, while God rests on the other. Israel must then choose between them. There is no such thing for Israel as freedom from both God and the nations, total autonomy and independence. There is only a choice of masters, a ruler on earth or a ruler in Heaven.

This is not to suggest that the eschatological teleology, with its Messiah symbol, in doctrine will have astonished or alarmed the framers of the Mishnah. To the contrary, with propositions such as these, the framers of the Mishnah will certainly have concurred. And why not? For the fundamental affirmations of the Mishnah about the centrality of Israel's perfection in stasis – sanctification – readily prove congruent to the attitudes at hand. Once the Messiah's coming had become dependent upon Israel's condition and not upon Israel's actions in historical time, then the Mishnah's system will have imposed its fundamental and definitive character upon the Messiah myth. An eschatological teleology framed through that myth then would prove wholly appropriate to the method of the larger system of the Mishnah. But, as a matter of fact, the Messiah, and, with him, the doctrine of history, through which the Yerushalmi's framers set forth their propositions in no way served the authorship of the Mishnah. That is why we are on firm ground in maintaining that utilization of the Messiah theme characterizes documents that stand in intellectual situation closer to the Yerushalmi. Treating the Messiah as a taxic indicator and that alone, not as a medium of expressing systemic teleology, places a document closer to the Mishnah.

What, specifically, the Yerushalmi's compilers wished to convey through the Messiah doctrine is seen in the answer to the question, What makes a messiah a false messiah? It is not his claim to save Israel, but his claim to save Israel without the help of God. The meaning of the true Messiah is Israel's total submission, through the Messiah's gentle rule, to God's yoke and service. So God is not to be manipulated through Israel's humoring of Heaven in rite and cult. The notion of keeping the commandments so as to please Heaven and get God to do what Israel wants is totally incongruent to the text at hand, and, as we shall see in Chapter Seven, contradicts the conception of *zekhut*, which is central to the system of the Yerushalmi. Keeping the commandments as a mark of submission, loyalty, humility before God is the rabbinic system of salvation. So Israel does not "save itself." Israel never controls its own destiny, either on earth or in Heaven. The only choice is whether to place one's fate into the hands of cruel, deceitful men, or to trust in the living God of mercy and love. We shall now see how this critical position is spelled out in the setting of discourse about the Messiah in the Talmud of the Land of Israel.

Bar Kokhba, above all, exemplifies arrogance against God. He lost the war because of that arrogance. In particular, he ignored the authority of sages:

Y. Taanit 4:5

X   J.   Said R. Yohanan, "Upon orders of Caesar Hadrian, they killed eight hundred thousand in Betar."

K.   Said R. Yohanan, "There were eighty thousand pairs of trumpeteers surrounding Betar. Each one was in charge of a number of troops. Ben Kozeba was there and he had two hundred thousand troops who, as a sign of loyalty, had cut off their little fingers.

L.   "Sages sent word to him, 'How long are you going to turn Israel into a maimed people.

M.   "He said to them, 'How otherwise is it possible to test them?'

N.   "They replied to him, 'Whoever cannot uproot a cedar of Lebanon while riding on his horse will not be inscribed on your military rolls.'

O.   "So there were two hundred thousand who qualified in one way, and another two hundred thousand who qualified in another way."

P.   When he would go forth to battle, he would say, "Lord of the world! Do not help and do not hinder us! 'Hast thou not rejected us, O God? Thou dost not go forth, O God, with our armies'"[Ps. 60:10].

Q.   Three-and-a-half years did Hadrian besiege Betar.

R.   R. Eleazar of Modiin would sit on sackcloth and ashes and pray every day, saying "Lord of the ages! Do not judge in accord with strict judgment this day! Do not judge in accord with strict judgment this day!"

S.   Hadrian wanted to go to him. A Samaritan said to him, "Do not go to him until I see what he is doing, and so hand over the city [of Betar] to you. [Make peace...for you.]"

T.   He got into the city through a drain pipe. He went and found R. Eleazar of Modiin standing and praying. He pretended to whisper something in his ear.

U.   The townspeople saw [the Samaritan] do this and brought him to Ben Kozeba. They told him, "We saw this man having dealings with your friend."

V.   [Bar Kokhba] said to him, "What did you say to him, and what did he say to you?"

W.   He said to [the Samaritan], "If I tell you, then the king will kill me, and if I do not tell you, then you will kill me. It is better that the king kill me, and not you.

X.   "[Eleazar] said to me, 'I should hand over my city.' ['I shall make peace....']"

Y.   He turned to R. Eleazar of Modiin. He said to him, "What did this Samaritan say to you?"

Z.   He replied, "Nothing."

AA.   He said to him, "What did you say to him?"

BB.   He said to him, "Nothing."

CC.   [Ben Kozeba] gave [Eleazar] one good kick and killed him.

DD.   Forthwith an echo came forth and proclaimed the following verse:

EE.   "Woe to my worthless shepherd, who deserts the flock! May the sword smite his arm and his right eye! Let his arm be wholly withered, his right eye utterly blinded! [Zech. 11:17].

FF.   "You have murdered R. Eleazar of Modiin, the right arm of all Israel, and their right eye. Therefore may the right arm of that man wither, may his right eye be utterly blinded!"

GG.   Forthwith Betar was taken, and Ben Kozeba was killed.

We notice two complementary themes. First, Bar Kokhba treats Heaven with arrogance, asking God merely to keep out of the way. Second, he treats an especially revered sage with a parallel arrogance. The sage had the power to preserve Israel. Bar Kokhba destroyed Israel's one protection. The result was inevitable.

The Messiah, the centerpiece of salvation history and hero of the tale, emerged as a critical figure. The historical theory of this Yerushalmi passage is stated very simply. In their view Israel had to choose between wars, either the war fought by Bar Kokhba or the "war for Torah." "Why had they been punished? It was because of the weight of the war, for they had not wanted to engage in the struggles over the meaning of the Torah" (Y. Ta. 3:9 XVI I). Those struggles, which were ritual arguments about ritual matters, promised the only victory worth winning. Then Israel's history would be written in terms of wars over the meaning of the Torah and the decision of the law.

The Mishnah's teleology beyond time and its capacity to posit an eschatology without a place for a historical Messiah take a position distinct from that of the Talmud of the Land of Israel and related Midrash compilations. In the Yerushalmi we witness, among the Mishnah's heirs, a striking reversion to biblical convictions about the centrality of history and therefore the critical role of the Messiah in the definition of Israel's ontology. The issue of the Messiah and the meaning of Israel's history framed through the Messiah myth in the system represented by those documents contrast with the representation of these same matters in the Mishnah.

When constructing a systematic account of Judaism – that is, the worldview and way of life for Israel presented in the Mishnah – the philosophers of the Mishnah did not make use of the Messiah myth in the construction of a teleology for their system. They found it possible to present a statement of goals for their projected life of Israel which was entirely separate from appeals to history and eschatology. Since they certainly knew, and even alluded to, long-standing and widely held convictions on eschatological subjects, beginning with those in Scripture, the framers thereby testified that, knowing the larger repertoire, they made choices different from others before and after them. Their document accurately and ubiquitously expresses these choices, both affirmative and negative.

The appearance of a messianic eschatology, with its stress on the viewpoints and prooftexts of Scripture, its interest in what was happening to Israel, its focus upon the national-historical dimension of the life of the group, differs from the treatment of the same subject in the mishnaic system. The Talmud of the Land of Israel approaches that subject in a way quite different in the aggregate from the mishnaic system, which had found little use for the Messiah myth. But, conforming to the Mishnah's interest in constructing an ahistorical and timeless ontology for Israel, the Yerushalmi's materials' authors transformed the Messiah myth in its totality into an essentially ahistorical force. If people wanted to reach the end of time, they had to rise above time, that is, history, and stand off at the side of great movements of political and military character. That is the message of the Messiah myth as it reaches full exposure in the first of the two Talmuds. At its foundation it is precisely the message of teleology without eschatology expressed by the Mishnah and its associated documents. Israel must turn away from time and change, submit to whatever happens, so as to win for itself the only government worth having, that is, God's rule, accomplished through God's anointed agent, the Messiah.

The evidence we seek in this context is both verbal and narrative. Do we find the word *Messiah,* or the Messiah theme, utilized to express the systemic teleology set forth by the so-called Tannaitic Midrashim? That is, do stories[1] or sayings appeal to the Messiah to explain what is going to happen when the system attains its full realization? Or do the so-called Tannaitic Midrashim treat the word or theme *Messiah* as a mere taxic indicator, for example, relevant to the differentiation among political authorities or among priests, as is the case in the Mishnah? We are not called upon to make systemic judgments but only to assess whether or not the Messiah theme plays a role in the documents under study.

2. Mekhilta Attributed to R. Ishmael

So far as I can discern, the Messiah theme plays no role in this document, even though there are passages of a teleological, and even eschatological, character.

---

[1]Since Maccoby refers to "the *aggadah,*" it is legitimate to ask for stories or the absence of stories to serve as a principal indicator of the systemic position of a document.

3. Sifra

Sifra's authorship invokes an eschatological teleology, to which the Messiah theme is entirely irrelevant. God, not the Messiah, is the principal actor in the eschatological teleology before us.

Sifra 263. Parashat Behuqotai Pereq 3

CCLXIII:I

3. A. "And I will make my abode among you:"
     B. This refers to the house of the sanctuary.

4. A. "And my soul shall not abhor you:"
     B. Once I shall redeem you, I shall never again reject you.

5. A. "And I will walk among you:"
     B. The matter may be compared to the case of a king who went out to stroll with his sharecropper in an orchard.
     C. But the sharecropper hid from him.
     D. Said the king to that sharecropper, "How come you're hiding from me? Lo, I am just like you."
     E. So the Holy One, blessed be He, said to the righteous, "Why are you trembling before me?"
     F. So the Holy One, blessed be He, is destined to walk with the righteous in the Garden of Eden in the coming future, and the righteous will see him and tremble before him,
     G. [and he will say to them,] "[How come you're trembling before me?] Lo, I am just like you."

8. A. "And I have broken the bars of your yoke:"
     B. The matter may be comapred to the case of a householder who had a cow for ploughing, and he lent it to someone else to plough with it.
     C. That man had ten sons. This one came and ploughed with it and went his way, and that one came and ploughed with it and went his way, so that the cow got tired and crouched down.
     D. All the other cows came back, but that cow did not enter the fold.
     E. The owner hardly agreed to accept consolation from that man, but he went and broke the yoke and cut off the carved ends of the yoke.
     F. So is Israel in this world.
     G. One ruler comes along and subjugates them and then goes his way, then another ruler comes along and subjugates them and goes his way, so that the furrow is very long.
     H. So it is said, "Plowman plowed across my back; they made long furrows. [The Lord, the righteous one, has snapped the cords of the wicked]" (Ps. 129:3-4).
     I. Tomorrow, when the end comes, the Holy One, blessed be He, will not say to the nations, "Thus and so have you done to my children!"
     J. Rather, he will immediately come and break the yoke and cut off the ends of the yoke.
     K. For it is said, "and I have broken the bars of your yoke."
     L. And further, "The Lord has snapped the cords of the wicked."

The eschatological focus is made sharp at No. 4. The polemic throughout is uniform: Israel is destined to be redeemed in the future, and when that happens, it will be for all time. Then the return to Zion and rebuilding of the Temple did not fulfill the prophecies of redemption; Israel will have a future redemption, of which the prophets, including Moses, spoke. The pertinence to our problem cannot be missed. Here we have a highly eschatological teleology, but the Messiah theme is entirely absent.

4. Sifré to Numbers 1-115

The Messiah theme does not arise in the chapters reviewed here, Nos. 1-115.

5. Sifré to Deuteronomy

The eschatological passages of Deuteronomy do not provoke comment that appeals to the Messiah theme for formulation and expression. The example of Sifra suffices to show what I mean. Numerous examples of a Messiah-less eschatology in Sifré to Deuteronomy will not make the point better than it has already been made. While Sifra and Sifré to Deuteronomy concur that, in the representation of the systemic teleology, eschatological issues must be introduced – and, after all, both biblical books, Leviticus and Deuteronomy, make that position necessary – their authorships find remarkably little use for the Messiah theme.[2]

---

[2]That is the conclusion of *Judaisms and their Messiahs in the beginning of Christianity*. New York, 1987: Cambridge University Press, which I edited with William Scott Green and Ernest S. Frerichs. When "Judaism" – meaning, all of the Judaisms of late antiquity – is represented as a messianic religion, "it" is simply misrepresented. Traits very important in some systems are imputed to them all.

V

The Nations.
Rome in Particular

1. The Mishnah as against the Yerushalmi

The Messiah theme draws us onward to a consideration of the contrasting theories of Israel and the nations put forth by the Mishnah, on the one side, and the Yerushalmi, on the other. We deal first with how each system, as represented by its principal document, treats "the nations" in general, Rome in particular, and then proceed to the contrasting systemic usages of "Israel" characteristic of the one and the other.

When the sages of the Mishnah and the Tosefta spoke of Edom and Edomites, they meant biblical Edom, a people in the vicinity of the Land of Israel.[1] By Rome they meant the city – that alone. When the sages of the Yerushalmi, Leviticus Rabbah, and Genesis Rabbah spoke of Rome, it was not a place, a city, a political Rome, but a messianic Rome that is at issue. Rome receives a supernatural standing as sibling and competitor and even surrogate for Israel, as well, of course, as the last obstacle to Israel's salvation and world-rule. For our purposes the point is a simple one. The document that treats Rome as undifferentiated, simply another nation, will stand closer to the Mishnah; the one that identifies Rome as special and imputes to Rome the status of Israel's opposite and counterpart will stand closer to the Yerushalmi's associated documents. And the document to which Rome

---

[1]Here we go over materials treated at greater length in the Appendix to this book. The reader is warned that there is some repetition between paragraphs of this part of the chapter and what is to come at the end.

is simply not an issue, whether systemic or indicative, will not come under the classification made possible by the indicator at hand.

In the successor system Rome of course is singled out, and that means, to begin with, nations are differentiated from one another. In the Mishnah, "the nations" are undifferentiated; all equally serve as taxic indicators of the same kind. As to cultic uncleanness, all nations are held to be in the status of the corpse. Any gentile produces the same effect as any other, and there is no interest in differentiating gentiles in any other way but as to uncleanness. In the Yerushalmi, by contrast, the gentiles are differentiated, and the differences are important not solely as to the homogeneous matter of cultic uncleanness.

The differentiation of course is important in particular because Rome is deemed in a category distinct from all other nations. Other nations, except for Rome, simply are unlike Israel; Rome is interstitial and liminal: like Israel in some ways, unlike Israel in other ways. That distinction is simply not present in the Mishnah. It forms part of the larger interest of the Yerushalmi and related Midrash compilations in history and historical narrative and forms a component in the eschatological teleology of those documents. Specifically, Rome is next-to-last cosmocrator or world ruler. Israel will succeed and mark the end of time. So the differentiation of Rome is not a trivial matter but forms a fundamental component of the system as a whole.

If we ask the Mishnah its principal view of the nations and the world beyond Israel, it answers with a simple principle: the framers of the document insist that the world beyond was essentially undifferentiated. Rome to them proved no more, and no less, important than any other place in that undifferentiated world.[2] So far as the epochs of human history were concerned, these emerged solely from within Israel, and, in particular, the history of Israel's cult, as M. Zeb. 14:4-9 lays matters out in terms of the cult's location, and M. R.H. 4:1-4

---

[2]As a matter of fact, if we turn to H. Y. Kosovsky, *Thesaurus Mishnae* (Jerusalem, 1956) I, II, IV, and look for Edom, Esau, Ishmael, and Rome, we come away disappointed. "Edom" in the sense of Rome does not occur. The word stands for the Edomites of biblical times (M. Yeb. 8:3) and the territory of Edom (M. Ket. 5:8). Ishmael, who like Edo m later stands for Rome, supplies a name of a sage, nothing more. As to Rome itself, the picture is not terribly different. There is a "Roman hyssop," (M. Par. 11:7, M. Neg. 14:6), and Rome occurs as a place name (M. A.Z. 4:7). Otherwise I see not a single passage indicated by Kosovsky in which Rome serves as a topic of interest, and, it goes without saying, in no place does "Rome" stand for an age in human history, let alone the counterpart to and opposite of Israel. Rome is part of the undifferentiated other, the outside world of death beyond. That fact takes on considerable meaning when we turn to the later fourth and fifth century compilations of scriptural exegeses.

in terms of the before and after of the destruction.[3] The undifferentiation of the outside world may be conveyed in a simple fact, to which I have already made reference. The entire earth outside of the Land of Israel in the Mishnah's law was held to suffer from contamination by corpses. Hence it was unclean with a severe mode of uncleanness, inaccessible to the holy and life-sustaining processes of the cult. If an Israelite artist were asked to paint a wall portrait of the world beyond the Land, he would paint the entire wall white, the color of death. The outside world, in the imagination of the Mishnah's law, was the realm of death. Among corpses, how are we to make distinctions?

When we come to the Tosefta, a document containing systematic and extensive supplements to the sayings of the Mishnah, we find ourselves entirely within the Mishnah's circle of meanings and values.[4] When, therefore, we ask how the Tosefta's authors incorporate and treat apocalyptic verses of Scripture, as they do, we find that they reduce to astonishingly trivial and local dimensions materials bearing for others world-historical meaning – including symbols later invoked by sages themselves to express the movement and meaning of history. No nation, including Rome, plays a role in the Tosefta's interpretation of biblical passages presenting historical apocalypse.[5]

If – along with Shmuel Krauss, author of a book with the same title – we were to propose a thesis on "Rome in the Talmud and Midrash" based on the evidence at hand in the Mishnah and the Tosefta, it

---

[3]In my *Messiah in Context, Israel's History and Destiny in Formative Judaism (Foundations of Judaism, Vol. II. Teleology)* (Philadelphia, 1983: Fortress) I dealt at some length with the larger question of the later reimagining of Israel's history. But that is not at issue here.

[4]Since the Tosefta is assuredly a document of the third century, it shows us how a document within the orbit of the Mishnah restates positions indicative of the system for which the Mishnah stands. When we examine the condition of other mediating documents, standing in time, it is generally assumed, between the Mishnah and the Yerushalmi and its related Midrash compilations, the Tosefta will provide us with a solid analogy for a compilation that works out the Mishnah's system's principal concerns – and not those of the Yerushalmi's system.

[5]Esau, Edom, Ishmael, and Rome in H. Y. Kosovsky [here: Chaim Josua Kasowski], *Thesaurus Thosephthae* (Jerusalem, I: 1932; III: 1942; VI, 1961), yield pretty much the same sort of usages, in the same proportions, as the Mishnah has already shown us. Specifically, Edom is a biblical people, T. Yeb. 8:1, Niddah 6:1, Qid. 5:4. Ishmael is a proper name for several sages. More important, Ishmael never stands for Rome. And Rome itself? We have Todor of Rome (T. Bes. 2:15), Rome as a place where people live, e. g., "I saw it in Rome" (T. Yoma 3:8), "I taught this law in Rome" (T. Nid. 7:1, T. Miq. 4:7). And that is all.

would not produce many propositions. Rome is a place, and no biblical figures or places prefigure the place of Rome in the history of Israel. That is so even though the authors of the Mishnah and the Tosefta knew full well who had destroyed the Temple and closed off Jerusalem and what these events had meant. To state the negative: Rome does not stand for Israel's nemesis and counterpart, Rome did not mark an epoch in the history of the world, Israel did not encompass Rome in Israel's history of humanity, and Rome did not represent one of the four monarchies – the last, the worst, prior to Israel's rule. To invoke a modern category, Rome stood for a perfectly secular matter: a place, where things happened. Rome in no way symbolized anything beyond itself. And Israel's sages did not find they had to take seriously the presence or claims of Christianity. Now to the Yerushalmi and its associated writings, beginning with Genesis Rabbah.

In Genesis Rabbah and Leviticus, which we take for this topic as the system's representative compilations, sages read the book of Genesis as if it portrayed the history of Israel and Rome – Rome not as representative of "the nations" in general, *but in particular.* Now Rome plays a role in the biblical narrative, with special reference to the counterpart and opposite of the patriarchs, first Ishmael, then Esau, and, always, Edom. For that is the single obsession binding sages of the document at hand to common discourse with the text before them. Why Rome in the form it takes in Genesis Rabbah? And how come the obsessive character of sages disposition of the theme of Rome? Were their picture merely of Rome as tyrant and destroyer of the Temple, we should have no reason to link the text to the problems of the age of redaction and closure. But now it is Rome as Israel's brother, counterpart, and nemesis, Rome as the one thing standing in the way of Israel's, and the world's, ultimate salvation. So the stakes are different, and much higher.

I give a simple example of how ubiquitous is the shadow of Ishmael/Esau/Edom/Rome. Wherever sages reflect on future history, their minds turn to their own day. They found the hour difficult, because Rome, now Christian, claimed that very birthright and blessing that they understood to be theirs alone. Christian Rome posed a threat without precedent. Now another dominion, besides Israel's, claimed the rights and blessings that sustained Israel. Wherever in Scripture they turned, sages found comfort in the iteration that the birthright, the blessing, the Torah, and the hope all belonged to them and to none other. From the womb Israel and Rome contended. The following suffices to prove the differentiation of Rome and the special status accorded to Rome: in its unique relationship to Israel:

Genesis Rabbah

LXIII:VI

1. A.   "And the children struggled together [within her, and she said, 'If it is thus, why do I live?' So she went to inquire of the Lord. And the Lord said to her, 'Two nations are in your womb, and two peoples, born of you, shall be divided; the one shall be stronger than the other, and the elder shall serve the younger']" (Gen. 25:22-23):

    B.   R. Yohanan and R. Simeon b. Laqish:

    C.   R. Yohanan said, "[Because the word *struggle* contains the letters for the word *run*,] this one was running to kill that one and that one was running to kill this one."

    D.   R. Simeon b. Laqish: "This one releases the laws given by that one, and that one releases the laws given by this one."

2. A.   R. Berekhiah in the name of R. Levi said, "It is so that you should not say that it was only after he left his mother's womb that [Esau] contended against [Jacob].

    B.   "But even while he was yet in his mother's womb, his fist was stretched forth against him: 'The wicked stretch out their fists [so Freedman] from the womb' (Ps. 58:4)."

3. A.   "And the children struggled together within her":

    B.   [Once more referring to the letters of the word *struggled*, with special attention to the ones that mean *run*,] they wanted to run within her.

    C.   When she went by houses of idolatry, Esau would kick, trying to get out: "The wicked are estranged from the womb" (Ps. 58:4).

    D.   When she went by synagogues and study houses, Jacob would kick, trying to get out: "Before I formed you in the womb, I knew you" (Jer. 1:5)."

4. A.   "...and she said, 'If it is thus, why do I live?'"

    B.   R. Haggai in the name of R. Isaac: "This teaches that our mother, Rebecca, went around to the doors of women and said to them, 'Did you ever have this kind of pain in your life?'"

    C.   "[She said to them,] '"If thus": If this is the pain of having children, would that I had not gotten pregnant.'"

    D.   Said R. Huna, "If I am going to produce twelve tribes only through this kind of suffering, would that I had not gotten pregnant."

5. A.   It was taught on Tannaite authority in the name of R. Nehemiah, "Rebecca was worthy of having the twelve tribes come forth from her. That is in line with this verse:

    B.   "'Two nations are in your womb, and two peoples, born of you, shall be divided; the one shall be stronger than the other, and the elder shall serve the younger.' When her days to be delivered were fulfilled, behold, there were twins in her womb. The first came forth red, all his body like a hairy mantle, so they called his name Esau. Afterward his brother came forth' (Gen. 25:23-24).

    C.   "'Two nations are in your womb': thus two.

    D.   "'and two peoples': thus two more, hence four.

    E.   "'...the one shall be stronger than the other': two more, so six.

    F.   "'...and the elder shall serve the younger': two more, so eight.

G.   "'When her days to be delivered were fulfilled, behold, there were twins in her womb': two more, so ten.

H.   "'The first came forth red': now eleven.

I.   "'Afterward his brother came forth': now twelve."

J.   There are those who say, "Proof derives from this verse: 'If it is thus, why do I live?' Focusing on the word for *thus*, we note that the two letters of that word bear the numerical value of seven and five respectively, hence, twelve in all."

6. A.   "So she went to inquire of the Lord":

B.   Now were there synagogues and houses of study in those days [that she could go to inquire of the Lord]?

C.   But is it not the fact that she went only to the study of Eber?

D.   This serves to teach you that whoever receives an elder is as if he receives the Presence of God.

Nos. 1-3 take for granted that Esau represents Rome, and Jacob, Israel. Consequently the verse underlines the point that there is natural enmity between Israel and Rome. Esau hated Israel even while he was still in the womb. Jacob, for his part, revealed from the womb those virtues that would characterize him later on, eager to serve God as Esau was eager to worship idols. The text invites just this sort of reading. No. 4 and No. 5 relate Rebecca's suffering to the birth of the twelve tribes. No. 6 makes its own point, independent of the rest and tacked on.

What we see in Leviticus Rabbah is consistent with what we have already observed in Genesis Rabbah: how sages absorb events into their system of classification. So it is sages that make history through the thoughts they think and the rules they lay down. In such a context, we find no interest either in the outsiders and their powers, or in the history of the empires of the world, or, all the more so, in redemption and the messianic fulfillment of time. What is the alternative to the use of the sort of symbols just now examined?

Let us turn immediately to the relevant passages of Leviticus Rabbah. I give only a single abstract of a much longer discussion.

Leviticus Rabbah

XIII:V

7. A.   [Gen. R. 42:2:] Abraham foresaw what the evil kingdoms would do [to Israel].

B.   "[As the sun was going down,] a deep sleep fell on Abraham; and lo, a dread and great darkness fell upon him]" (Gen. 15:12).

C.   "Dread" ('YMH) refers to Babylonia, on account of the statement, "Then Nebuchadnezzar was full of fury (HMH)" (Dan. 3:19).

D.   "Darkness" refers to Media, which brought darkness to Israel through its decrees: "to destroy, to slay, and to wipe out all the Jews" (Est. 7:4).

E.   "Great" refers to Greece.

F.   Said R. Judah b. R. Simon, "The verse teaches that the kingdom of Greece set up one hundred twenty-seven governors, one hundred and twenty-seven hyparchs and one hundred twenty-seven commanders."

G.   And rabbis say, "They were sixty in each category."

H.   R. Berekhiah and R. Hanan in support of this position taken by rabbis: "'Who led you through the great terrible wilderness, with its fiery serpents and scorpions and thirsty ground where there was no water]' (Deut. 8:15).

I.   "Just as the scorpion produces eggs by sixties, so the kingdom of Greece would set up its administration in groups of sixty."

J.   "Fell on him" (Gen. 15:12).

K.   This refers to Edom, on account of the following verse: "The earth quakes at the noise of their [Edom's] fall" (Jer. 49:21).

L   There are those who reverse matters.

M.   "Fear" refers to Edom, on account of the following verse: "And this I saw, a fourth beast, fearful, and terrible" (Dan. 7:7).

M.   "Darkness" refers to Greece, which brought gloom through its decrees. For they said to Israel, "Write on the horn of an ox that you have no portion in the God of Israel."

O.   "Great" refers to Media, on account of the verse: "King Ahasuerus made Haman [the Median] great" (Est. 3:1).

P.   "Fell on him" refers to Babylonia, on account of the following verse: "Fallen, fallen is Babylonia" (Isa. 21:9).

8.   A   Daniel foresaw what the evil kingdoms would do [to Israel].

B.   "Daniel said, I saw in my vision by night, and behold, the four winds of Heaven were stirring up the great sea. And four great beasts came up out of the sea, [different from one another. The first was like a lion and had eagles' wings. Then as I looked, its wings were plucked off....And behold, another beast, a second one, like a bear....After this I looked, and lo, another, like a leopard....After this I saw in the night visions, and behold, a fourth beast, terrible and dreadful and exceedingly strong; and it had great iron teeth]" (Dan. 7:3-7).

C.   If you enjoy sufficient merit, it will emerge from the sea, but if not, it will come out of the forest.

D.   The animal that comes up from the sea is not violent, but the one that comes up out of the forest is violent.

E   Along these same lines: "The boar out of the wood ravages it" (Ps. 80:14).

F.   If you enjoy sufficient merit, it will come from the river, and if not, from the forest.

G.   The animal that comes up from the river is not violent, but the one that comes up out of the forest is violent.

H.   "Different from one another" (Dan. 7:3).

I.   Differing from [hating] one another.

J.   This teaches that every nation that rules in the world hates Israel and reduces them to slavery.

K.   "The first was like a lion [and had eagles' wings]" (Dan. 7:4).

L   This refers to Babylonia.

M.   Jeremiah saw [Babylonia] as a lion. Then he went and saw it as an eagle.

N.   He saw it as a lion: "A lion has come up from his thicket" (Jer. 4:7).

O.   And [as an eagle:] "Behold, he shall come up and swoop down as the eagle" (Jer. 49:22).

P.   People said to Daniel, "What do you see?"

Q.   He said to them, "I see the face like that of a lion and wings like those of an eagle: 'The first was like a lion and had eagles' wings. Then, as I looked, its wings were plucked off, and it was lifted up from the ground [and made to stand upon two feet like a man and the heart of a man was given to it]' (Dan. 7:4).

R.   R. Eleazar and R. Ishmael b. R. Nehemiah:

S.   R. Eleazar said, "While the entire lion was smitten, its heart was not smitten.

T.   "That is in line with the following statement: 'And the heart of a man was given to it' (Dan. 7:4)."

U.   And R. Ishmael b. R. Nehemiah said, "Even its heart was smitten, for it is written, 'Let his heart be changed from a man's' (Dan. 4:17).

V.   "And behold, another beast, a second one, like a bear. [It was raised up one side; it had three ribs in its mouth between its teeth, and it was told, Arise, devour much flesh]" (Dan. 7:5).

W.   This refers to Media.

X.   Said R. Yohanan, "It is like a bear."

Y.   It is written, "similar to a wolf" (DB); thus, "And a wolf was there."

Z.   That is in accord with the view of R. Yohanan, for R.Yohanan said, "'Therefore a lion out of the forest [slays them]' (Jer. 5:6) – this refers to Babylonia.

AA.   "'A wolf of the deserts spoils them' (Jer. 5:6) refers to Media.

BB.   "'A leopard watches over their cities' (Jer. 5:6) refers to Greece.

CC.   "'Whoever goes out from them will be savaged' (Jer. 5:6) refers to Edom.

DD.   "Why so? 'Because their transgressions are many, and their backslidings still more' (Jer. 5:6)."

EE.   "After this, I looked, and lo, another, like a leopard [with four wings of a bird on its back; and the beast had four heads; and dominion was given to it]" (Dan. 7:6).

FF.   This [leopard] refers to Greece, which persisted impudently in making harsh decrees, saying to Israel, "Write on the horn of an ox that you have no share in the God of Israel."

GG.   "After this I saw in the night visions, and behold, a fourth beast, terrible and dreadful and exceedingly strong; [and it had great iron teeth; it devoured and broke in pieces and stamped the residue with its feet. It was different from all the beasts that were before it; and it had ten horns]" (Dan. 7:7).

HH.   This refers to Edom [Rome].

II.   Daniel saw the first three visions on one night, and this one he saw on another night. Now why was that the case?

JJ.   R. Yohanan and R. Simeon b. Laqish:

KK.   R. Yohanan said, "It is because the fourth beast weighed as much as the first three."

LL. And R. Simeon b. Laqish said, "It outweighed them."

MM. R. Yohanan objected to R. Simeon b. Laqish, "'Prophesy, therefore, son of man, clap your hands [and let the sword come down twice; yea, thrice. The sword for those to be slain; it is the sword for the great slaughter, which encompasses them]' (Ezek. 21:14-15). [So the single sword of Rome weighs against the three others]."

NN. And R. Simeon b. Laqish, how does he interpret the same passage? He notes that [the threefold sword] is doubled (Ezek. 21:14), [thus outweighs the three swords, equally twice their strength].

9. A. Moses foresaw what the evil kingdoms would do [to Israel].

B. "The camel, rock badger, and hare" (Deut. 14:7). [Compare: "Nevertheless, among those that chew the cud or part the hoof, you shall not eat these: the camel, because it chews the cud but does not part the hoof, is unclean to you. The rock badger, because it chews the cud but does not part the hoof, is unclean to you. And the hare, because it chews the cud but does not part the hoof, is unclean to you, and the pig, because it parts the hoof and is cloven-footed, but does not chew the cud, is unclean to you" (Lev. 11:4-8).]

C. The camel (GML) refers to Babylonia, [in line with the following verse of Scripture: "O daughter of Babylonia, you who are to be devastated!] Happy will be he who requites (GML) you, with what you have done to us" (Ps. 147:8).

D. "The rock badger" (Deut. 14:7) – this refers to Media.

E. Rabbis and R. Judah b. R. Simon.

F. Rabbis say, "Just as the rock badger exhibits traits of uncleanness and traits of cleanness, so the kingdom of Media produced both a righteous man and a wicked one."

G. Said R. Judah b. R. Simon, "The last Darius was Esther's son. He was clean on his mother's side and unclean on his father's side."

H. "The hare" (Deut 14:7) – this refers to Greece. The mother of King Ptolemy was named "Hare" [in Greek: lagos].

I. "The pig" (Deut. 14:7) – this refers to Edom [Rome].

J. Moses made mention of the first three in a single verse and the final one in a verse by itself [(Deut. 14:7, 8)]. Why so?

K. R. Yohanan and R. Simeon b. Laqish:

L. R. Yohanan said, "It is because [the pig] is equivalent to the other three."

M. And R. Simeon b. Laqish said, "It is because it outweighs them."

N. R. Yohanan objected to R. Simeon b. Laqish, "'Prophesy, therefore, son of man, clap your hands [and let the sword come down twice, yea thrice]' (Ezek. 21:14)."

O. And how does R. Simeon b. Laqish interpret the same passage? He notes that [the threefold sword] is doubled (Ezek. 21:14).

10. A. [Gen. R. 65:1:] R. Phineas and R. Hilqiah in the name of R. Simon: "Among all the prophets, only two of them revealed [the true evil of Rome], Assaf and Moses.

B. "Assaf said, 'The pig out of the wood ravages it' (Ps. 80:14).

C.   "Moses said, 'And the pig, [because it parts the hoof and is cloven-footed but does not chew the cud]' (Lev. 11:7).

D.   "Why is [Rome] compared to a pig?

E.   "It is to teach you the following: Just as, when a pig crouches and produces its hooves, it is as if to say, 'See how I am clean [since I have a cloven hoof],' so this evil kingdom takes pride, seizes by violence, and steals, and then gives the appearance of establishing a tribunal for justice."

F.   There was the case of a ruler in Caesarea, who put thieves, adulterers, and sorcerers to death, while at the same time telling his counsellor, "That same man [I] did all these three things on a single night."

13. A.   Another interpretation [now treating "bring up the cud" (GR) as "bring along in its train" (GRR)]:

B.   "The camel" (Lev. 11:4) – this refers to Babylonia.

C.   "Which brings along in its train" – for it brought along another kingdom after it.

D.   "The rock badger" (Lev. 11:5) – this refers to Media.

E.   "Which brings along in its train" – for it brought along another kingdom after it.

F.   "The hare" (Lev. 11:6) – this refers to Greece.

G.   "Which brings along in its train" – for it brought along another kingdom after it.

H.   "The pig" (Lev. 11:7) – this refers to Rome.

I.   "Which does not bring along in its train" – for it did not bring along another kingdom after it. [Only Israel will follow Rome, and Israel will succeed as cosmocrator after Rome.]

J.   And why is it then called "pig" (HZYR)? For it restores (MHZRT) the crown to the one who truly should have it [namely, Israel, whose dominion will begin when the rule of Rome ends].

K.   That is in line with the following verse of Scripture: "And saviors will come up on Mount Zion to judge the Mountain of Esau [Rome], and the kingdom will then belong to the Lord" (Ob. 1:21).

To stand back and consider this apocalyptic vision of Israel's history, we first review the message of the construction as a whole. This comes in two parts, first, the explicit, then the implicit. As to the former, the first claim is that God had told the prophets what would happen to Israel at the hands of the pagan kingdoms, Babylonia, Media, Greece, Rome.   These are further represented by Nebuchadnezzar, Haman, Alexander for Greece, Edom or Esau, interchangeably, for Rome.   The same vision came from Adam, Abraham, Daniel, and Moses.   The same policy toward Israel – oppression, destruction, enslavement, alienation from the true God – emerged from all four.

How does Rome stand out? First, it was made fruitful through the prayer of Isaac in behalf of Esau. Second, Edom is represented by the fourth and final beast. Rome is related through Esau, as Babylonia, Media, and Greece are not. The fourth beast was seen in a vision separate from the first three. It was worst of all and outweighed the rest. In the apocalypticizing of the animals of Lev. 11:4-8/Deut. 14:7, the camel, rock badger, hare, and pig, the pig, standing for Rome, again emerges as different from the others and more threatening than the rest. Just as the pig pretends to be a clean beast by showing the cloven hoof, but in fact is an unclean one, so Rome pretends to be just but in fact governs by thuggery. Edom does not pretend to praise God but only blasphemes. It does not exalt the righteous but kills them. These symbols concede nothing to Christian monotheism and biblicism. Of greatest importance, while all the other beasts bring further ones in their wake, the pig does not: "It does not bring another kingdom after it." It will restore the crown to the one who will truly deserve it, Israel. Esau will be judged by Zion, so Obadiah 1:21.

Now how has the symbolization delivered an implicit message? It is in the treatment of Rome as distinct, but essentially equivalent to the former kingdoms. This seems to me a stunning way of saying that the now-Christian empire in no way requires differentiation from its pagan predecessors. Nothing has changed, except matters have gotten worse. Beyond Rome, standing in a straight line with the others, lies the true shift in history, the rule of Israel and the cessation of the dominion of the (pagan) nations. Leviticus Rabbah came to closure, it is generally agreed, around A.D. 400, that is, approximately a century after the Roman Empire in the east had begun to become Christian, and half a century after the last attempt to rebuild the Temple in Jerusalem had failed – a tumultuous age indeed. Accordingly, we have had the chance to see how distinctive and striking are the ways in which, in the text at hand, the symbols of animals that stand for the four successive empires of humanity and point towards the messianic time, serve for the framers' message.

A striking shift in the treatment of Rome does appear to take place in the period from the Mishnah to Genesis Rabbah and Leviticus Rabbah. In earlier times Rome symbolized little beyond itself, and Edom, Esau (absent in the Mishnah, a singleton in Tosefta), and Ishmael were concrete figures. In later times these figures bore traits congruent to the fact of Christian rule. The correspondence between the modes of symbolization – the pig, the sibling – and the facts of the Christian challenge to Judaism – the same Scripture, read a new way, the same messianic hope, interpreted differently – turns out to be remarkable and significant when we compare what the earlier compilers of canonical writings, behind the Mishnah and the Tosefta, produced to the writings of the later ones, behind the two Rabbah compilations. I have dwelt at great length on this matter, to make possible the reading of the evidence of the so-called Tannaite Midrashim.

Now to the task at hand. The evidence we seek, first, is narrative. Do we find in the so-called Tannaitic Midrashim stories[6] that differentiate among the nations, for example, Rome as against Babylonia or Persia or Media? Or are "the nations" regarded as an undifferentiated and homogenized mass, so that stories distinguishing one from another of the nations, or contrasting Israel with one or another of the nations, are not told? If the former, then we stand closer to the Yerushalmi and related compilations of Midrash exegeses, if the latter, we find ourselves in communion with the Mishnah. There can be a second sort of evidence as well, not narrative but propositional: are "the nations" encompassed within a single, undifferentiated classification for the purposes of making a point having little or nothing to do with "the nations" in particular? Or, when people wish to refer to gentiles in a propositional composition, do they appeal to "the evil kingdom" or "the fourth monarchy" or "Rome" or "Esau" or "Ishmael" or "Edom" in particular? If the former, then, we stand closer to the Mishnah and its circle, if the latter, then to the Yerushalmi, Genesis Rabbah, and Leviticus Rabbah.

2. Mekhilta Attributed to R. Ishmael

Shirata   Chapter   Thirty-Three
XXXIII:I
1.   A.   "Who is like you, O Lord, among gods? [Who is like you, majestic in holiness, terrible in glorious deeds, doing wonders?]":

     B.   When the Israelites saw that Pharaoh and his host had perished at the Red Sea, the dominion of the Egyptians was over, and judgments were executed on their idolatry, they all opened their mouths and said, "Who is like you, O Lord, among gods? [Who is like you, majestic in holiness, terrible in glorious deeds, doing wonders?]"

     C.   And not the Israelites alone said the song, but also the nations of the world said the song.

     D.   When the nations of the world saw that Pharaoh and his host had perished at the Red Sea, the dominion of the Egyptians was over, and judgments were executed on their idolatry, they all renounced their idolatry and opened their mouths and confessed their faith in the Lord and said, "Who is like you, O Lord, among gods? [Who is like you, majestic in holiness, terrible in glorious deeds, doing wonders?]"

---

[6]Since Maccoby refers to "the *aggadah*," it is legitimate to ask for stories or the absence of stories to serve as a principal indicator of the systemic position of a document.

E.　　So too you find that in the age to come the nations of the world will renounce their idolatry: "O Lord, my strength and my stronghold and my refuge, in the day of affliction to you the nations shall come...shall a man make himself gods" (Jer. 16:19-20); "In that day a man shall cast away his idols of silver...to go into the clefts of the rocks" (Isa. 2:20-21);. "And the idols shall utterly perish" (Isa. 20:18).

The important points are two.　First, the nations are undifferentiated, and Rome is not identified for special consideration. Second, there is an eschatological dimension to the theory of the nations, who in that day will confess to the worship of one God. But here again, we find an eschatology without resort to the messiah theme. Both of these traits place the statement at hand closer to the Mishnah than to the Yerushalmi.

Shirata Chapter Nine

XXXIV:I

12.　A.　　"The peoples have heard, they tremble":
　　　B.　　When the nations of the world heard that Pharaoh and his troops had perished in the sea and that the monarchy of Egypt had come to an end and that judgments had been carried out on their idols, they began to tremble.
　　　C.　　That is why it is said, "The peoples have heard, they tremble."
13.　A.　　Another interpretation of the phrase, "The peoples have heard, they tremble":
　　　B.　　When the nations of the world heard that the Omnipresent had raised up the horn of Israel and was bringing them into the land, they began to tremble.
　　　C.　　Said to them the Omnipresent, "Idiots of the world! How many of your kings have ruled, without Israel's taking umbrage?
　　　D.　　"For it is said, 'And these are the kings that reigned in the land of Edom' (Gen. 36:31).
　　　E.　　"And how many of your rulers have governed, without Israel's taking umbrage?
　　　F.　　"For it is said, 'The chief of Lotan' (Gen. 36:39).
　　　G.　　"Now you are taking umbrage! I for my part will take umbrage with you, for which there is no reconciliation: 'The Lord reigns, let the people tremble' (Ps. 99:1).

Here we see no differentiation among the nations. In the passages that follow, Scripture refers to specific nations, on account of which several of them are differentiated.

Shirata Chapter Nine

XXXIV:I

14.　A.　　"Pangs have seized the inhabitants of Philistia":
　　　B.　　When the inhabitants of Philistia heard that the Israelites were entering the land, they said, "Now they are going to come to take vengeance for the Ephraimites [whom we defeated in their premature exodus from Egypt]."

C.   For it is said, "And the sons of Ephraim, Shuthelah, and Bered was his son" (1 Chr. 7:20);

D.   "The children of Ephraim were archers, handling the bow, they turned back in the day of battle" (Ps. 78:9). Why? "Because they did not keep the covenant of God and would not walk in his Torah" (Ps. 78:10).

E.   That is, it was they transgressed the specified time limit [trying to gain redemption sooner than it was supposed to take place] and violated the terms of the oath.

16. A.   "Now are the chiefs of Edom dismayed":

B.   Should you suppose that [it was because they thought that] "they are coming to inherit our land," it is in fact stated, "You are to pass through the border of your brethren...take care not to contend with them" (Dt. 2:4-5).

C.   So why is it that "Now are the chiefs of Edom dismayed"?

D.   It was on account of [fear of their imposing] taxes.

17. A.   Another comment on the verse, "Now are the chiefs of Edom dismayed":

B.   It was because they thought, "Now the Israelites are coming to arouse the strife between their father and ours."

C.   "Esau hated Jacob" (Gen. 27:41).

The appeal to Esau/Edom is precipitated by Scripture, not by a special interest in distinctive aspects of Israelite-Roman relations, to which I see no appeal at all. This is shown in the very next passage.

Shirata Chapter Nine

XXXIV:I

18. A.   "The leaders of Moab, trembling seizes them":

B.   Should you suppose that [it was because they thought that] "they are coming to inherit our land," it is in fact stated, "Do not distress Moab" (Dt. 2:9); "And when you come near against the children of Ammon" (Dt. 2:19).

C.   So why is it that "Now are the chiefs of Edom dismayed"?

D.   It was on account of [fear of their imposing] taxes.

19. A.   Another comment on the verse, "the leaders of Moab, trembling seizes them":

B.   It was because they thought, "Now the Israelites are coming to arouse the strife between their father and ours."

C.   "And there was strife between the herdsmen of Abram's cattle" (Gen. 13:7).

20. A.   "All the inhabitants of Canaan have melted away":

B.   When the inhabitants of Canaan heard that the Omnipresent had said to Moses, "Only as to the cities of those nations...but you shall utterly destroy them" (Dt. 20:16-17), they thought, "These and those were afraid only on account of their capital and their property, but as to us, they are coming against us only to annihilate us and to inherit our land."

C.   They began to take fright: "All the inhabitants of Canaan have melted away,"

      D.   "Melting away" meaning only, "take fright": "And every heart shall lose courage" (Ezek. 21:12); "When the earth and all the inhabitants thereof are dissolved" (Ps. 75:4); "That their heart may melt" (Ezek. 21:20).

21. A.   "Terror and dread fall upon them":

      B.   "Terror" on the distant, "dread" on the nearby ones.

      C.   Thus: "And it came to pass when all the kings of the Amorites heard" (Josh. 5:1).

      D.   So Rahab said to the messengers of Joshua: "For we have heard how the Lord dried up the water of the Red Sea...and as soon as we had heard it our hearts melted" (Josh. 2:10-11).

The theme is the same throughout, and if I had to invoke the criterion of differentiation or uniform treatment, I would say that the intent of the compositor or author is to treat all the nations in exactly the same way and to say one thing about them all.

The foregoing passages play no role in Genesis Rabbah and Leviticus Rabbah. By contrast, the following passage, shared with Leviticus Rabbah and Genesis Rabbah, singles out Rome in the differentiation of the empires that subjugate Israel.

Mekhilta attributed to R. Ishmael

LV:I

13. A.   He showed him [Abraham] the four monarchies which are destined to subjugate his children:

      B.   "And it came to pass, as the sun was going down,] lo, a deep sleep fell on Abram, and lo, a dread and great darkness fell upon him" (Gen. 15:12).

      C.   "...lo, a dread" refers to Babylonia, [as it is written, "Then was Nebuchadnezzar filled with fury" (Gen. 3:19)].

      D.   "...and darkness" refers to Media, [which darkened the eyes of Israel by making it necessary for the Israelites to fast and conduct public mourning].

      E.   "...great..." refers to Greece.

      F.   "...fell upon him" refers to Edom, [as it is written, "The earth quakes at the noise of their fall" (Jer. 49:21)].

      G.   Some reverse matters:

      H.   "...fell upon him" refers to Babylonia, since it is written, "Fallen, fallen is Babylonia" (Isa. 21:9).

      I.   "...great..." refers to Media, in line with this verse: "King Ahasuerus did make great" (Est. 3:1).

      J.   "...and darkness" refers to Greece, which darkened the eyes of Israel by its harsh decrees.

      K.   "...lo, a dread" refers to Edom, as it is written, "After this I saw...a fourth beast, dreadful and terrible" (Dan. 7:7).

I do not think we can make much of the appearance of a singleton of this sort, when, we realize, it has traveled from one document to another. But it does represent a different conception of Rome among the nations, and it does accomplish that differentiation among the nations that is otherwise uncommon in the document at hand.

3. Sifra

Sifra Parashat Behuqotai Pereq 3
CCLXIII:I
8. A.   "And I have broken the bars of your yoke":
    B.   The matter may be compared to the case of a householder who had a cow for ploughing, and he lent it to someone else to plough with it.
    C.   That man had ten sons. This one came and ploughed with it and went his way, and that one came and ploughed with it and went his way, so that the cow got tired and crouched down.
    D.   All the other cows came back, but that cow did not enter the fold.
    E.   The owner hardly agreed to accept consolation from that man, but he went and broke the yoke and cut off the carved ends of the yoke.
    F.   So is Israel in this world.
    G.   One ruler comes along and subjugates them and then goes his way, then another ruler comes along and subjugates them and goes his way, so that the furrow is very long.
    H.   So it is said, "Plowman plowed across my back; they made long furrows. [The Lord, the righteous one, has snapped the cords of the wicked]" (Ps. 129:3-4).
    I.   Tomorrow, when the end comes, the Holy One, blessed be He, will not say to the nations, "Thus and so have you done to my children!"
    J.   Rather, he will immediately come and break the yoke and cut off the ends of the yoke.
    K.   For it is said, "and I have broken the bars of your yoke."
    L.   And further, "The Lord has snapped the cords of the wicked."

Here again when we deal with the government of the nations, it is without that differentiation that singles out Rome as last, worst, strangest, or whatever. The nations are pretty much the same throughout; they bear in common the single and sole important trait that they impose their yoke on Israel. True, the Mishnah's interest in the nations does not encompass that point; but our point of interest – the issue of differentiation – is made once more. We also note, by the way, that when we introduce the eschatological dimension of Israel's subjugation to the nations, we hear nothing of the Messiah theme; God, not the Messiah, does these things.

4. Sifré to Numbers 1-115

Sifré to Numbers 1-115
LXXXIV:I.IV
1.   A.   "...and let them that hate you flee before you":
     B.   And do those who hate [come before] him who spoke and brought
             the world into being?
     C.   The purpose of the verse at hand is to say that whoever hates
             Israel is as if he hates him who spoke and by his word brought the
             world into being.
     D.   Along these same lines: "In the greatness of your majesty you
             overthrow your adversaries" (Ex. 15:7).
     E.   And are there really adversaries before him who spoke and by his
             word brought the world into being? But Scripture thus indicates
             that whoever rose up against Israel is as if he rose up against the
             Omnipresent.
     F.   Along these same lines: "Do not forget the clamor of your foes,
             the uproar of your adversaries, which goes up continually" (Ps.
             74:23).
     G.   "For lo, your enemies, O Lord" (Ps. 92:10).
     H.   "For those who are far from you shall perish, you put an end to
             those who are false to you" (Ps. 73:27)
     I.   "For lo, your enemies are in tumult, those who hate you have
             raised their heads" (Ps. 83:2). On what account? "They lay crafty
             plans against your people, they consult together against your
             protected ones" (Ps. 83:3).
     J.   "Do I not hate those who hate you, O Lord? And do I not loathe
             them that rise up against you? I hate them with perfect hatred, I
             count them my enemies" (Ps. 139:21-22)
     K.   And so too Scripture says, ""For whoever lays hands on you is as if
             he lays hands on the apple of his eye" (Zech. 2:12).

The nations are undifferentiated; those who hate Israel hate God,
and that is without singling out any one of them for special
consideration.

5. Sifré to Deuteronomy

Sifré to Deuteronomy Pisqa
CCCXXII:III
1.   A.   "...their enemies who might misjudge":
     B.   In the time of Israel's trouble, the nations of the world treat them
             as strangers and act as though they do not know them at all.
     C.   And so we find that they wanted to flee toward the north, but they
             would not gather them in, rather closing the gates against them,
             in line with this verse:

D.   "For three sins of Tyre, and even for four, I shall not grant them a reprieve, because, forgetting the ties of kinship, they delivered a whole band of exiles to Edom" (Amos 1:9).

E.   They wanted to flee to the south but they shut them out:

F.   "Thus says the Lord, For three sins of Gaza, even for four, I shall grant them no reprieve, because they deported a whole band of exiles and delivered them up to Edom" (Amos 1:6).

G.   They wanted to flee to the east, but they shut them out:

H.   "Thus says the Lord, For three sins of Damascus" (Amos 1:3).

I.   They wanted to flee to the west, but they shut them out:

J.   "With the Arabs: an oracle. You caravans of Dedan, that camp in the scrub with the Arabs, bring water to meet the thirsty. You dwellers in Tema, meet the fugitives with food, for they flee from the sword, the sharp edge of the sword, from the bent bow, and from the press of battle" (Isa. 21:13-15).

K.   When things go well with Israel, the nations of the world try to deceive them and pretend that they are brothers, and so Esau said to Jacob, "I have more than enough, keep what is yours, my brother" (Gen. 33).

L.   And so did Hiram say to Solomon, "What are these forests, which you have given to me, my brother" (1 Kgs. 9:13).

The result is the same as before. The nations are the same, act the same, treat Israel in the same way, and in no way are differentiated. No occasion at which Rome might be introduced is exploited for that purpose. The so-called Tannaite Midrashim all fall within the orbit of the Mishnah in failing to address the special role of Rome (or Ishmael, Edom, and Esau).[7]

---

[7]This result is odd for a number of reasons. What Chapters Four and Five suggest is that the system adumbrated by the Yerushalmi and closely aligned documents is rather more "special" than I have appreciated; but it became normative.

VI

Israel

1. The Mishnah as against the Yerushalmi

From "the nations" we move on to "Israel," an important systemic variable – all Judaisms require a doctrine of "Israel" – and indicator. For the Mishnah, "Israel" served as a taxic indicator in two dimensions. It classified persons within Israel. It classified nations vis-à-vis Israel. For when the system of the Mishnah invoked the category, "Israel," it invariably meant to call forth, also, the opposite of "Israel," and "Israel" has in the Mishnah only two opposites: "Israel" versus the nations, without, and "Israel" versus Levite, versus Priest, within. Both usages, then, treat "Israel" as transitive and taxonomic, helping to sort out both persons and social entities. For the Yerushalmi and related documents, by contrast, "Israel" served intransitively, to speak of a particular family. "Israel" invoked a genealogy, for all Israelites were deemed part of the extended family of a single couple, Abraham and Sarah. "Israel," further, referred to a social entity lacking all analogy: an entity that, in societies, was *sui generis* and beyond all comparisons. These definitions of "Israel" – metaphorizations, really – are distinct from one another. Each, as a matter of fact, carried forward the systemic program of the system that made use of it.

Two metaphors, scarcely explored in the writings of the first stage – the Mishnah's – in the formation of the Judaism of the Dual Torah, in the second stage came to prominence, first, the view of "Israel" as a family, the children and heirs of the man, Israel; second, the conception of "Israel" as *sui generis*. This second sense may be expressed in emphasis upon "Israel" as holy, wholly other and different from the nations. While "Israel" in the first phase of the formation of Judaism perpetually finds definition in relationship to its opposite, "Israel" in the second phase constituted an intransitive entity, defined in its own terms and not solely or mainly in relationship to other comparable entities. The enormous investment in the conception of "Israel" as *sui generis* makes that point blatantly.

But "Israel" as family bears that same trait of autonomy and self-evident definition. In the first phase, just as "gentile" was an abstract category, so was "Israel." "*Kohen*" was a category, and so too "Israel." When we see "Israel" as classifier and taxonomic category, we confront an abstraction in a system of philosophy. "Israel" in the second stratum of the literature of the Dual Torah by contrast bears a socially vivid sense. The contrast is clear. "Israel" when viewed in the this-worldly framework of most of the Mishnah's discussions emerges through a series of contrasts and comparisons, not as intrinsically important, systemically determinative facts. We know in that literature what "Israel" or "an Israel" is mainly when we can specify the antonym. In the successor system, by contrast, Israel is not defined by not-Israel but by appeal to other dimensions of social being altogether.

This social entity, this Israel, therefore, may constitute a family of a particular order, that is, all Jews descend from Abraham, Isaac, and Jacob, Sarah, Rebecca, Leah, and Rachel. Then we invoke the metaphor of family. Or, it may be held, Israel constitutes a people or a nation, in which case to be "Israel" is to be part of a political unit of one kind or another, comparable to other such social groups based on, or in, a shared political being, and that will dictate thought on the nature of Israel, whether or not the Jews at a given time and place constituted a political entity at all. We find, furthermore, the claim that the social entity at hand simply is not like any other, a genus unto itself. "Israel" as unique has no counterpart among the nations; on one side of the social equation of humanity are all the nations all together, on the other side, Israel, all alone. These and other metaphors serve as the vehicles for the social thought of the Judaic systems, or Judaisms, of the ages. These abstract observations have now to be made concrete for our particular experiment.

We come to identify the data that will distinguish one system from another, hence tell us, by their presence of absence, the intellectual location of the mediating documents. These data derive from those social metaphors by which Judaisms express their systemic statement on what they understand by (an) "Israel." A social metaphor tells a group how to identify itself, and this in two ways. First, the metaphor identifies the type or genus of social group at hand, the genus, and, second, it will consequently define the species of the genus, or type, at hand. Is the social entity a family? Then how does it compare to other families? Is it a nation? Then in what way does it differ from other nations, and in what context does the category, nation, take on its definitive sense and meaning? Or a social group may declare itself *sui generis*, not like any other social group at all, but a genus unto itself, for example, a third possibility as between two available choices.

The kind of metaphors that come into use, then, dictate our differentiation among systems. Metaphors of two basic classifications occur. First of all, some held that the Jews – Israel – were *sui generis*, of a type of social entity lacking all counterpart, and thus not of a type into which all other social groups could be classified. These then generate the usage of "Israel" as taxic indicator: like this, utterly unlike that. Then, as I said at the outset, "Israel" will precipitate the appeal to its opposite, either "gentile" or "priest/Levite." Second, others maintained that Israel formed a distinct species of a common genus, whether family or nation or people. That metaphor accounts for the identification of "Israel" with the children of Abraham and Sarah. These two indicators intertwine in the successor system. But the primary usage of "Israel" in the initial one is, as I said, taxonomic, and in the mediating documents, we shall want to know how, exactly, "Israel" is metaphorized.

To understand the meaning of "Israel" as the Mishnah and its friends sort matters out, we revert to the sense of "gentile." Specifically, does the authorship of the Mishnah differentiate when speaking of gentiles? The answer is no, for the gentiles represent an undifferentiated mass. To the system of the Mishnah, whether or not a gentile is a Roman or an Aramaean or a Syrian or a Briton does not matter (except, for example, at M. Neg. 2:2, as to skin tone, an Ethiopian is different from a German). And, it is also the fact, to the system of the Mishnah, that in the relationship at hand, "Israel" is not differentiated either. The upshot is that just as "gentile" is an abstract category, so is "Israel." *"Kohen"* is a category, and so is "Israel." For the purposes for which Israel/priest are defined, no further differentiation is undertaken. That is where matters end. But, as we shall see, to the Judaic system represented by the Yerushalmi and its associated writings, "gentile" may be Roman or other-than-Roman, for instance, Babylonian, Median, or Greek. That act of further differentiation – we may call it "speciation" – makes a considerable difference in the appreciation of gentile.

"Israel" in the first system of Judaism finds definition in relationship to its opposite. The entire process of thought pursues philosophical lines, defining matters and sorting them out as do the scientists in natural philosophy, through comparison and contrast of traits. Only when the traits of mind shift, as they do in the second phase of the formation of Judaism portrayed in its canonical writings, and sages turn to categories of history, therefore also to storytelling and other forms of narrative, does the poetry of metaphor and analogy come into play. Then we see those powerful metaphors that impart to the data at hand the color and life that, in the Judaism at hand, "Israel" has displayed from then to now.

In the system adumbrated by the Yerushalmi and related writings "Israel" circulated not as an abstraction but as a concrete and palpable social fact: a real group of people thoughtfully imagined, profoundly loved, intimately known. And that is why "Israel" found definition in its own terms, meaning, what "we" are, that is absolutely and not principally in terms of who, or what, an "Israel" – an "it" – was not. "Israel" as against "not-Israel," "Israel" as against Levite or priest had defined categories which portray "Israel" not in relationship to "not-Israel," for example, family formed by a common genealogy and sustained by the shared inheritance of the merit of the ancestors, Israel as *sui generis* and – in the nature of things – therefore a supernatural entity – categories served discourse only at severely limited points. Now we find these traits of thought and definition: the definition of "Israel" in its own terms, the representation of "Israel" as a concrete and material society or nation or family, the protracted account of "Israel" in the social world of nations and not solely in the theoretical and abstract world of classifying things, including, incidentally, nations, the attention to the history and eschatological salvation of this "Israel."

The evidence we seek is narrative[1] and verbal alike. Do we find usages of "Israel" or stories about "Israel" as not merely taxic indicator, vis-à-vis the nations without, the castes within, but intransitive social entity: a family? Stories about "Israel" as the extended family of Abraham, Isaac, and Jacob place us closer to the position of the Yerushalmi and associated writings and their conception of what is important about "Israel." So too the treatment of Israel as different in genus from the nations, wholly other, will situate us nearer the Yerushalmi than the Mishnah, since that Israel by its nature is represented as intransitive. References to "Israel, not gentiles," or "Israel, Levite, priest" place us closer to the utilization of "Israel" in characteristic of the Mishnah. We deal, of course, with tendencies and aggregates, not with precise and one-sided evidence in favor of one or another of the possibilities at hand.

---

[1]What I said about the appropriate character of this kind of evidence in response to Maccoby's allegation needs no further repetition.

2. Mekhilta Attributed to R. Ishmael

The following links Israel's conduct at the Sea with Israel's ancestors, Abraham, Isaac, and Jacob, who had taught them to worship God. I give only a small part of the whole, which laboriously makes this one point, defining Israel genealogically in the manner of the Yerushalmi.

Mekhilta attributed to R. Ishmael

XXI:I

7. A. "And they were in great fear. And the people of Israel cried out to the Lord":
    B. They reverted to their ancestors' profession, the profession of Abraham, Isaac, and Jacob.
    C. What does Scripture say of Abraham? "Having Beth-el on the west and Ai on the east, he built an altar to the Lord and called on the name of the Lord" (Gen. 12:8); "And Abraham planted a tamarisk tree in Beer Sheba and called on the name of the Lord, the everlasting God" (Gen. 21:33).
    D. Isaac: "And Isaac went out to meditate in the field" (Gen. 24:63), and meditation bears the meaning of prayer: "Evening and morning and at noonday I will complain and moan, and he has heard my voice" (Ps. 55:18); "I pour out my complaint before him' (Ps. 142:3); "A prayer of the afflicted, when he faints and pours out his complaint before the Lord" (Ps. 102:1).
    E. Jacob: "And he lighted upon the place" (Gen. 28:11), and the word for "lighting upon" means only prayer: "Therefore do not pray for this people or lift up cry or prayer for them nor make intercession to me" (Jer 7:16); "Let them now make intercession to the Lord of hosts" (Jer. 27:18).

The passage goes on to speak of others out of the past who taught Israel to pray. The passage is not critical to my argument but seems to me relevant. What follows is a more direct characterization of Israel as different from all the nations, uniquely loved by God.

Mekhilta attributed to R. Ishmael

XXVIII:I

4. A. Another interpretation of "my strength":
    B. [Israel speaks:] "You help and support everyone in the world, but me most of all.
5. A. "The Lord is [my strength] and my song":
    B. [Israel speaks:] "You are a song for everyone in the world, but me most of all.
    C. "He made me particular, and I made him particular.
    D. "He made me particular: 'The Lord has today made you special' (Dt. 26:18).
    E. "And I made him particular: 'And you have made the Lord particular this day' (Dt. 26:17)."

F.   "True, lo, the nations of the world also declare the praise of the One who spoke and brought the world into being.

G.   "But mine is very pleasing before him: 'But sweet are the songs of Israel' (2 Sam. 23:1)."

6.   A.   [Continuing the foregoing:] Israel says, "Hear, Israel, the Lord our God, the Lord is one" (Dt. 6:4).

B.   And the Holy Spirit cries out from Heaven, "And who is like your people Israel, a unique nation in the earth" (1 Chr. 17:21).

C.   Israel says, "Who is like you Lord among the mighty" (Ex. 15:11).

D.   And the Holy Spirit cries out from Heaven, "Happy are you, Israel, who is like you" (Dt. 33:29).

E.   Israel says, "As the Lord our God is whenever we call on him" (Dt. 4:7).

F.   And the Holy Spirit cries out from Heaven, "And what great nation is there that has statutes and ordinances so righteous" (Dt. 4:8).

G.   Israel says, "For you are the glory of their strength" (Ps. 89:18).

H.   And the Holy Spirit cries out from Heaven, "Israel in whom I will be glorified" (Isa. 49:3).

7.   A.   "And he has become my salvation":

B.   "You are the salvation of everyone in the world but me most of all.

8.   A.   Another interpretation of the clause, "and he has become my salvation":

B.   "He was, and he will be [my salvation],

C.   "He was in times past, and he will be, in the age to come."

The point throughout is the uniqueness of Israel, attested by the Song, with the special emphasis upon the "my." The same point is made in the next passage, which has the fate of Israel intertwined with that of God, the treatment of Israel identified with the nations' attitude toward God.

Mekhilta attributed to R. Ishmael
XXXI:I
15.   A.   And whoever helps Israel is as if he helped the One who spoke and brought the world into being,

B.   for it is said, "Curse Meroz, said the angel of the Lord, curse bitterly the dwellers therein, because they did not come to the help of the Lord, to the help of the Lord against the mighty" (Judg. 5:23).

16.   A.   ["In the greatness of your majesty you overthrow those who rose up against you":] "You have greatly taken pride over those who rose up against you."

B.   And who are those who rose up against you? They are the ones you rose up against your children.

C.   How so?

D.   "Against Chedorlaomer, king of Elam" (Gen. 14:9); "And he divided himself against them by night" (Gen. 14:15); "Who has raised up one from the east...his sword makes them as the dust" (Isa. 41:2).

E.   And what follows? "He pursues them and passes on safely" (Isa. 41:3).

F.   So too: "The Lord says to my lord, the rod of your strength the Lord will send out of Zion; your people offer themselves willingly in the day of your warfare...the Lord has sworn and will not repent..." (Ps. 110:1-4).

G.   And what follows? "The Lord as your right hand" (Ps. 110:5).

17. A.   ["In the greatness of your majesty you overthrow those who rose up against you":] "You have greatly taken pride over those who rose up against you."

B.   And who are those who rose up against you? They are the ones who rose up against your children.

C.   That is, against Pharoah and all his hosts.

D.   "And they took six hundred chosen chariots" (Ex. 14:7); "Pharaoh's chariots and his hosts has he cast into the sea" (Ezek. 15:4).

18. A.   ["In the greatness of your majesty you overthrow those who rose up against you":] "You have greatly taken pride over those who rose up against you."

B.   And who are those who rose up against you? They are the ones who rose up against your children.

C.   That is, against Sisera and all his chariots:

D.   "And Sisera gathered together all his chariots" (Judg. 4:13); "They fought from Heaven" (Judg. 5:20).

19. A.   ["In the greatness of your majesty you overthrow those who rose up against you":] "You have greatly taken pride over those who rose up against you."

B.   And who are those who rose up against you? They are the ones who rose up against your children.

C.   That is, against Sennacherib and all his troops:

D.   "By your servants you have taunted..." (Isa. 37:24); "And the Lord sent an angel who cut off all the mighty men of valor" (2 Chr. 32:21).

20. A.   ["In the greatness of your majesty you overthrow those who rose up against you":] "You have greatly taken pride over those who rose up against you."

B.   And who are those who rose up against you? They are the ones who rose up against your children.

C.   That is, against Nebuchadnezzar and all his multitude:

D.   And you said in your heart, I will ascend to Heaven" (Isa. 14:13).

E.   Nebuchadnezzar had said, "I will make a little cloud for myself and will live in it," so: "I will ascend above the heights of the clouds" (Isa. 14:14).

F.   Said to him the Holy One, blessed be He, "You wanted to distinguish yourself from other people, so in the end people will be distinguished from you: 'At the end of twelve months...the king spoke and said, Is not this great Babylon....While the word was in the king's mouth,...and you shall be driven from men....The same hour the thing was fulfilled upon Nebuchadnezzar" (Dan. 4:26-40). "All this came upon the king Nebuchadnezzar" (Dan. 4:25).

G.   "Belshazzar the king made a great feast; Belshazzar, while he tasted the wine, commanded...then they brought the golden

vessels...they drank wine...in the same hour fingers came
forth....Then the king's face was changed." (Dan. 5:1-6).

H.   Further: "Woe to him who gives his neighbor drink...you are filled
with shame instead of glory" (Hab. 2:15-16); "In that night
Belshazzar, the Chaldean king, was slain" (Dan. 5:30).

21. A.   "You overthrow those who rose up against you":

B.   What is written here is not "you have overthrown" but "you will
overthrow those that rise up against you,"

C.   which is to say, in the age to come.

D.   So it is written: "Break their teeth, God, in their mouth" (Ps. 58:7),
"Because they give no heed to the works of the Lord nor to the
workings of his hands; he will break them down and not build
them up" (Ps. 28:5).

E.   "He will break them down": in this world,

F.   "And not build them up": in the world to come.

While protracted and repetitive, the composition really does make
a single point, which is that those who oppose Israel are as though
they oppose God, and those who help Israel help God. Israel then is
absolutely unique and *sui generis*, not to be compared to the nations, just
as the Yerushalmi and associated writings maintain.

3. Sifra

Sifra Parashat Tazria Parashah 1
CXXI:I
1. A.   ["The Lord spoke to Moses, saying, 'Speak to the Israelite people
thus: When a woman at childbirth bears a male, she shall be
unclean seven days'":]

B.   "Israelite people":

C.   In this matter, the Israelite people are engaged, but idolators are
not engaged in this matter.

The specification of Israelites is understood to exclude gentiles. In
the following we ask the same question, with a different result.

Sifra Parashat Aharé Mot Pereq 13
CXCIV:I
1. A.   "None of you [shall come near anyone of his own flesh to uncover
nakedness; I am the Lord]":

B.   [Since the Hebrew for "none of you" is, "a man, a man,"] why is it
that Scripture says, "a man, a man"?

C.   It serves to encompass gentiles, who are admonished against
incest like Israelites.

The clarification of the language here yields an inclusive result.
Gentiles are not to practice incest. These two passages and the many, in
Sifra, that go over the same ground, treat Israel and the nations as
comparable, Israel as transitive, and in such passages Israel by

definition is not unique. The following likewise represent Israel as subject to the same conditions as the gentiles and not fundamentally different from them.

Sifra
CXCIV:II

7. A.   "You shall not copy the practices of the land of Egypt where you dwelt":

    B.   Scripture makes the point that the practices of the Egyptians were the most corrupt of those of all peoples,

    C.   and that place in which Israel dwelt was the most corrupt in the land of Egypt.

8. A.   "Or of the land of Canaan to which I am taking you":

    B.   Now was it not perfectly well known that they were coming to the land of Canaan?

    C.   Why does Scripture make this point, saying "or of the land of Canaan to which I am taking you"?

    D.   But Scripture so makes the point that the practices of the Canaanites were the most corrupt of those of all peoples,

    E.   and that place to which the Israelites were planning to go was the most corrupt of all.

9. A.   "You shall not copy the practices of the land of Egypt where you dwelt, or of the land of Canaan to which I am taking you":

    B.   Scripture thereby treats as analogous the practices of the Egyptians and the practices of the Canaanites.

    C.   What were the practices of the Canaanites?

    D.   They were flooded with idolatry, fornication, murder, pederasty, and bestiality.

    E.   So the practices of the Egyptians were the same.

    F.   Then why did the Egyptians receive their punishment forty years ahead of the Canaanites?

    G.   It was as a reward for their paying honor to that righteous man, as it is said, 'Hear us, my lord, you are the elect of God among us' (Gen. 23:6).

    H.   and further: "[The name of Hebron was formerly Kiriath-arba;] he was the great man among the Anakites. And the land had rest from war" (Josh. 14:15).

10. A.   "nor shall you follow their laws":

    B.   Now [in making this inclusive statement,] what is it that Scripture has neglected to say?

    C.   Has it not already been said, "Let no one be found among you who consigns his son or daughter to the fire, or who is an augur, a soothsayer, a diviner, a sorcerer, one who casts spells, or one who consults ghosts or familiar spirits, or one who inquires of the dead" (Dt. 18:10)?

    D.   Why then does Scripture say, "nor shall you follow their laws"?

    E.   It is that you should not follow their customs in matters that are established by law for them, for example, going to their theaters, circuses, and playing fields.

F.   R. Meir says, "These are forbidden under the rubric of 'the ways of the Amorites,' which sages have specified."

G.   R. Judah b. Betera says, "The meaning is that you should not grow your hair as they do, you should not make your show-fringes long, you should not get a haircut in the manner of their priests."

H.   And should you argue, "For them they are laws, for us they are not laws?"

I.   Scripture says, "My rules alone shall you observe and faithfully follow my laws: I the Lord am your God."

J.   Still, the impulse to do evil can still quibble and say, "Theirs are nicer than ours"!

K.   Scripture says, "You shall keep and do it, for it is your wisdom and your understanding" (Dt. 4:6).

11.   A.   "You shall keep my laws":

B.   This refers to matters that are written in the Torah.

C.   But if they had not been written in the Torah, it would have been entirely logical to write them,

D.   for example, rules governing thievery, fornication, idolatry, blasphemy, murder,

E.   examples of rules that, had they not been written in the Torah, would have been logical to include them.

F.   Then there are those concerning which the impulse to do evil raises doubt, the nations of the world, idolators, raise doubt,

G.   for instance, the prohibition against eating pork, wearing mixed species, the rite of removing the shoe in the case of the deceased childless brother's widow, the purification-rite for the person afflicted with the skin ailment, the goat that is sent forth –

H.   cases in which the impulse to do evil raises doubt, the nations of the world, idolators, raise doubt.

I.   In this regard Scripture says, "I the Lord have made these ordinances, and you have no right to raise doubts concerning them."

12.   A.   "[My rules alone shall you observe] and faithfully follow [my laws]":

B.   Treat them as principal and do not treat them as peripheral.

13.   A.   "And faithfully follow":

B.   Your give and take should be only in them.

C.   You should never mix up with them other matters,

D.   for instance, you should not say, "I have learned the wisdom of Israel, not I shall learn the wisdom of the nations."

E.   Scripture says, "...and faithfully follow,"

F.   You do not have the right to take your leave of them.

G.   And so Scripture says, "Tie them over your heart always, bind them around your throat. When you walk it will lead you; when you lie down it will watch over you; and when you are awake it will talk with you" (Prov. 6:21-22).

H.   "When you walk it will lead you": in this world.

I.   "When you lie down it will watch over you": in the hour of death.

J.   "And when you are awake it will talk with you": in the age to come.

K. And so Scripture says, "Awake and shout for joy, you who dwell in the dust, for your dew is like the dew on fresh growth, you make the land of the shades to come to life" (Isa. 26:19).

L. And might you say, "My hope is lost, my prospects are lost"?

M. Scripture says, "I am the Lord":

N. "I am your hope, I am your prospects, in me is your trust."

O. And so Scripture says, "Till you grow old, I will be the same; when you turn gray, it is I who will carry; I was the Maker and I will be the Bearer; and I will carry and rescue you" (Isa. 46:4).

P. And so Scripture says, "Thus said the Lord, the King of Israel, their redeemer, the Lord of hosts: I am the first and I am the last, and there is no god but me" (Isa. 44:6).

Q. And further: ""Who has wrought and achieved this? He who announced the generations from the start – I the Lord who was first and will be with the last as well" (Isa. 41:4).

15. A. "By the pursuit of which man shall live":

B. R. Jeremiah says, "How do I know that even a gentile who keeps the Torah, lo, he is like the high priest?

C. "Scripture says, 'by the pursuit of which man shall live.'"

D. And so he says, "'And this is the Torah of the priests, Levites, and Israelites,' is not what is said here, but rather, 'This is the Torah of the man, O Lord God' (2 Sam. 7:19)."

E. And so he says, "'Open the gates and let priests, Levites, and Israelites enter it' is not what is said, but rather, 'Open the gates and let the righteous nation, who keeps faith, enter it' (Isa. 26:2)."

F. And so he says, "'This is the gate of the Lord. Priests, Levites, and Israelites...' is not what is said, but rather, 'the righteous shall enter into it' (Ps. 118:20).

G. And so he says, "'What is said is not, 'Rejoice, priests, Levites, and Israelites,' but rather, 'Rejoice, O righteous, in the Lord' (Ps. 33:1)."

H. And so he says, "It is not, 'Do good, O Lord, to the priests, Levites, and Israelites,' but rather, 'Do good, O Lord, to the good, to the upright in heart' (Ps. 125:4)."

I. "Thus, even a gentile who keeps the Torah, lo, he is like the high priest."

16. A. "by the pursuit of which man shall live":

B. not that he should die by them.

C. R. Ishmael would say, "How do you know that if people should say to someone when entirely alone, 'Worship an idol and do not be put to death,' the person should worship the idol and not be put to death?

D. "Scripture says, 'By the pursuit of which man shall live,' not that he should die by them."

E. "But even if it is in public should he obey them?

F. "Scripture says, '[You shall faithfully observe my commandments; I am the Lord.] You shall not profane my holy name, that I may be sanctified in the midst of the Israelite people – I the Lord who sanctify you, I who brought you out of the land of Egypt to be your God, I the Lord' (Lev. 22:31-32).

G. "If you sanctify my name, then I shall sanctify my name through you.

H.   "For that is just as Hananiah, Mishael, and Azariah did.

I.   "When all of the nations of the world at that time were prostrate before the idol, while they stood up like palm trees.

J.   "And concerning them it is stated explicitly in tradition: 'Your stately form is like the palm' (Song 7:8).

K.   "'I say, let me climb the palm, let me take hold of its branches; [let your breasts be like clusters of grapes, your breath like the fragrance of apples, and your mouth like choicest wine]' (Ps. 7:9).

L.   "'This day I shall be exalted through them in the sight of the nations of the world, who deny the Torah.

M.   "'This day I shall exact vengeance for them from those who hate them.

N.   "'This day I shall resurrect the dead among them.'

O.   "I am the Lord":

P.   "I am Judge to exact punishment and faithful to pay a reward.

The overall theme is the conduct of the nations and the relationship of Israelites to prevailing practice in the world at large. The point throughout is that Israel must not copy the ways of the gentiles. And that point is precisely what the base verse says. So what we have is a kind of scrapbook of diverse materials, all of them pertinent to a fundamental proposition, if not particular to the details of the formulation of that proposition in the passage at hand. From our perspective what is important is the comparability of Israel to the nations, which is far more the Mishnah's than the Yerushalmi's perspective on matters. All of Sifra's materials utilize "Israel" for taxic purposes, and Israel is transitive throughout.

4. Sifré to Numbers 1-115

In the surveyed passages I find nothing relevant.

5. Sifré to Deuteronomy

Sifré to Deuteronomy

XXXI:I

1.   A.   "Hear, O Israel! The Lord is our God, the Lord alone" (Dt. 6:4-9):

      B.   Why is this matter stated?

      C.   It is because it is said, "Speak to the children of Israel" (Ex. 25:2).

      D.   "Speak to the children of Abraham," "Speak to the children of Isaac," is not written here, but rather, "Speak to the children of Israel."

      E.   Our father Jacob had the merit that the act of speech should be addressed to his children [in particular], because our father, Jacob, lived in fear all his life, saying, "Woe is me, perhaps some chaff should come forth from me, as it came forth from my fathers.

F.   "From Abraham came forth Ishmael, from Isaac issued Esau. But as to me, may no chaff ever issue from me as came forth from my fathers."

Israel as family, defined by a common genealogy and governed by that, is the paramount metaphor before us here. My sense is that Rome as Esau plays a role too, but that is not compelling, since the context is what requires a reference to Esau. So for our purpose the paramount metaphor for Israel, the Yerushalmi's, is what governs.

Sifré to Deuteronomy
XXXI:III

1.   A.   "The Lord is our God":
     B.   Why is this stated? Is it not said in any event, "The Lord is one"?
     C.   Why then does Scripture say, "is our God"?
     D.   Because the name of God rests upon us in greatest measure.
2.   A.   Along these same lines: "Three times in the year shall all your males appear before the Lord God, *the God of Israel* " (Ex. 34:23):
     B.   Why is it necessary to say matters in this way? Does it not in fact say, "before the Lord God"?
     C.   Because the name of God rests upon Israel in greatest measure.
3.   A.   Along these same lines: "Thus says the Lord of hosts, *the God of Israel*" (Jer. 32:14).
     B.   Why is it necessary to say matters in this way? Does it not in fact say, "Behold I am the Lord, the God of all flesh, is there anything too hard for me" (Jer. 32:27)?
     C.   Why then does Scripture say, *"the God of Israel "*?
     D.   Because the name of God rests upon Israel in greatest measure.
4.   A.   Along these same lines: "Hear, O my people, and I will speak, O Israel, and I will testify against you. God, your God, I am" (Ps. 50:7):
     B.   Because the name of God rests upon you in greatest measure.

Sifré to Deuteronomy
XXXI:IV

1.   A.   "The Lord, our God": – for us.
     B.   "the Lord is one: " – for everyone in the world.
     C.   "the Lord, our God": – in this world.
     D.   "the Lord is one": – in the world to come.
     E.   And so Scripture says, "The Lord shall be king over all the earth. In that day shall the Lord be one and his name one" (Zech. 14:9).

Intransitive Israel is the paramount metaphor, but, we note, an eschatological point is made as well. At this time, God's name rests in greatest measure upon Israel. But in the age to come, God's name will achieve that unity that derives from the confession of all humanity. All of this leaves us entirely within the framework of the Yerushalmi's reading of Israel.

Sifré to Deuteronomy

CCCXXVI:I

1. A.   ["For the Lord will vindicate his people and repents himself [JPS:
           take revenge] for his servants, when he sees that their might is
           gone, and neither bond nor free is left"(Dt. 32:36):]
    B.   "For the Lord will vindicate his people":
    C.   When the Holy One, blessed be He, judges the nations, it is a joy
           to him, as it is said, ""For the Lord will vindicate his people."
    D.   But when the Holy One, blessed be He, judges Israel, it is – as it
           were – a source of grief to him.
    E.   For it is said, "…and repents himself [JPS: take revenge] for his
           servants.
    F.   Now "repents" can only mean "regret, for it is said, "For I regret
           that I made them" (Gen. 6:7),
    G.   and further, "I regret that I made Saul king" (1 Sam. 15:11).

Here is a standard way of invoking the definition of Israel as *sui
generis*, utterly beyond comparison with the nations. The following
makes the same point, that Israel on earth is unique as God in Heaven
is unique.

Sifré to Deuteronomy

CCCLV:XVII

1. A.   ["O Jeshurun, there is none like God" (Dt. 33:24):]
    B.   "O Jeshurun, there is none like God":
    C.   The Israelites say, "There is none like God,"
    D.   and the Holy Spirit says, "O Jeshurun."
2. A.   The Israelites say, "Who is like you, O Lord among the mighty"
           (Ex. 15:11).
    B.   And the Holy Spirit says, "Happy are you, Israel, who is like you"
           (Isa. 33:29).
3. A.   The Israelites say, "Hear O Israel, the Lord our God, the Lord is
           one" (Dt. 56:4).
    B.   And the Holy Spirit says, "And who is like your people, Israel, a
           unique nation in the earth" (1 Chr. 17:21).
4. A.   The Israelites say, "As an apple tree among the trees of the wood"
           (Song 2:3).
    B.   And the Holy Spirit says, "As a lily among thorns" (Song 2:2).
5. A.   The Israelites say, "This is my God and I will glorify him" (Ex. 15:2).
    B.   And the Holy Spirit says, "The people which I formed for myself"
           (Isa. 43:21).
6. A.   The Israelites say, "For you are the glory of their strength" (Ps.
           89:18).
    B.   And the Holy Spirit says, "Israel, in whom I will be glorified" (Isa.
           49:3)

Once more we find ourselves well within the framework of the
Yerushalmi's treatment of Israel as unique and beyond compare with
the nations of the world.

VII

Zekhut

1. The Mishnah as against the Yerushalmi

From systemic indicators – the doctrines of Torah, Messiah and history, and Israel and the nations – we move on to two episodic items, first, the concept of *zekhut*, second, the issue of woman. The former bears an indeterminate sense in the Mishnah, a well-framed definition in the circle of writings around the Mishnah, but a systemically critical role in the Yerushalmi. It is a point at which the two systems are connected, while remaining autonomous. The latter is important because the treatment of woman is readily classified: taxically in the Mishnah, substantively in the Yerushalmi. In both cases the system expresses its character through its utilization of the indicators at hand, even while the two indicators, for the Mishnah, are tangential and merely representative of prevailing systemic attitudes.

The word *zekhut* stands for the empowerment of a supernatural character that derives from the virtue of one's ancestry or from one's own virtuous deeds of a very particular order.[1] *Zekhut* is a key concept in the system of the Yerushalmi. In the Mishnah the concept may have been present; by the closure of Avot fifty years after the Mishnah was concluded it certainly had reached the definition that was paramount later on. But in the prior system *zekhut* was systemically inert. The difference between the Mishnah and the Yerushalmi's respective systems in regard to *zekhut* therefore is systemic. The former writings

---

[1]*Zekhut* is a native category and ultimately untranslatable by a single word into English. As I explain in the next note, "merit," the word usually used, is precisely the wrong choice and conveys the opposite of the meaning from that to be assigned to *zekhut* in the contexts in which *zekhut* appears.

occasionally, and episodically, referred to the matter; the latter regularly and systemically invoked it as the centerpiece of the system.

No single word in English bears the same meaning, nor can I identify a synonym for *zekhut* in the canonical writings in the original either. *Zekhut* is to be defined as "the heritage of virtue and its consequent entitlements." *Zekhut* may be gained as an inheritance from prior generations, or under certain circumstances it may be acquired through one's own action. The following story shows the meaning of the entitlement of *zekhut* and how *zekhut* is acquired by one's own action:

Y. Taanit 3:11

IV

C. There was a house that was about to collapse over there [in Babylonia], and Rab set one of his disciples in the house, until they had cleared out everything from the house. When the disciple left the house, the house collapsed.

D. And there are those who say that it was R. Adda bar Ahwah.

E. Sages sent and said to him, "What sort of good deeds are to your credit [that you have that much merit]?"

F. He said to them, "In my whole life no man ever got to the synagogue in the morning before I did. I never left anybody there when I went out. I never walked four cubits without speaking words of Torah. Nor did I ever mention teachings of Torah in an inappropriate setting. I never laid out a bed and slept for a regular period of time. I never took great strides among the associates. I never called my fellow by a nickname. I never rejoiced in the embarrassment of my fellow. I never cursed my fellow when I was lying by myself in bed. I never walked over in the marketplace to someone who owed me money.

G. "In my entire life I never lost my temper in my household."

H. This was meant to carry out that which is stated as follows: "I will give heed to the way that is blameless. Oh, when wilt thou come to me? I will walk with integrity of heart within my house" (Ps. 101:2).

What I find striking in this story is that mastery of the Torah is only one means of attaining the *zekhut* that had enabled the sage to keep the house from collapsing. And Torah study is not the primary means of attaining *zekhut*. The question at E provides the key, together with its answer at F. For what the sage did to gain such remarkable *zekhut* is not to master such-and-so many tractates of the Mishnah. It was rather acts of courtesy, consideration, gentility, restraint. These produced *zekhut*, all of them acts of self-abnegation or the avoidance of power over others and the submission to the will and the requirement of self-esteem of others. Torah study is simply an item on a list of actions or attitudes that generate *zekhut*.

Zekhut, scarce or common as our capacity for uncoerced action dictated, puissant or supine as our strength to refrain from deeds of worldly power decided, formed into a cogent political economy for the social order of Israel that economics and that politics that made powerlessness into power, disinheritance into wealth. Acts of will consisting of submission, on one's own, to the will of Heaven endowed Israel with a lien and entitlement upon Heaven. What we cannot by will impose, we can by will evoke. What we cannot accomplish through coercion, we can achieve through submission. God will do for us what we cannot do for ourselves, when we do for God what God cannot make us do. In a wholly concrete and tangible sense, love God with all the heart, the soul, the might, we have. That systemic statement justifies classifying the successor system as religious in as profound and complete a way as the initial system had been wholly and restrictedly philosophical.

Even though a man was degraded, one action sufficed to win for him that heavenly glory to which rabbis in lives of Torah study aspired. The mark of the system's integration around *zekhut* lies in its insistence that all Israelites, not only sages, could gain *zekhut* for themselves (and their descendants). A single remarkable deed, exemplary for its deep humanity, sufficed to win for an ordinary person the *zekhut* that elicits supernatural favor enjoyed by some rabbis on account of their Torah study. The centrality of *zekhut* in the systemic structure, the critical importance of the heritage of virtue together with its supernatural entitlements therefore emerge in a striking claim. Even though a man was degraded, one action sufficed to win for him that heavenly glory to which rabbis in general aspired. The rabbinical storyteller as we shall now see identifies with this lesson.

In all three instances that follow, defining what the individual must do to gain *zekhut,* the point is that the deeds of the heroes of the story make them worthy of having their prayers answered, which is a mark of the working of *zekhut.* It is deeds beyond the strict requirements of the Torah, and even the limits of the law altogether, that transform the hero into a holy man, whose holiness served just like that of a sage marked as such by knowledge of the Torah. The following stories should not be understood as expressions of the mere sentimentality of the clerks concerning the lower orders, for they deny in favor of a single action of surpassing power sages' lifelong devotion to what the sages held to be the highest value, knowledge of the Torah:

Y. *Taanit* 1:4

I

    F.   A certain man came before one of the relatives of R. Yannai. He said to him, "Rabbi, attain *zekhut* through me [by giving me charity]."

    G.   He said to him, "And didn't your father leave you money?"

    H.   He said to him, "No."

    I.   He said to him, "Go and collect what your father left in deposit with others."

    J.   He said to him, "I have heard concerning property my father deposited with others that it was gained by violence [so I don't want it]."

    K.   He said to him, "You are worthy of praying and having your prayers answered."

The point of K, of course, is self-evidently a reference to the possession of entitlement to supernatural favor, and it is gained, we see, through deeds that the law of the Torah cannot require but must favor: what one does on one's own volition, beyond the measure of the law. Here I see the opposite of sin. A sin is what one has done by one's own volition beyond all limits of the law. So an act that generates *zekhut* for the individual is the counterpart and opposite: what one does by one's own volition that also is beyond all requirements of the law.

    L.   A certain ass driver appeared before the rabbis [the context requires: in a dream] and prayed, and rain came. The rabbis sent and brought him and said to him, "What is your trade?"

    M.   He said to them, "I am an ass driver."

    N.   They said to him, "And how do you conduct your business?"

    O.   He said to them, "One time I rented my ass to a certain woman, and she was weeping on the way, and I said to her, 'What's with you?' and she said to me, 'The husband of that woman [me] is in prison [for debt], and I wanted to see what I can do to free him.' So I sold my ass and I gave her the proceeds, and I said to her, 'Here is your money, free your husband, but do not sin [by becoming a prostitute to raise the necessary funds].'"

    P.   They said to him, "You are worthy of praying and having your prayers answered."

The ass driver clearly has a powerful lien on Heaven, so that his prayers are answered, even while those of others are not. What he did to get that entitlement? He did what no law could demand: impoverished himself to save the woman from a "fate worse than death."

    Q.   In a dream of R. Abbahu, Mr. Pentakaka ["Five sins"] appeared, who prayed that rain would come, and it rained. R. Abbahu sent and summoned him. He said to him, "What is your trade?"

R.   He said to him, "Five sins does that man [I] do every day, [for I am a pimp:] hiring whores, cleaning up the theater, bringing home their garments for washing, dancing, and performing before them."

S.   He said to him, "And what sort of decent thing have you ever done?"

T.   He said to him, "One day that man [I] was cleaning the theater, and a woman came and stood behind a pillar and cried. I said to her, 'What's with you?' And she said to me, 'That woman's [my] husband is in prison, and I wanted to see what I can do to free him,' so I sold my bed and cover, and I gave the proceeds to her. I said to her, 'Here is your money, free your husband, but do not sin.'"

U.   He said to him, "You are worthy of praying and having your prayers answered."

Q moves us still further, since the named man has done everything sinful that one can do, and, more to the point, he does it every day. So the singularity of the act of *zekhut*, which suffices if done only one time, encompasses its power to outweigh a life of sin – again, an act of *zekhut* as the mirror image and opposite of sin. Here again, the single act of saving a woman from a "fate worse than death" has sufficed.

V.   A pious man from Kefar Imi appeared [in a dream] to the rabbis. He prayed for rain and it rained. The rabbis went up to him. His householders told them that he was sitting on a hill. They went out to him, saying to him, "Greetings," but he did not answer them.

W.   He was sitting and eating, and he did not say to them, "You break bread too."

X.   When he went back home, he made a bundle of faggots and put his cloak on top of the bundle [instead of on his shoulder].

Y.   When he came home, he said to his household [wife], "These rabbis are here [because] they want me to pray for rain. If I pray and it rains, it is a disgrace for them, and if not, it is a profanation of the Name of Heaven. But come, you and I will go up [to the roof] and pray. If it rains, we shall tell them, 'We are not worthy to pray and have our prayers answered.'"

Z.   They went up and prayed and it rained.

AA.   They came down to them [and asked], "Why have the rabbis troubled themselves to come here today?"

BB.   They said to him, "We wanted you to pray so that it would rain."

CC.   He said to them, "Now do you really need my prayers? Heaven already has done its miracle."

DD.   They said to him, "Why, when you were on the hill, did we say hello to you, and you did not reply?"

EE.   He said to them, "I was then doing my job. Should I then interrupt my concentration [on my work]?"

FF.   They said to him, "And why, when you sat down to eat, did you not say to us 'You break bread too'?"

GG.   He said to them, "Because I had only my small ration of bread. Why would I have invited you to eat by way of mere flattery [when I knew I could not give you anything at all]?"

HH.   They said to him, "And why when you came to go down, did you put your cloak on top of the bundle?"

II.   He said to them, "Because the cloak was not mine. It was borrowed for use at prayer. I did not want to tear it."

JJ.   They said to him, "And why, when you were on the hill, did your wife wear dirty clothes, but when you came down from the mountain, did she put on clean clothes?"

KK.   He said to them, "When I was on the hill, she put on dirty clothes, so that no one would gaze at her. But when I came home from the hill, she put on clean clothes, so that I would not gaze on any other woman."

LL.   They said to him, "It is well that you pray and have your prayers answered."

The pious man of V, finally, enjoys the recognition of the sages by reason of his lien upon Heaven, able as he is to pray and bring rain. What has so endowed him with *zekhut*? Acts of punctiliousness of a moral order: concentrating on his work, avoiding an act of dissimulation, integrity in the disposition of a borrowed object, his wife's concern not to attract other men and her equal concern to make herself attractive to her husband. None of these stories refers explicitly to *zekhut*; all of them tell us about what it means to enjoy not an entitlement by inheritance but a lien accomplished by one's own supererogatory acts of restraint.

Now how shall we relate this important, systemically integrating conception to the task at hand? The answer is somewhat complicated. On the one side, the evidence of the Mishnah shows that the sense of *zekhut* paramount in the successor documents is not original to them. On the other hand, no account of the system of the Mishnah can situate *zekhut* in the systemic center. But *zekhut* forms the heart of the Judaic system attested by the Yerushalmi and associated documents. So here the criterion of documentary situation must be a systemic judgment upon whether or not *zekhut* forms a considerable, or an episodic, consideration; it is a formative and definitive category, or a mere presence.

Here is clear indication of the presence of a conception of an entitlement deriving from some source other than one's own deed of the moment:

Mishnah-tractate Sotah 3:4-5

3:4

E.   There is the possibility that *zekhut* suspends the curse for one year, and there is the possibility that *zekhut* suspends the curse

> for two years, and there is the possibility that *zekhut* suspends the curse for three years.

F. On this basis Ben Azzai says, "A man is required to teach Torah to his daughter.

G. "For if she should drink the water, she should know that [if nothing happens to her], *zekhut* is what suspends [the curse from taking effect]."

3:5

A. R. Simeon says, "*Zekhut* does not suspend the effects of the bitter water.

B. "And if you say, '*Zekhut* does suspend the effects of the bitter water,' you will weaken the effect of the water for all the women who have to drink it.

C. "And you give a bad name to all the women who drink it who turned out to be pure.

D. "For people will say, 'They are unclean, but *zekhut* suspended the effects of the water for them."

E. Rabbi says, "*Zekhut* does suspend the effects of the bitter water. But she will not bear children or continue to be pretty. And she will waste away, and in the end she will have the same [unpleasant] death."

Now if we insert for *zekhut* at each point, "the heritage of virtue and its consequent entitlements," (thus instead of "For people will say, 'They are unclean, but *zekhut* suspended the effects of the water for them,'" then, "For people will say, 'They are unclean, but the heritage of virtue and its consequent entitlements suspended the effects of the water for them)'" we have good sense. That is to say, the woman may not suffer the penalty to which she is presumably condemnable, not because her act or condition (e.g., her innocence) has secured her acquittal or nullified the effects of the ordeal, but because she enjoys some advantage extrinsic to her own act or condition. She may be guilty, but she may also possess a benefice deriving by inheritance, hence, heritage of virtue, and so be entitled to a protection not because of her own, but because of someone else's action or condition.

The evidence of tractate Avot is consistent with that of the Mishnah. The juridical sense of *zekhut* occurs at 1:6, "Judge everybody as though to be acquitted," more comprehensibly translated, "And give everybody the benefit of the doubt," forming a reasonably coherent unit with the usages important in Mishnah-tractate Sanhedrin. In Avot, however, we have clear evidence for the sense of the word that seems to me demanded later on. At M. Avot 2:2 we find the following:

Tractate Avot

2:2

C. "And all who work with the community – let them work with them for the sake of Heaven.

D.   "For the [1] *zekhut* of their fathers strengthens them, and their
        [fathers'] [2] righteousness stands forever.
E.   "And as for you, I credit you with a great reward, as if you had
        done [all of the work required by the community on your own
        merit alone]."

Here we find not merely *zekhut*, but *zekhut avot*, the lien upon Heaven
received by reason of inheritance from the ancestors, and, it follows,
there is no meaning possible other than that I have given above: "the
heritage of virtue and its consequent entitlements." The reference to an
advantage that one gains by reason of inheritance out of one's fathers'
righteousness is demanded by the parallel between *zekhut* of clause [1]
and *righteousness* of clause [2]. Whatever the conceivable ambiguity of
the Mishnah, none is sustained by the context at hand, which is
explicit in language and pellucid in message. That the sense is exactly
the same as the one I have proposed is shown at the following
passages, which seem to me to exhibit none of the possible ambiguity
that characterized the usage of *zekhut* in the Mishnah:

Tractate Avot
5:18
A.   He who causes *zekhut* to the community never causes sin.
B.   And he who causes the community to sin – they never give him a
        sufficient chance to attain penitence.

Here the contrast is between causing *zekhut* and causing sin, so *zekhut* is
the opposite of sin. The continuation is equally clear that a person
attained *zekhut* and endowed the community with *zekhut*, or sinned
and made the community sin:

C.   Moses attained *zekhut* and bestowed *zekhut* on the community.
D.   So the *zekhut* of the community is assigned to his [credit],
E.   as it is said, "He executed the justice of the Lord and his
        judgments with Israel" (Dt. 33:21).
F.   Jeroboam sinned and caused the community to sin.
G.   So the sin of the community is assigned to his [debit],
H.   as it is said, "For the sins of Jeroboam which he committed and
        wherewith he made Israel to sin" (I Kgs. 15:30).

The appropriateness of interpreting the passage in the way I have
proposed will now be shown to be self-evident. All that is required is to
substitute for *zekhut* the proposed translation:

C.   Moses attained *zekhut* and bestowed its consequent entitlements
        on the community.
D.   So the heritage of virtue end its entitlements enjoyed by the
        community are assigned to his [credit],

The sense then is simple. Moses through actions of his own (of an unspecified sort) acquired *zekhut*, which is the credit for such actions that accrued to him and bestowed upon him certain supernatural entitlements; and he for his part passed on as an inheritance that credit, a lien on Heaven for the performance of these same supernatural entitlements: *zekhut*, pure and simple.

If we may now define *zekhut* as the initial system explicated in how tractate Avot has used the word, we must pay close attention to the antonymic structure before us. The juridical opposites are guilty as against innocent, the religious ones, sin as against the opposite of sin. That seems to me to require our interpreting *zekhut* as [1] an action, as distinct from a (mere) attitude; that [2] is precisely the opposite of a sinful one; it is, moreover, an action that [3] may be done by an individual or by the community at large, and one that [4] a leader may provoke the community to do (or not do). The contrast of sin to *zekhut* requires further attention. Since, in general, two classes that are compared to begin with, if different, must constitute opposites, the ultimate definition of *zekhut* requires us to ask how *zekhut* is precisely the opposite of sin. For one thing, as we recall, Scripture is explicit that the burden of sins cannot be passively inherited, willy-nilly, but, to form a heritage of guilt, must be actively accepted and renewed; the children cannot be made to suffer for the sins of the parents, unless they repeat them. Then *zekhut*, being a mirror image, can be passively inherited, not by one's own merit[2] but by one's good fortune alone.

The single distinctive trait of *zekhut* is its transitive quality: one need not earn or merit the supernatural power and resource represented by the things you can do if you have *zekhut* but cannot do if you do not have it. One can inherit that entitlement from others, dead or living.

---

[2]Indeed, the conception of merit is so alien to the concept of *zekhut*, which one enjoys whether or not one personally has done something to merit it, that I am puzzled on how merit ever seemed to anyone to serve as a translation of the word *zekhut*. If I can inherit the entitlements accrued by my ancestors, then these entitlements not only cannot be classed as merit(ed by me), they must be classed as a heritage bestowed by others and not merited by me at all. And, along these same lines, the *zekhut* that I gain for myself may entitle me to certain benefits, but it may also accrue to the advantage of the community in which I live (as is made explicit by Avot for Moses's *zekhut*) and also of my descendants. The transitive character of *zekhut*, the power we have of receiving it from others and handing it on to others, serves as the distinctive trait of this particular entitlement, and, it must follow from that definitive characteristic, *zekhut* is the opposite of merit, as I said, and its character is obscured by the confusion created through that long-standing and conventional, but wrong translation of the word.

Moses not only attains *zekhut* but he also imparts *zekhut* to the community of which he is leader, and the same is so for any Israelite. That conception is broadened in the successor documents into the deeply historical notion of *zekhut avot*, empowerment of a supernatural character to which Israel is entitled by reason of what the patriarchs and matriarchs in particular did long ago. That conception forms the foundation for the paramount sense of *zekhut* in the successor system: that Israel possesses a lien upon Heaven by reason of God's love for the patriarchs and matriarchs, his appreciation for certain things they did, and his response to those actions not only in favoring them but also in entitling their descendants to do or benefit from otherwise unattainable miracles. *Zekhut*, as we noted earlier, explains the present – particularly what is odd and unpredictable in the presence – by appeal to the past, hence forms a distinctively historical conception.

Zekhut speaks of not legitimate but illegitimate violence, not power but weakness. *Zekhut* is the power of the weak, people who through their own merit and capacity can accomplish nothing, but through what others do for them in leaving a heritage of *zekhut*, or have done for them, can accomplish miracles. And, not to miss the stunning message of the triplet of stories cited above, *zekhut* also is what the weak and excluded and despised can do that outweighs in power what the great masters of the Torah have accomplished. In the context of a system that represents Torah as supernatural, that claim of priority for *zekhut* represents a considerable transvaluation of power, as much as of value. And, by the way, *zekhut* also forms the inheritance of the disinherited: what you receive as a heritage when you have nothing in the present and have gotten nothing in the past, that scarce resource that is free and unearned but much valued. So let us dwell upon the definitive character of the transferability of *zekhut* in its formulation, *zekhut avot*, the *zekhut* handed on by the ancestors, the transitive character of the concept and its standing as a heritage of entitlements.

This brings us back to our question, what are the indicators, vis-à-vis *zekhut*, that tell us whether a document falls close to the Mishnah, where the word may or may not bear its later meaning, exposed definitively only in Avot, or to the Yerushalmi, where the concept is critical? What gives *zekhut* its systemic centrality not in the initial, but only in the successor system? It is a simple linguistic criterion that serves the present purpose, if not a definitive one over all. In the successor documents the concept of *zekhut* is joined with *avot*, that is, the *zekhut* that has been left as Israel's family inheritance by the patriarchs or ancestors, yielding the very specific notion, defining the systemic politics, its theory of the social entity, of Israel not as a (mere) community (e.g., as in tractate Avot's reference to Moses's bestowing *zekhut* upon the community) but as a family, with a history that takes the form of a genealogy, precisely as Genesis has represented that history.

Now *zekhut* was joined to the metaphor of the genealogy of patriarchs and matriarchs and served to form the missing link, explaining how the inheritance and heritage were transmitted from them to their heirs. Consequently, the family, called "Israel," could draw upon the family estate, consisting of the inherited *zekhut* of matriarchs and patriarchs in such a way as to benefit today from the heritage of yesterday. This notion involved very concrete problems. If "Israel, the family" sinned, it could call upon the "*zekhut*" accumulated by Abraham and Isaac at the binding of Isaac (Genesis 22) to win forgiveness for that sin. True, "fathers will not die on account of the sin of the sons," but the children may benefit from the *zekhut* of the forebears. That concrete expression of the larger metaphor imparted to the metaphor a practical consequence, moral and theological, that was not at all neglected.

The systemic statement made in the successor documents by the usages of *zekhut* speaks of relationship, function, the interplay of humanity and God. One's store of *zekhut* derives from a relationship, that is, from one's forebears. That is one dimension of the relationships in which one stands. *Zekhut* also forms a measure of one's own relationship with Heaven, as the power of one person, but not another, to pray and so bring rain attests. What sort of relationship does *zekhut*, as the opposite of sin, then posit? It is not one of coercion, for Heaven cannot force us to do those types of deeds that yield *zekhut*, and that, story after story suggests, is the definition of a deed that generates *zekhut:* doing what we ought to do but do not have to do. But then, we cannot coerce Heaven to do what we want done either, for example, by carrying out the commandments. These are obligatory, but do not obligate Heaven.

Whence then our lien on Heaven? It is through deeds of a supererogatory character – to which Heaven responds by deeds of a supererogatory character: supernatural favor to this one, who through deeds of ingratiation of the other or self-abnegation or restraint exhibits the attitude that in Heaven precipitates a counterpart attitude, hence generating *zekhut*, rather than to that one, who does not. The simple fact that rabbis cannot pray and bring rain, but a simple ass driver can, tells the whole story. The relationship measured by *zekhut* – Heaven's response by an act of uncoerced favor to a person's uncoerced gift, for example, act of gentility, restraint, or self-abnegation – contains an element of unpredictability for which appeal to the *zekhut* inherited from ancestors accounts. So while I cannot coerce Heaven, I can through *zekhut* gain acts of favor from Heaven, and that is by doing what Heaven cannot require of me. Heaven then responds to my attitude in carrying out my duties – and more than my duties. That act of pure disinterest – giving the woman my means of livelihood – is the one that gains for me Heaven's deepest interest, *zekhut* as the power of the powerless, the riches of the disinherited, the valuation and valorization of the will of those who have no right to will.

The evidence we seek is partly verbal, partly systemic. Do we find in the so-called Tannaitic Midrashim references to the fully exposed conception of *zekhut* as a lien upon Heaven that can be inherited or gained for oneself through deeds of a supererogatory character? If we do find the word in that sense, than, at least as a preliminary guess, does it seem that *zekhut* plays a systemically important role in the document's structure? One key indicator will be usages of merit of the ancestors, *zekhut avot*, and that will be our principal point of inquiry.

2. Mekhilta Attributed to R. Ishmael

Mekhilta attributed to R. Ishmael
XXII:I
3.   A.   R. Ishmael says, "On account of the *zekhut* of Jerusalem I shall divide the sea for them:
     B.   "'Awake, awake, put on your strength O Zion, put on your beautiful garments, O Jerusalem, the holy city; for henceforth the uncircumcised and the unclean will not come into you any more' (Isa. 52:1).

This does not seem to me to provide pertinent evidence, one way or the other. The sense of *zekhut* as "by reason of," is systemically not indicative, as I have explained. For the present purpose, therefore, we must limit our inquiry to usages in which the *zekhut* accrued by the exceptional virtue of ancestors and handed on to descendants is the clear meaning of a passage, whether or not *zekhut avot* occurs at all.

Mekhilta attributed to R. Ishmael
XXII:I
4.   A.   Another interpretation [of the verse, "Why do you cry to me? Tell the people of Israel to go forward":]
     B.   [God said,] "I am going to carry out the promise that I made to their ancestors that I shall divide the sea for them:
     C.   "'And your seed shall be as the dust of the earth and you shall spread abroad to the seaward and to the east' (Gen. 28:14), [meaning,] break through the sea."

5. A.   R. Judah b. Beterah says, "Said the Holy One, blessed be he, to him, 'I have already kept the promise that I made to their ancestors:

    B.   "'And he made the sea dry land" (Ex. 16:18); "But the children of Israel walked upon dry land in the midst of the sea" (Ex. 14:29).'"

7. A.   R. Banaah says, "'On account of the merit attained by the religious duty that Abraham, their ancestor, carried out, I shall divide the sea for them':

    B.   "'He cleaved the wood for the burnt-offering' (Gen. 22:3).

    C.   "And here: 'And the waters were cleft."

8. A.   Simeon of Teman says, "'On account of the merit gained by circumcision, I shall split the sea for them':

    B.   "'Thus says the Lord, if not for my covenant of day and night, I would not have appointed the ordinances of Heaven and earth' (Jer. 33:25). Now go and find out what is the covenant which applies by day and by night? You shall find only the religious duty of circumcision."

Here are fine examples of what *zekhut avot* does not mean: simply carrying out promises to ancestors. The sense of "by what reason," is present as well.

Mekhilta (Shirata Chapter Nine)
XXXIV:I

2. A.   [Since it says, "The earth swallowed them," Scripture indicates that they reached final burial.] On account of what *zekhut* was a burial place given to them?

    B.   It was by the *zekhut* of their having said, "The Lord is righteous" (Ex. 9:27).

    C.   Said to them the Holy One, blessed be He, "You have accepted for yourselves the righteousness of the judgment that is meted out to you, so I shall not hold back your reward, but I shall give you a burial place."

    D.   So it is said, "The earth swallowed them."

5. A.   "You have led in your steadfast love [the people whom you have redeemed]":

    B.   It was an act of steadfast love that you did with us, for we did not have to our credit deeds [to gain for us the *zekhut* that would make us worthy of being redeemed]:

    C.   "I will make mention of the mercies of the Lord" (Isa. 63:7); "I will sing of the mercies of the Lord for ever" (Ps. 68:2).

    D.   And to begin with the world was created only by steadfast love:

    E.   "For I have said, the world shall be built by mercy" (Ps. 89:3).

6. A.   "[You have led in your steadfast love] the people whom you have redeemed":

    B.   For the whole of the world belongs to you, and you have as a people only Israel:

    C.   "The people which I formed for myself' (Isa. 43:21).

9. A.   "you have guided them by your strength":

    B.   This was on account of the *zekhut* produced by the Torah, which they were destined to receive.

C.   For "your strength" refers only to the Torah: "The Lord will give strength to his people" (Ps. 29:11); "The strength also of the king who loves justice" (Ps. 99:4).

10. A   Another comment on the verse, "you have guided them by your strength":

B.   It was on account of the *zekhut* accruing to the kingdom of the house of David, which they were destined to accept.

C.   For "your strength" refers only to the monarchy:

D.   "O Lord, in your strength the king rejoices" (Ps. 21:2); "And he will give strength to his king" (1 Sam. 2:10).

11. A   "To your holy abode":

B.   It was on account of the *zekhut* accruing to the house of the sanctuary that they were destined to build.

C.   For "abode" refers only to the house of the sanctuary:

D.   "And laid waste his habitation" (Ps. 79:7); "Look upon Zion, the city of our solemn gatherings. Your eyes shall see Jerusalem a peaceful habitation" (Isa. 33:20).

The matter of *zekhut* is ambiguous here; the sense is that through certain actions or persons *zekhut* is to be gained, but whether or not this sense of the word conforms to the usage important in the successor system is not obvious to me. The very distinctive sense of *zekhut*, as distinct from a generalized meaning of doing what one has promised in the past, is not present in a passage such as the foregoing. But in the same passage, the following units explicitly invoke the besought concept:

Mekhilta attributed to R. Ishmael
XXII:I
14. A   R. Eleazar b. Azariah says, "'For the sake of their father, Abraham, I shall divide the sea for them:

B.   "'For he remembered his holy word to Abraham his servant' (Ps. 105:42).

C.   "'And he brought forth his people with joy' (Ps. 105:43)."

15. A   R. Eleazar b. Judah of Kefar Tota says, "'For the sake of the tribal progenitors I shall divide the sea for them:

B.   "'You have pierced through because of his tribes' (Hab. 3:14).

C.   "'To him who divided the Red Sea into parts' (Ps. 136:13)."

16. A   Abtalyon says, "The faith that they trusted in me is so worthy that I should divide the sea for them.'

B.   "For it is said, 'And they believed' (Ex. 4:31).

17. A   Simeon of Qitron says, "It is on account of the merit attained by tending to the bones of Joseph that I shall divide the sea for them:

B.   "'And he left his garment in her hand and fled' (Gen. 39:12). 'The sea saw it and fled' (Ps. 114:3)."

Here is a very explicit utilization of the conception of *zekhut* in the formulation critical to the system of the Yerushalmi and related documents.

In Mekhilta in general, Kosovsky's *Concordance* indicates, we find the senses of "to be found innocent," "to acquire possession of," and "by reason of." The usage, "by reason of the lien upon Heaven inherited from the ancestors on account of remarkable deeds of self-abnegation," such as the presence of the language of *zekhut avot* would represent, is further to be located at these passages: Beshellah 2:5 to Ex. 14:22; Bo 1 to Ex. 12:1, *zekhut avot* used explicitly; Ba 16 to Ex. 13:4, the *zekhut* of Abraham our father; and so on. We must therefore conclude that the usage emblematic of the Yerushalmi and associated documents is well represented in Mekhilta.

3. Sifra

The following passage, which we have met in the Introduction and also in our consideration of the myth of the Dual Torah, further joins the two themes of the uniqueness of Israel and the differentiation of the nations, typical then of the Yerushalmi's system's treatment of both matters. It further introduces the conception of *zekhut* inherited from the tribal progenitors and the myth of the Dual Torah.

Sifra Parashat Behuqotai Pereq 8

CCLXIX:I

12. A.   "[Yet for all that, when they are in the land of their enemies,] I will not spurn them, neither will I abhor them so as to destroy them utterly":

     B.   Now what is left for them, but that they not be spurned nor abhorred? For is it not the fact that all the good gifts that had been given to them were now taken away from them?

     C.   And were it not for the Scroll of the Torah that was left for them, they were in no way be different from the nations of the world!

     D.   But "I will not spurn them": – in the time of Vespasian.

     E.   "neither will I abhor them": – in the time of Greece.

     F.   "So as to destroy them utterly and break my covenant with them": – in the time of Haman.

     G.   "For I am the Lord their God": – in the time of Gog.

13. A.   And how do we know that the covenant is made with the tribal fathers?

     B.   As it is said, "But I will for their sake remember the covenant with their forefathers whom I brought forth out of the land of Egypt":

     C.   This teaches that the covenant is made with the tribal fathers.

14. A.   "These are the statutes and ordinances and Torahs":

     B.   "the statutes": this refers to the exegeses of Scripture.

     C.   "and ordinances": this refers to the laws.

     D.   "and Torahs": this teaches that two Torahs were given to Israel, one in writing, the other oral.

     E.   Said R. Aqiba, "Now did Israel have only two Torahs? And did they not have many Torahs given to them? 'This is the Torah of burnt-offering (Lev. 6:2),' 'This is the Torah of the meal-offering

(Lev. 6:27),' 'This is the Torah of the guilt-offering (Lev. 7:1),' 'This is
the Torah of the sacrifice of peace-offerings (Lev. 7:11) 'This is the
Torah: when a man dies in a tent (Num. 19:1).'"

15.   A.   "Which the Lord made between him and the people of Israel [on
           Mount Sinai by Moses]":
      B.   Moses had the merit of being made the intermediary between
           Israel and their father in Heaven.
      C.   "on Mount Sinai by Moses":
      D.   This teaches that the Torah was given, encompassing all its laws,
           all its details, and all their amplifications, through Moses at Sinai.

It would be difficult to locate a better integration of a variety of
emblematic ideas in a single statement than the passage at hand,
which has the Dual Torah, the uniqueness of Israel (by reason of the
Torah), the differentiation of the nations, and *zekhut avot*, all
explicitly joined together. Not only so, but the same passage identifies
the myth of the two Torahs and says it explicitly. I find no other
pertinent evidence in Sifra, and Kosovsky's catalogue does not indicate
there is any.

4. Sifré to Numbers 1-115

Apart from extensions of the matter of *zekhut* used in relationship
with the wife accused of adultery, parallel to the usages in Mishnah-
tractate Sota, I find nothing relevant.

5. Sifré to Deuteronomy

"All things by reason of the *zekhut* of your fathers" and equivalent
usages occur at Sifré to Deuteronomy 96, 144, 145, 319. One example
suffices:

Sifré to Deuteronomy Pisqa
XCVI:II

> ["...in order that the Lord may turn from his blazing anger [and
> show you compassion, and in his compassion increase you as he
> promised your fathers on oath, for you will be heeding the Lord
> your God, obeying all his commandments that I enjoin upon you
> this day, doing what is right in the sight of the Lord your God]" (Dt.
> 13:13-19)]:

4.   A.   "...[increase you] as he promised your fathers on oath":
     B.   all is on account of the *zekhut* of the ancestors.

The besought usage is represented here. I do not find a great deal of
pertinent evidence in Sifré to Deuteronomy.

VIII

Woman

1. The Mishnah as against the Yerushalmi

The Mishnah treats the subject of the woman as it treats most other topics on which it concentrates, as a problem of hierarchical classification. In the case of woman, the problem is to set that classification into correct relationship with man. The woman, as much as Israel, therefore serves as a taxic indicator, representing the abnormal to which the man is normal. The successor system endows woman with flesh and blood, presenting not woman, a taxic category, but *a* woman as a principal actor in stories, for instance. We dwell on the Mishnah's distinctive treatment of woman, since the principal concern for this indicator is whether or not the mediating documents come within the orbit of the Mishnah. No study of woman, or women, in the successor system having been accomplished, we cannot know whether or not those documents represent women as they are systemically treated in the later compilations; indeed, we do not at this point even know whether women are systemically active or inert. But in the Mishnah, woman is an absolutely critical systemic component. Once we recognize how that is the case and know the marks of the mishnaic system, we can readily identify in the mediating writings traits coherent with the Mishnah's systemic treatment of the subject.

The indicative characteristic of the Mishnah's theory of woman is the view of woman as anomalous, man as the norm. An anomaly is for this system a situation requiring human intervention so that affairs may be brought into stasis, that is, made to conform with the Heavenly projections of the created world. That quest for stasis, order and regulation, which constitute wholeness and completeness, in the division of Women takes up yet another circumstance of uncertainty.

141

This it confronts at its most uncertain. The system subjects the anomaly of women to the capacity for ordering and regulating, which is the skill of the Mishnah's system's framers.

The anomaly of woman is addressed at its most anomalous, that is, disorderly and dangerous, moment, the point at which women move from one setting and status to another. The very essence of the anomaly, woman's sexuality, is scarcely mentioned. But it always is just beneath the surface. For what defines the woman's status – what is rarely made explicit in the division of Women – is not whether or not she may have sexual relations, but with whom she may have them and with what consequence. It is assumed that, from long before the advent of puberty, a girl may be married and in any event is a candidate for sexuality. From puberty onward she will be married. But what is selected for intense and continuing concern is with whom she may legitimately do so, and with what economic and social effect. There is no sexual deed without public consequence; and only rarely will a sexual deed not yield economic results, in the aspect of the transfer of property from one hand to another. So what is anomalous is the woman's sexuality, which is treated in a way wholly different from man's. And the goal and purpose of the Mishnah's division of Women are to bring under control and force into stasis all of the wild and unruly potentialities of sexuality, with their dreadful threat of uncontrolled shifts in personal status and material possession alike.

The Mishnah invokes Heaven's interest in this most critical moment for individual and society alike. Its conception is that what is rightly done on earth is confirmed in Heaven. A married woman who has sexual relations with any man but her husband has not merely committed a crime on earth. She has sinned against Heaven. It follows that when a married woman receives a writ of divorce and so is free to enter into relationships with any man of her choosing, the perceptions of that woman are affected in Heaven just as much as are those of man on earth. What was beforehand a crime and a sin afterward is holy, not subject to punishment at all. The woman may contract a new marriage on earth which Heaven, for its part, will oversee and sanctify.

What is stated in these simple propositions is that those crucial and critical turnings at which a woman changes hands produce concern and response in Heaven above as much as on earth below. And the reason, as I suggested at the beginning, is that Heaven is invoked specifically at those times, and in those circumstances, in which the Mishnah confronts a situation of anomaly or disorder and proposes to effect suitable regulation and besought order. Woman in the Mishnah therefore defines an important component of the Mishnah's system as a whole, an organizing category being framed around that subject. Facts that can be seen as inert, such as that a woman receives a marriage contract when she is betrothed and wed, and that she receives a writ of divorce when she is sent away, indeed prove systemically expressive. The mishnaic system of women defines the position of women in the social economy of Israel's supernatural and natural reality. That position acquires definition wholly in relationship to men, who impart form to the Israelite social economy. It is effected through both supernatural and natural, this-worldly action. What man and woman do on earth provokes a response in Heaven, and the correspondences are perfect. So the position of women is defined and secured both in Heaven and here on earth, and that position is always and invariably relative to men.

The principal interest for the Mishnah is the point at which a woman becomes, and ceases to be, *holy* to a particular man, that is, enters and leaves the marital union. These transfers of women are the dangerous and disorderly points in the relationship of woman to man, therefore, as I said, to society as well. Attention to the details of the tractates underscores that fact. Five of the seven tractates of the division on Women are devoted to the formation and dissolution of the marital bond. Of them, three treat what is done by man here on earth, that is, formation of a marital bond through betrothal and marriage contract and dissolution through divorce and its consequences: Qiddushin,[1] Ketubot,[2] and Gittin.[3] One of them is devoted to what by woman is done here on earth: Sotah.[4] And Yebamot,[5] greatest of the seven in size and in formal and substantive brilliance, deals with the corresponding Heavenly intervention into the formation and end of a marriage: the effect of death upon the marital bond and the dissolution, through death, of that bond. The other two tractates, Nedarim[6] and Nazir,[7] draw into one the two realms of reality, Heaven and earth, as they work out the effects of vows taken by women and subject to the confirmation or abrogation of the father or husband. These vows make a deep impact upon the marital life of the woman

---

[1] Betrothals.

[2] Marriage contracts and the settlement thereof; the transfer of property in connection with the transfer of a woman from the father's to the husband's domain.

[3] Writs of divorce.

[4] The wife suspected of adultery and the rite of drinking the bitter water described in Numbers 5.

[5] Levirate marriages, in accord with the rule of Deut. 25:10-15.

[6] Vows.

[7] The vow of the Nazirite, as in Numbers 6.

who has taken such a vow. So, in all, the division and its system delineate the natural and supernatural character of the woman's role in the social economy framed by man: the beginning, end, and middle of that relationship.

The mishnaic system of women thus focuses upon the two crucial stages of the transfer of women and of property from one domain to another: the leaving of the father's house at its dissolution through divorce or through the husband's death. There is yet a third point of interest, though it is much less important than these first two stages: the duration of the marriage. Finally, included within the division and at a few points relevant to women in particular are rules of vows in general and of the special vow to be a *Nazir*, the former included because, in the scriptural treatment of the theme, the rights of the father or husband to annul the vows of a daughter or wife form the central problematic, and the latter included for no very clear reason except that it is a species of which the vow is the genus.

To the message and the purpose of the mishnaic system of women, woman is essential and central. But she is not critical, and that explains why, when a woman (not woman in the abstract) plays an active role, for example, in a narrative or in a law, we find ourselves outside of the orbit of the Mishnah's system. For in that system she sets the stage for the processes of the sacred. It is she who can be made sacred to man. It is she who ceases to stand within a man's sacred circle. But God, through supernature, and man, through the documentary expression of his will and intention, possess the active power of sanctification. Like the Holy Land of the Mishnah's division of Agriculture, the Holy Temple of the division of Sacrifices, and the potentially holy realm of the clean of the division of Purities, women for the division of Women define a principal components of the Mishnah's orderly conception of reality. Women form a chief component of the six-part realm of the sacred.

It is, as I said, their position in the social economy of the Israelite reality, natural and supernatural, which is the subject of the division and its tractates. But the whole – this six-part realm – is always important in *relationship* to man on earth and God in Heaven. Sanctification is effected through process and through relationship. The center of logical tension is critical relationship. The problematic of the subject is generated *at* the critical points of the relationship. The relationship, that is, *the process*, is what makes holy or marks as profane. God and man shape and effect that process. Earth, woman, cult, and the cult-like realm of the clean – these foci of the sacred form that inert matter made holy or marked as profane by the will and deed of God and of man, who is like God. This, I conceive, is the problematic so phrased as to elicit the desired response in our division. *The system shapes the problematic which defines how the topic will be explored and made consequential.* The Mishnah's is a system of sanctification through the word of God and through that which corresponds to God's word on earth, which is the will of man. If, as I have said, the division yields no propositions of encompassing and fundamental importance but merely legal facts about documents and relationships signified through documents, it still says a great deal both as a system and also in behalf of the Mishnah's system as a whole.

Accordingly, in the system of the Mishnah, women are abnormal; men are normal.[8] I am inclined to think that the reason they chose to work out a division on women flows from that fact. And, when we recall that the only other systems of women worthy of the name come to us under priestly auspices, in the Priestly Code (Lev. 1-15) and in the Holiness Code (Lev. 17ff.), we can hardly be surprised at the selection of women, for the men before us create the Mishnah as a scribal-priestly document. Women in the priestly perspective on the holy life are excluded from the centers of holiness. They cannot enter the sensitive domain of the cult, cannot perform the cultic service, and cannot participate even in the cultic liturgy. They are abnormal and excluded, something out of the ordinary. That is why they form a focus of sanctification: restoration of the extraordinary to the ordinary and the normal.

The Mishnah cannot make women into men. It can provide for a world in which it is normal for woman to be subject to man – father or husband – and a system which regularizes the transfer of women from the hand of the father to that of the husband. The regulation of the transfer of women is the Mishnah's way of effecting the sanctification of what, for the moment, disturbs and disorders the orderly world. The work of sanctification *becomes* necessary in particular at the point of danger and disorder. An order of women must be devoted, therefore, to just these things, so as to preserve the normal modes of creation ("how these things really are") so that maleness, that is, normality, may encompass all, even and especially at the critical point of transfer.

About woman as wife the Mishnah has little to say; about woman as mother, I cannot think of ten relevant lines in the Mishnah's division of Women[!]. These are not the topics to which the Mishnah will devote itself. The three systemically anomalous tractates from this perspective are not so far out of line. Sotah, of course, attends to the wife who is not a good wife. Nedarim, bearing *Nazir* in its wake,

---

[8]On the notion of the woman as anomalous see Simone de Beauvoir, *The Second Sex*, trans. and ed. by H. M. Parshley (New York: Knopf, 1953).

treats those moments specified by Scripture as especially important in
the daughter's relationship to the father or the wife's to the husband.
These are moments at which the father or the husband may intervene
in the relationship of daughter or wife to God. In the present context,
that relationship is unruly and dangerous, exactly like the
relationship of daughter leaving father or of wife leaving husband,
that is, at the critical moment of betrothal and consummation of the
marriage, with attendant property settlement; or divorce or husband's
death, at the critical moment of the dissolution of the marriage, with
attendant property settlement.

So it is to a situation which is so fraught with danger as to threaten
the order and regularity of the stable, sacred society in its perfection
and at its point of stasis that the Mishnah will devote its principal
cognitive and legislative efforts. For that situation, the Mishnah will
invoke Heaven and express its most vivid concern for sanctification.
What breaks established routine or what is broken out of established
routine is what is subject to the fully articulated and extensive
reflections of a whole division of the Mishnah, or, in Hebrew, a *seder*,
a division, of the whole. The anomaly of woman is worked out – that
is, held in stasis – by assigning her to man's domain. It follows that the
stasis is disturbed at the point when she changes hands. Then the
Mishnah's instincts for regulating and thereby restoring the balance
and order of the world are aroused. So from the recognition of the
anomalous character of women, we find ourselves moving toward the
most profound and fundamental affirmations of the Mishnah about the
works of sanctification: the foci and the means. Women are sanctified
through the deeds of men. So too are earth and time, the fruit of the
herd and of the field, the bed, chair, table, and hearth – but, in the
nature of things, women most of all.

The evidence we seek in the so-called Tannaite Midrashim is
narrative. Do we find stories, such as those we have in the Yerushalmi
and related Midrash compilations, in which woman, that is, *a woman*,
plays an active role in the narrative? Or is woman a mere abstraction,
a taxic indicator, a passive bystander, to be classified or treated as
merely an abnormality? If the former, we stand closer to the general
worldview, encompassing women, of the Yerushalmi, and if the latter,
then we are nearer the Mishnah and its system.

2. Mekhilta Attributed to R. Ishmael

The story that follows treats Miriam not as a person, for the
occasion at which she is prominent does not precipitate deep thought
about her individual traits, for example, as heroine. For an example of

what can have been done, I point to the treatment of woman in *Zekhut-stories*, "He said to them, "When I was on the hill, she put on dirty clothes, so that no one would gaze at her. But when I came home from the hill, she put on clean clothes, so that I would not gaze on any other woman." Here the wife receives not pro-forma praise but quite specific recognition for her wit and intelligence and virtue; she is a person with striking qualities, not merely a symbol or a classification of biped. Contrast Miriam in the following:

Mekhilta (Shirata Chapter Ten)
XXXV:II.

1. A. "Then Miriam, the prophetess, the sister of Aaron, took [a timbrel in her hand; and all the women went out after her with timbrels and dancing. And Miriam said to them, 'Sing to the Lord, for he has triumphed gloriously; the horse and his rider he has thrown into the sea]":
   B. Where do we find that Miriam prophesied?
   C. She said to her father, "You are going to produce a son who will arise and save Israel from the power of Egypt."
   D. Forthwith: "There went a man of the house of Levi and took a wife...and the woman conceived and bore a son...and when she could not hide him any longer" (Ex. 2:1-3).
   E. Her father berated her: "What has become of your prophecy?"
   F. But she held fast to her prophecy: "And his sister stood afar off, to know what would be done to him" (Ex. 2:4).
2. A. ["And his sister stood afar off, to know what would be done to him" (Ex. 2:4):] The sense of "standing" is only the Holy Spirit.
   B. For so it is said, "I saw the Lord standing beside the altar" (Amos 9:4); "And the Lord came and stood" (1 Sam. 3:10); "Call Joshua and stand" (Dt. 31:14).
3. A. "[And his sister stood] afar off, [to know what would be done to him]" (Ex. 2:4):
   B. The sense of "afar" is only the Holy Spirit:
   C. "From afar the Lord appeared to me" (Jer. 31:2).
4. A. "[And his sister stood afar off,] to know [what would be done to him]" (Ex. 2:4):
   B. The sense of "know" is only the Holy Spirit:
   C. "For the earth shall be full of the knowledge of the Lord" (Isa. 11:9); For the earth shall be filled with the knowledge of the glory of the Lord, as the waters cover the sea" (Hab.. 2:14).
5. A. "[And his sister stood afar off, to know] what would be done to him" (Ex. 2:4):
   B. The sense of "what would be done to him" is only the Holy Spirit:
   C. "For the Lord will do nothing without revealing his counsel to his servants the prophets" (Amos 3:7).
6. A. "The sister of Aaron":
   B. Was she not sister of both of them? Why does Scripture call her only "sister of Aaron"?

C.   It is because he was prepared to give his life for his sister that she bore his name.

8. A.   Along these same lines: "In the matter of Cozbi, daughter of the prince of Midian, their sister" (Num. 25:18).

B.   Was she really their sister? Was she not one of the chiefs of her nation: "Cozbi, daughter of Zur; he was head of the people of a father's house in Midian" (Num. 25:15). So why "their sister" only?

C.   It is because she was prepared to give her life to her nation that the whole nation is called by her name.

9. A.   "Took a timbrel in her hand":

B.   Where did the Israelites get timbrels and flutes in the wilderness?

C.   The righteous were entirely confident, knowing that the Omnipresent would do wonders and acts of might when they went forth from Egypt,

D.   so they readied for themselves timbrels and flutes.

10. A.   "And Miriam said to them":

B.   Scripture indicates that just as Moses recited the song to the men, so Miriam recited the song to the women: "Sing to the Lord, for he has triumphed gloriously; the horse and his rider he has thrown into the sea."

Beyond No. 1, nothing in this mélange treats Miriam as a personality, requiring the development of individual traits; she is not given inner thoughts or a distinctive role. No. 1 is the only passage at which she forms the center of discussion. There she does show the virtue of holding fast to her own prophecy, and this is regarded as distinctive. From that point on she is scarcely an actor in the expansion of the narrative. We surely find ourselves closer to the Mishnah's than to the Yerushalmi's representation of matters.

3. Sifra

Sifra Parashat Vayyiqra Dibura Denedabah Parashah 2
III:II
1. A.   "[Speak to the Israelite people and say to them, 'When any (Hebrew: Adam) of you presents an offering of cattle to the Lord, he shall choose his offering from the herd or from the flock":

B.   [The reference to sons of Israel, translated Israelite people, but now understood to mean men, serves to exclude women, with the result:] male Israelites lay on hands, and female Israelites do not lay on hands.

C.   R. Yosé and R. Simeon say, "As an optional matter women indeed are permitted to lay on hands."

D.   Said R. Yosé, "Abba Eleazar said to me, 'We had a calf that fell into the classification of a sacrifice of peace-offerings, and we brought it out to the Women's Courtyard, so that the women laid hands on it. Now is there any valid laying on of hands in the

Women's Courtyard? Obviously not. But it was so as to please the women."'

2. A. Might one suppose that women should not lay hands on burnt-offerings, for burnt-offerings also do not require waving,

B. but they may indeed lay hands on peace-offerings, for peace-offerings do require waving?

C. Scripture says, "...and you will say to them,"

D. which serves to encompass everything stated in the passage within the fundamental rule, namely,

E. just as women do not lay hands on burnt-offerings, so they do not lay hands on peace-offerings.

Here is an example of the treatment of women as a mere classification of animate beings. The exclusion of women is based on the specific statement that the sons, that is, males, do thus and so – understood, then, to intend the elimination of women. But women in some cases may indeed do the action. No. 2 introduces the distinction between one classification and another of offering, specifically, with reference to the act of waving.

Sifra Parashat Qedoshim Parashah 1

CXCV:I.II

1. A. "Every one [Hebrew: man] [of you shall revere his mother and his father, and you shall keep my sabbaths]":

B. I know only that a man [is subject to the instruction].

C. How do I know that a woman is also involved?

D. Scripture says, "...shall revere" [using the plural].

E. Lo, both genders are covered.

2. A. If so, why does Scripture refer to "man"?

B. It is because a man controls what he needs, while a woman does not control what she needs, since others have dominion over her.

3. A. It is said, "Every one of you shall revere his mother and his father," and it is further said, "The Lord your God you shall fear" (Dt. 6:13).

B. Scripture thereby establishes an analogy between the reverence of father and mother and the reverence of the Omnipresent.

C. It is said, "Honor your father and your mother" (Ex. 20:12), and it is further said, "Honor the Lord with your wealth" (Prov. 3:9).

D. Scripture thereby establishes an analogy between the honor of father and mother and the honor of the Omnipresent.

E. It is said, "He who curses his father or his mother will certainly die" (Prov. 20:20), and it is said, "Any person who curses his God will bear his sin" (Lev. 24:15).

F. Scripture thereby establishes an analogy between cursing father and mother and cursing the Omnipresent.

G. But it is not possible to refer to smiting Heaven [in the way in which one is warned not to hit one's parents].

H. And that is entirely reasonable, for all three of them are partners [in a human being].

4. A. R. Simeon says, "Sheep take precedence over goats in all circumstances.

B.   "Is it possible that that is because they are more choice?

C.   "Scripture says, 'If he brings a sheep as his offering for sin' (Lev. 4:32), teaching that both of them are of equivalent *zekhut*.

D.   "Pigeons take precedence over turtledoves under all circumstances.

E.   "Might one suppose that that is because they are more choice?

F.   "Scripture says, 'Or a pigeon or a turtledove for a sin-offering' (Lev. 12:6), teaching that both of them are of equivalent *zekhut*.

G.   "The father takes precedence over the mother under all circumstances.

H.   "Is it possible that the honor owing to the father takes preference over the honor owing to the mother?

I.   "Scripture says, 'Every one of you shall revere his mother and his father,' teaching that both of them are of equivalent *zekhut*."

J.   But sages have said, "The father takes precedence over the mother under all circumstances, because both the son and the mother are liable to pay respect to his father."

5. A.   What is the form of reverence that is owing?

B.   The son should not sit in his place, speak in his place, contradict him.

C.   What is the form of honor that is owing?

D.   The son should feed him, give him drink, dress him, cover him, bring him in and take him out.

Once again we see how woman forms a classification to be set into hierarchical relationship to other classifications of the same kind. The interest in comparison and contrast exhausts the matter.

4. Sifré to Numbers 1-115

The same focus of interest characterizes the treatment of women in this document.

Sifré to Numbers 1-115

II:II

1. A.   R. Josiah says, "'...a man or a woman....' Why are matters formulated so as to refer to both man and woman?

B.   "Since it is said, 'When a man leaves a pit open, or when a man digs a pit...' (Ex. 21:33).

C.   "I know only that a man is covered by the law. How do I know that a woman is equally culpable?

D.   "Scripture states, '....a man or a woman....'

E.   "That statement serves to encompass both a woman and a man in respect to all actions subject to sin-offerings and to all torts that are listed in the Torah."

F.   R. Jonathan says, "It is hardly necessary to supply such a proof, for, in that same context, it is stated in any event: 'the *owner* of the pit shall make it good,' and it says, '*the one* that kindled the fire shall make full restitution' (Ex. 22:6). [These formulations encompass both genders.]

G.   "Why then does Scripture state, '...a man or a woman...'? Merely to provide yet another occasion for the exercise of learning."

The sole point of concern is to discover whether or not woman falls under the law at hand.

Sifré to Numbers 1-115

XXI:I
1.   A.   "[This is the law in cases of jealousy, when a wife, though under her husband's authority, goes astray and defiles herself,] or when the spirit of jealousy comes upon a man and he is jealous of his wife; [then he shall set the woman before the Lord, and the priest shall execute upon her all this law. The man shall be free from iniquity, but the woman shall bear her iniquity]" (Num. 5:29-31).
      B.   Why is this clause stated [namely, "and he is jealous of his wife"]?
      C.   Since it says, "when the spirit of jealousy comes upon a man and he is jealous of his wife; [then he shall set the woman before the Lord,]" might one maintain that, just as prior to his expressing jealousy, it is a matter of optional concern [whether or not he does so and imposes the rite], so even after he has expressed jealousy, it remains an optional matter [whether or not he imposes the rite],
      D.   Scripture states, "when the spirit of jealousy comes upon a man and he is jealous of his wife," as a matter not of an option but of an obligation. [Once he has commenced the rite, he cannot cancel it.]

XXI:II
1.   A.   "...then he shall set the woman before the Lord, and the priest shall execute upon her all this law. The man shall be free from iniquity, but the woman shall bear her iniquity]" (Num. 5:29-31).
      B.   If he has carried out the rite, he is free of sin, but if he has not carried out the rite, he is not going to be free of sin.

XXI:III
1.   A.   "...The man shall be free from iniquity " (Num. 5:29-31):
      B.   [The husband should not feel guilty if the wife dies, and he should not say,] "Woe is me, for I have put an Israelite woman to death.
      C.   "Woe is me, for I have caused the humiliation of an Israelite woman.
      D.   "Woe is me, for I used to have sexual relations with a woman who was in fact unclean."
      E.   Therefore it is said, "...The man shall be free from iniquity."
      F.   Ben Azzai says, "Scripture speaks of a case in which the woman emerges as clean. Since she has brought herself into this affair, she too should not escape some sort of punishment. Therefore it is said, 'The man shall be free from iniquity, but the woman shall bear her iniquity.'"
      G.   R. Aqiba says, "Scripture comes to teach you the lesson that the end of the matter is death: 'Her body shall swell and her thigh shall fall away' (Num. 5:27).
      H.   "Why then is it said, 'The man shall be free from iniquity, but the woman shall bear her iniquity'?
      I.   "The man is free of sin, but that woman will bear her sin.

J. "It is then not in accord with the statement, 'I shall not visit your daughters when they turn into prostitutes, nor your daughters-in-law when they commit adultery, for men themselves go aside with harlots and sacrifice with cult prostitutes, and a people without understanding shall come to ruin' (Hos. 4:14).

K. "He said to them, 'Since you run after whores, the bitter water will not put your wives to the test.'

L. "That is why it is said, 'The man shall be free from iniquity' – that is with reference to that sin [of which Hosea spoke. The husband is not guilty of having had sexual relations with a whore, though his wife is guilty, because he did not realize it, and, when he did, he took the correct action.]"

The points of interest remain the same as before: distinguishing the man from the woman as to the applicability of the law. The topic elicits only an entirely predictable response, which accords with that of the Mishnah's framers, both in general and in their discussion of the wife accused of adultery in Mishnah-tractate Sotah in particular.

5. Sifré to Deuteronomy

I find nothing relevant to this issue here.

IX

The Intellectual Situation of the Tannaitic Midrashim and the Dating of Documents

We now review the results attained for each of our seven indicator categories, document by document.

1. Mekhilta Attributed to R. Ishmael

i. The Dual Torah

The myth of the Dual Torah makes no appearance in this document.

ii. The Gnostic Torah

The conception of study of the Torah as a source of salvation, transformation and regeneration, makes no appearance in Mekhilta. I identify no passage in which Torah study is recommended as the means of knowing God.

iii. The Messiah

While setting forth an eschatological teleology, this document does not utilize the Messiah theme in doing so.

iv. The Nations. Rome in Particular

The nations are undifferentiated, and Rome is not singled out. Here again, moreover, we find an eschatological teleology without resort to the Messiah theme. Rome is singled out only in a passage shared with Genesis Rabbah or Leviticus Rabbah.

v. Israel

Israel is identified as the family of Abraham, Isaac, and Jacob, and its exemplary conduct at the sea was on account of its origin as their children. Israel is particular, distinctive, unlike all other nations. Israel celebrates the uniqueness of God, and God celebrates the uniqueness of Israel. Whoever attacks Israel attacks God.

vi. Zekhut

The systemically consequential sense, *zekhut avot*, does occur in this document. Whether or not the system set forth by Mekhilta utilizes the conception in the way in which it is central to the Yerushalmi's system we cannot know, since, as I have argued in my Introduction to Mekhilta, the document to begin with can scarcely be described as the statement of a cogent system; it is, rather, an encyclopaedia. But in the context of an encyclopaedic statement of many things, we most certainly do find a clear expression of the matter.

vii. Woman

Where a scriptural passage invites the characterization of a woman as a real person, the compilers of this document do not include materials that take advantage of the opportunity. Miriam is a name; only one passage suggests she has qualities beyond her classification as woman.

2. Sifra

i. The Dual Torah

I find a fully exposed account of the myth of the Dual Torah in Sifra. Not only so, but, as noted earlier, the composition in which the myth makes its appearance rings the changes on a number of our other indicator categories. Since the passage is a singleton, we do not know whether it was included in the document when it attained closure, the manuscript tradition being parlous at best. But the character of Sifra as a whole registers, and my judgment on that matter is worked out in great detail in my *Uniting the Dual Torah: Sifra and the Problem of the Mishnah* (Cambridge, 1989: Cambridge University Press).

ii. The Gnostic Torah

Sifra endows Torah study with supernatural value. Israelites' relationship with God depends upon their Torah study; that does more than merely inform the disciple, Torah study changes him.

iii. The Messiah

While setting forth an eschatological teleology, this document does not utilize the Messiah theme in doing so.

iv. The Nations. Rome in Particular

"One ruler comes along and subjugates them and then goes his way, then another ruler comes along and subjugates them and goes his way," which means that the nations are undifferentiated.

v. Israel

Sifra's authorship treats Israel and the nations as comparable, Israel as transitive, and in such passages Israel by definition is not unique. The doctrine of the uniqueness of Israel, by itself or as a by-product of its descent from the patriarchs, plays no role I can discern in the document. Israel is a taxic indicator, distinguished from the gentiles, pure and simple.

vi. Zekhut

There can be no doubt that *zekhut* in the sense of *zekhut avot* does make an appearance in this document.

vii. Woman

Woman is solely a taxic indicator in this document.

3. Sifré to Numbers

i. The Dual Torah

The myth of the Dual Torah is absent from the 115 passages of this document that I examined.

ii. The Gnostic Torah

This document gives no hint that its authorship regards Torah study as a critical action of salvific consequence.

iii. The Messiah

The Messiah theme does not occur.

iv. The Nations. Rome in Particular

Whoever hates Israel hates God; there is no distinction between Rome and any other nation.

v. Israel

No passages permit classifying the document in regard to its theory of Israel.

vi. Zekhut

The usage of *zekhut* in this document is exactly the same as in the Mishnah, and the one point of pertinence comes in the treatment of the wife accused of adultery, which is to say, the same context as in the Mishnah.

vii. Woman

The sole point at which woman makes an appearance in 1-115 is in the story of the wife accused of adultery; nothing in the treatment of that theme diverges from the Mishnah's framing of the issues.

4. Sifré to Deuteronomy

i. The Dual Torah

While the myth of the Dual Torah is not explicitly stated, we do find a detailed account of varieties of canonical documents, Mishnah, Talmud, and so on. So implicitly the document recognizes components of the Torah beyond Scripture. On the other hand at the point at which the Torah is celebrated as what is unique to Israel, there is no appeal to the myth at hand. I am therefore inclined to assign both Sifrés to the category of writings that do not utilize the myth of the Dual Torah.

ii. The Gnostic Torah

Study of the Torah is more valued than practice of religious duties, a more abundant reward pertains to learning, whatever one learns changes his standing or status, and the simplest Torah teaching transforms the man who has mastered it. Teachings of Torah guide a person's intellect to know the Omnipresent. Study of the Torah is equivalent to making sacrifices in the Temple. The stakes of Torah study are very high: study of Torah transforms, purifies, sanctifies. All of these statements form the proposition that Torah study provides more than mere illumination. We stand entirely within the framework of the Yerushalmi's assessment of the matter.

iii. The Messiah

While setting forth an eschatological teleology, this document does not utilize the Messiah theme in doing so.

iv. The Nations. Rome in Particular

The nations are all alike, when Israel needs them. There is no interest whatsoever in identifying Edom or Ishmael or Esau as different or special.

v. Israel

Israel occurs in the two complementary ways: [1] defined by genealogy; [2] unique among nations. Israel is intransitive and beyond all comparison with the nations, though that will change at the end of time. Israel and God are comparable, in that each is unique in its classification; Israel proclaims God's uniqueness, God proclaims Israel's.

vi. Zekhut

This document makes explicit that "all is on account of the *zekhut* of the ancestors." More than that we cannot ask. But the concept is scarcely critical to the program of the compilation overall.

vii. Woman

Nothing relevant to this issue comes to hand.

5. The Position of the So-Called Tannaitic Midrashim

Let me now characterize each of our documents and then offer a judgment upon the results of the experiment that is now complete.

i. Mekhilta attributed to R. Ishmael

In my introduction, I characterized Mekhilta Attributed to R. Ishmael as the first scriptural encyclopaedia of Judaism. A scriptural encyclopaedia joins together expositions of topics, disquisitions on propositions, in general precipitated by the themes of scriptural narrative or the dictates of biblical law, and collects and arranges in accord with Scripture's order and program the exegeses – paraphrases which address an urgent question and, seen whole, set forth a cogent and compelling response to that question. But that is not the case here. The other Midrash compilations, moreover, intersect at a few places but not over the greater part of their territory. For, unlike Mekhilta Attributed to R. Ishmael, they are not compilations but free-standing compositions. They emerge as sharply differentiated from one another and clearly defined, each through its distinctive viewpoint and particular polemic, on the one side, and formal and aesthetic qualities, on the other. By contrast, in assembling conventions and banalities of the faith, Mekhilta Attributed to R. Ishmael has made a canonical statement, one with which, I take for granted, all of the faithful adhered, and therefore which none will have identified as a distinctive and particular program at all.

A sustained address to approximately half of the book of Exodus, Mekhilta Attributed to R. Ishmael seen whole and in the aggregate presents a composite of three kinds of materials. The first is a set of ad hoc and episodic exegeses of some passages of Scripture. The second is a group of propositional and argumentative essays in exegetical form, in which theological principles are set forth and demonstrated. The third is a set of topical articles, some of them sustained, many of them well crafted, about important subjects of the Judaism of the Dual Torah. Providing this encyclopaedia of information concerning theology and normative behavior, however, for the authorship of Mekhilta Attributed to R. Ishmael has not required a sustained demonstration of a position, whether whole or even in part, distinctive to that authorship and distinct from positions set forth by other authorships. This is indicated in two ways. First of all, our authorship has not composed an argument, prevailing through large tracts of the document, that is cogent in all details and accomplishes a main and overriding purpose. Nor, second, has that authorship set forth a statement of important propositions through most of the information, whether topical or exegetical, that it lays out. That is not to suggest, however, that here we have a mere conglomerate of unrelated facts. Quite to the contrary, there is no understanding the facts before us without ample access to a complete system, which is to say, the system of the Judaism of the Dual Torah of the canon of which our writing forms a principal part. Accordingly, the document before us participates in a system, but its authorship in no way proposes to shape or contribute to the setting forth of the system other than by rehearsing a corpus of inert facts.

Two considerations make me certain that we deal not with a systemically active and generative statement but only with a document that has been generated by a system. The first is that when facts – even set forth as well-composed essays of information – remain inert and contribute to the making of no point beyond themselves, we deal, not with a philosophy, but with what I call, by way of metaphor, an encyclopaedia. And a document that collects and rehearses facts but does not shape them in the service of important propositions serves a purpose all its own. It is to lay out and impart information needed for a system, but it is not to lay out the system. So far as a document presents an argument of its own, reshaping information to its purposes, we may characterize it as systemic, which is to say, argumentative and propositional. When a document serves the purpose of preserving and laying out received information, taking for granted the sense and meaning of that information but in no way reshaping that information for purposes of propositional argument, we may call such a document traditional.

Keenly interested in setting forth what there is to know about a variety of topics, the sages who stand behind Mekhilta Attributed to R. Ishmael preserve and transmit information necessary for the reader to participate in an ongoing tradition, that is to say, a system well beyond the nascent and formative stage. For framers such as these, important questions have been settled or prove null. For it is a system that is perceived to be whole, complete, fully in place, that the information collected and set forth by our authorship attests. When facts serve not for arguing in favor of a proposition but principally for informing a readership of things it must know, then we confront not a systemic exercise but a traditional rite: repeating the received facts so as to restate and reenforce the structure served by said facts. That accounts for my characterizing the document, assuming a provenance in late antiquity, as the first encyclopaedia of Judaism. And if it is, as some maintain, a writing of a later age, then while not first among the works of encyclopaedists, it is still first among encyclopaedias of its type. Yet encyclopaedists also make important points, and, in the case of the document before us, I find a stunning apologetic in the very laconic and commonplace character of the rhetoric and propositions assembled here.

In this context our findings prove coherent with the character of the document as a whole. We find no interest in the myth of the Dual Torah, no concern for the study of Torah as a salvific action, no expression of the Messiah theme, no interest in Rome as special, and no interest in woman as person. On the other hand, we do find Israel defined genealogically and as unique, and we do find the concomitant conception of *zekhut avot*. These results, by the definitions offered of what differentiates the Mishnah from the Yerushalmi, prove contradictory. But when we consider that our document forms not a systemic statement but a mass of information deemed relevant to the exposition of the selected passages of the book of Exodus, any results will have proven equally irrelevant to the question at hand. The encyclopaedists collected what they collected.

ii. Sifra

A document unlike Mekhilta in every important trait, Sifra, an address to the book of Leviticus, is as systemic and systematic as Mekhilta is encyclopaedic and haphazard. The authorship of Sifra employs a well-defined and restricted program of formal and rhetorical conventions to set forth within a single system of logical cogency an encompassing argument and determinate proposition. A framer of a pericope used in Sifra's final compilation could make use of one or more of three forms but no others. Not only so, but he ordinarily appealed to one paramount mode of logical coherence to make an intelligible point, but rarely to the other three that were available. And in the aggregate, when seen over all, the document that the framer helped to formulate again and again made a single stunning and encompassing point. I can think of no more probative case of the contrast between a well-crafted, propositional document and a haphazard compilation of commonplaces. While the framers of pericopes in Mekhilta's nine tractates used a variety of forms, appealed to all sorts of logics, and made a vast number of episodic points, or none at all, their counterparts in Sifra invoked a limited repertoire of rhetorical patterns, made cogent by a single logic of coherent discourse, to make one point, many times over. The match among rhetoric, logic, and proposition contrasts with the indifference to rhetorical, logical, and propositional congruity characteristic of Mekhilta Attributed to R. Ishmael and its nine tractates, severally and jointly.

Let us now revert to the formal conventions characteristic of Sifra in particular. What were the three forms? The first, the dialectical, is the demonstration that if we wish to classify things, we must follow the taxa dictated by Scripture rather than relying solely upon the traits of the things we wish to classify. The second, the citation form, invokes the citation of passages of the Mishnah or the Tosefta in the setting of Scripture. The third is what I call commentary form, in which a phrase of Scripture is followed by an amplificatory clause of some sort. The forms of the document admirably expressed the polemical purpose of the authorship at hand. What they wished to prove was that a taxonomy resting on the traits of things without reference to Scripture's classifications cannot serve. They further wished to restate the Oral Torah in the setting of the Written Torah. And, finally, they wished to accomplish the whole by rewriting the Written Torah.[1] The dialectical form accomplishes the first purpose, the citation form the second, and the commentary form the third.

The simple commentary form is familiar in Mekhilta Attributed to R. Ishmael, in which a verse, or an element of a verse, is cited and then a very few words explain the meaning of that verse. Second come the complex forms, in which a simple exegesis is augmented in some important way, commonly by questions and answers, so that we have more than simply a verse and a brief exposition of its elements or of its meaning as a whole. The authorship of the Sifra time and again wishes to show that prior documents, Mishnah or Tosefta, cited verbatim, require the support of exegesis of Scripture for important propositions, presented in the Mishnah and the Tosefta not on the foundation of exegetical proof at all. In the main, moreover, the authorship of Sifra tends not to attribute its materials to specific authorities, and most of the pericopae containing attributions are shared with Mishnah and Tosefta. As we should expect, just as in Mekhilta Attributed to R. Ishmael, Sifra contains a fair sample of pericopae which do not make use of the forms common in the exegesis of

---

[1]I have spelled out this matter in *Uniting the Dual Torah: Sifra and the Problem of the Mishnah* (Atlanta, 1988: Scholars Press for Brown Judaic Studies).

specific scriptural verses and, mostly do not pretend to explain the meaning of verses, but rather resort to forms typical of Mishnah and Tosefta. When Sifra uses forms other than those in which its exegeses are routinely phrased, it commonly, though not always, draws upon materials also found in Mishnah and Tosefta. It is uncommon for Sifra to make use of nonexegetical forms for materials peculiar to its compilation. As a working hypothesis, to be corrected presently, the two forms of rhetorical patterning of language in Sifra are two, simple and complex.

The rhetorical plan of Sifra leads us to recognize that the exegetes, while working verse by verse, in fact have brought a considerable program to their reading of the book of Leviticus. It concerns the interplay of the Oral Torah, represented by the Mishnah, with the Written Torah, represented by the book of Leviticus. That question demanded, in their view, not an answer comprising mere generalities. They wished to show their results through details, masses of details, and, like the rigorous philosophers that they were, they furthermore argued essentially through an inductive procedure, amassing evidence that in its accumulation made the point at hand. The syllogism I have identified about the priority of the revelation of the Written Torah in the search for truth is nowhere expressed in so many words, because the philosopher exegetes of the rabbinic world preferred to address an implicit syllogism and to pursue or to test that syllogism solely in a sequence of experiments of a small scale. Sifra's authorship therefore finds in the Mishnah and Tosefta a sizable laboratory for the testing of propositions. We have therefore to ask, at what points do Sifra and Mishnah and Tosefta share a common agenda of interests, and at what points does one compilation introduce problems, themes, or questions unknown to the other? The answer to these questions will show that Sifra and Mishnah and Tosefta form two large concentric circles, sharing a considerable area in common. Sifra, however, exhibits interests peculiar to itself. On the criterion of common themes and interests, Mishnah and Tosefta and Sifra exhibit a remarkable unity. If I had to compare the rhetorical program of Sifra's authorship with that of their counterparts in our document, I should say that the latter group has taken over and vastly expanded the program selected by the former. More to the point, the two documents intersect, but, for Sifré to Deuteronomy, the rhetorical intersection covers only a small segment of the whole plan governing the formulation of the document. In that sense, we have to say that our authorship has made choices and has not simply repeated a restricted program available to all rabbinic authorships and utilized at random by each.

Just as a limited and fixed pattern of formal preferences characteristic of the document as a whole, so a simple logical program, consisting of three logics of cogent discourse, served for every statement. The operative logics are mainly propositional, approximately 82%, inclusive of propositional, teleological, and methodical-analytical compositions. An authorship intending what we now call a commentary will have found paramount use for the logic of fixed association. That logic clearly served only a modest purpose in the context of the document as a whole. Our authorship developed a tripartite program. It wished to demonstrate the limitations of the logic of hierarchical classification, such as predominates in the Mishnah; that forms a constant theme of the methodical analytical logic. It proposed, second, to restate the Mishnah within the context of Scripture, that is, to rewrite the Written Torah to make a place for the Oral Torah. This is worked out in the logic of propositional discourse. And, finally, it wished in this rewriting to re-present the whole Torah as a cogent and unified document. Through the logic of fixed association it in fact did re-present the Torah. What the authorship of Sifra wished to prove was that a taxonomy resting on the traits of things without reference to Scripture's classifications cannot serve. They further wished to restate the Oral Torah in the setting of the Written Torah. And, finally, they wished to accomplish the whole by rewriting the Written Torah. The dialectical form accomplished the first purpose, the citation form the second, and the commentary form the third.

For its topical program the authorship of Sifra takes the book of Leviticus. For propositions Sifra's authorship presents episodic and ad hoc sentences. In general I fail to see a topical program distinct from that of Scripture, nor do I find it possible to set forth important propositions that transcend the cases at hand. Sifra remains wholly within Scripture's orbit and range of discourse, proposing only to expand and clarify what it found within Scripture. Where the authorship moves beyond Scripture, it is not toward fresh theological or philosophical thought, but rather to a quite different set of issues altogether, concerning Mishnah and Tosefta. When we describe the topical program of the document, the blatant and definitive trait of Sifra is simple: the topical program and order derive from Scripture. Just as the Mishnah defines the topical program and order for Tosefta, the Yerushalmi, and the Bavli, so Scripture does for Sifra. It follows that Sifra takes as its structure the plan and program of the Written Torah, by contrast to decision of the framers or compilers of Tosefta and the two Talmuds.

It follows that the three basic and definitive traits of Sifra, are, first, its total adherence to the topical program of the Written Torah for order and plan; second, its very common reliance upon the phrases or verses of the Written Torah for the joining into coherent discourse of discrete thoughts, for example, comments on, or amplifications of, words or phrases; and third, its equally profound dependence upon the Oral Torah for its program of thought: the problematic that defines the issues the authorship wishes to explore and resolve. Sifra in detail presents no paramount propositions. Sifra as a whole demonstrates a highly distinctive and vigorously demonstrated proposition. While in detail we cannot reconstruct a topical program other than that of Scripture, viewed in its indicative and definitive traits of rhetoric, logic, and implicit proposition, Sifra does take up a well-composed position on a fundamental issue, namely, the relationship between the Written Torah, represented by the book of Leviticus, and the Oral Torah, represented by the passages of the Mishnah deemed by the authorship of Sifra to be pertinent to the book of Leviticus. In a simple and fundamental sense, Sifra joins the two Torahs into a single statement, accomplishing a re-presentation of the Written Torah in topic and in program and in the logic of cogent discourse, and within that rewriting of the Written Torah, a re-presentation of the Oral Torah in its paramount problematic and in many of its substantive propositions. Stated simply, the Written Torah provides the form, the Oral Torah, the content. What emerges is not merely a united, Dual Torah, but *The* Torah, stated whole and complete, in the context defined by the book of Leviticus. Here the authorship of Sifra presents, through its re-presentation, The Torah as a proper noun, all together, all at once, and, above all, complete and utterly coherent. In order to do so our authorship has constructed through its document, first, the sustained critique of the Mishnah's *Listenwissenschaft*, then, the defense of the Mishnah's propositions on the foundation of scriptural principles of taxonomy, hierarchical classification in particular.

These general observations on the character of Sifra permit us to interpret the results in hand. Since Sifra's authorship has in hand the Mishnah and proposes to respond to that document, we cannot find surprising the points at which Sifra's authorship takes its own view of matters, such as we find, with such powerful emphasis, in the matters of the Dual Torah, the gnostic Torah, the definition of Israel, and the matter of *zekhut*. Sifra is not only post-mishnaic, it also stands alongside the Yerushalmi at four of the most characteristic traits of the system attested by the Yerushalmi. But with its interest in the Mishnah, we cannot find surprising the rather limited agendum that pertains to woman, on the one side, and the nations, on the other. The surprising point of departure from the Yerushalmi's system's program is at the Messiah theme, which is heavily utilized for the eschatological system set forth by the Yerushalmi, but not at all addressed in Sifra. In the aggregate, however, by the indicators set forth here we must deem Sifra to stand very close to the Yerushalmi and related documents.

iii. Sifré to Numbers

Sifré to Numbers constitutes a sustained commentary to the passages of the book of Numbers that its authors have chosen. The forms of the document all serve the purpose of conveying ad hoc comments on individual verses. The most common form, commentary form, consists of the citation of an opening verse, followed by an issue stated in terms extrinsic to the cited verse. The formal traits: [1] citation of a base verse from Numbers, [2] a generalization ignoring clauses or words in the base verse, [3] a further observation without clear interest in the verse at hand. The form yields a syllogism proved by a list of facts beyond all doubt. A secondary development involves dialectical exegesis, where we find a sequence of arguments about the meaning of a passage, in which the focus is upon the base verse and the meaning of the base verse. Logic pursues the sense of a verse, but the results of logic are tested, forthwith and one by one, against the language at hand, for example, why is this stated? or: you say it means X but why not Y? Or, if X, then what about Y? if Y, then what about Z?

All of these rather nicely articulated exegetical programs impose a scriptural test upon the proposals of logic. Yet another form, familiar from Sifra, demonstrates the fallacy of logic uncorrected by exegesis of Scripture. The formal indicator is the presence of the question, in one of several versions: is it not a matter of logic? The exegesis of the verse at hand plays no substantial role. Alongside is the inquiry into the scriptural basis for a passage of the Mishnah. What we have here is simply a citation of the verse plus a law in prior writing (Mishnah, Tosefta) which the verse is supposed to sustain. The Mishnah's or the Tosefta's rule then cannot stand as originally set forth, that is, absent any exegetical foundation. On the contrary, the rule, verbatim, rests on a verse of Scripture, given with slight secondary articulation: verse, then Mishnah sentence. That suffices, the point is made.

The recurrent polemic is that Scripture supplies hard facts, which, properly classified, generate syllogisms. By collecting and classifying facts of Scripture, therefore, we may produce firm laws of history, society, and Israel's everyday life. The diverse compositions in which verses from various books of the Scriptures are compiled in a list of evidence for a given proposition – whatever the character or purpose of that proposition – make that one point. And given their power and cogency, they make the point stick. Scripture alone supplies reliable basis for speculation. Laws cannot be generated by reason or logic unguided by Scripture.

When extrinsic issues intervene in the exegetical process, they coalesce to make a single point. It is that Scripture stands paramount, logic, reason, analytical processes of classification and differentiation, secondary. Reason not built on scriptural foundations yields uncertain results. The Mishnah itself demands scriptural bases. Scripture is complete, harmonious, perfect. Logic not only does not generate truth beyond the limits of Scripture but also plays no important role in the harmonization of difficulties yielded by what appear to be duplications or disharmonies.

There is a further, complementary point in the compilation. While Scripture stands paramount, logic, reason, analytical processes of classification and differentiation, secondary, nonetheless, man's mind joins God's mind when man receives and sets forth the Torah. Reason unaided by Scripture produces uncertain propositions. Reason operating within the limits of Scripture produces truth.

It is not at all clear to me that my seven indicator issues are important in this document. The evidence we have pursued leaves Sifré to Numbers entirely in the framework of the Mishnah. But that may tell us only that when commenting on the book of Numbers, the authorship before us was guided by the program of that book, which, so it would appear, did not precipitate deep thought on the indicator issues I have identified for our experiment. The upshot is that Sifré to Numbers is certainly post-mishnaic, on the one side, but not at all formulated within the orbit of the Yerushalmi's system, on the other. The correct point of comparison and contrast is between Sifra and Sifré to Numbers; both documents wish to make the same point about the Mishnah, but the authorship of the one had in mind issues that clearly did not concern the authorship of the other. Beyond that simple observation, I cannot go.

iv. Sifré to Deuteronomy

The fundamental rhetorical structure of Sifré to Deuteronomy, from beginning to end, is defined by verses of the book of Deuteronomy. These will be cited, and then whole verses or clauses will systematically dictate the arrangement of materials. The structure of the document, therefore, finds its definition in verses of the book of Deuteronomy. But the "commentary form" as structure plays a misleadingly paramount role. For that structure that dictates a form, a language pattern, in fact sustains and holds together a wide variety of forms. Once the overall arrangement of a given sequence of units of thought is established through the base verse -- that is, the verse of the book of Deuteronomy that stands at the head – we may find a variety of formalized patterns.

Nine recurrent patterns prove dominant in Sifré to Deuteronomy. Because of the close relationship between rhetorical conventions and logical necessities for coherent discourse, we distinguish among them by the presence of propositions, explicit, and then implicit, and how these are argued or proved:

i. Propositions Stated Explicitly and Argued Philosophically (by Appeal to Probative Facts):
1. The Proposition and its Syllogistic Argument
2. The Proposition Based on the Classification of Probative Facts
3. The Proposition Based on the Recurrent Opinions of Sages
4. The Narrative and its Illustrated Proposition: Parable
5. Narrative and its Illustrated Proposition: Scriptural Story

ii. Propositions Stated Implicitly but Argued Philosophically (as Above):
6. The (Implicit) Proposition Based on Facts Derived from Exegesis
7. The Priority of Exegesis and the Limitations of Logic

iii. Facts That Do Not Yield Propositions Beyond Themselves:
8. Exegetical Form with No Implicit Proposition. This is one form with a clear counterpart in Sifra.

iv. Facts That Do Not Yield Propositions Particular to the Case at Hand:
9. Dialectical Exegesis with No Implicit Proposition Pertinent to the Case at Hand but with Bearing on Large-Scale Structural Issues.

Two such patterns are, first, the systematic analytical exercise of restricting or extending the application of a discrete rule, ordinarily signified through stereotyped language; second, the demonstration that logic without revelation in the form of a scriptural formulation and exegesis produces unreliable results. There are other recurrent patterns of complex linguistic formation matched by sustained thought that conform to the indicative traits yielded by these two distinct ones. The form invariably involves either the exercise of generalization through extension or restriction of the rule to the case given in Scripture, or the demonstration that reason unaided by Scripture is not reliable. The formal traits are fairly uniform, even though the intent – the upshot of the dialectical exegesis – varies from instance to instance. Very often these amplifications leave the base verse far behind, since they follow a program of their own, to which the base verse and its information is at best contributory.

As to the paramount logic of cogent discourse, most units appeal for cogency to propositions, not to fixed associations, such as characterize commentaries and other compilations of exegeses of verses of Scripture. The logic is sustained, propositional, mostly philosophical, and not that of commentary. Sifré to Deuteronomy is unlike Mekhilta Attributed to R. Ishmael and Sifré to Numbers. What holds things together for our authorship does not rely upon the verse at hand to impose order and cogency upon discourse. To the contrary, the authorship of this document ordinarily appeals to propositions to hold two or more sentences together. If, by definition, a commentary appeals for cogency to the text that the commentators propose to illuminate, then ours is a document that is in no essential way a commentary. The logic is not that of a commentary, and the formal repertoire shows strong preference for other than commentary form.

The basic proposition of Sifré to Deuteronomy is that Israel stands in a special relationship with God, and that relationship is defined by the contract, or covenant, that God made with Israel. The covenant comes to particular expression, in our document, in two matters, first, the land, second, the Torah. Each marks Israel as different from all other nations, on the one side, and as selected by God, on the other. In these propositions, sages situate Israel in the realm of Heaven, finding on earth the stigmata of covenanted election and concomitant requirement of loyalty and obedience to the covenant.

The possession of the Torah imposes a particular requirement, involving an action. The most important task of every male Israelite is to study the Torah, which involves memorizing, and not forgetting, each lesson. This must go on every day and all the time. Study of the Torah should be one's main obligation, prior to all others. The correct motive is not for the sake of gain, but for the love of God and the desire for knowledge of God's will. People must direct heart, eyes, ears, to teachings of the Torah. Study of the Torah transforms human relationships, so that strangers become the children of the master of the Torah whom they serve as disciples. However unimportant the teaching or the teacher, all is as if on the authority of Moses at Sinai. When a person departs from the Torah, that person becomes an idolator. Study of the Torah prevents idolatry. The Torah's verses may be read in such a way that different voices speak discrete clauses of a single verse. One of these will be the Holy Spirit, another, Israel, and so on.

The covenant, through the Torah of Sinai, governs not only the on-going life of Israel but also the state of human affairs universally. The history of Israel forms a single, continuous, cycle, in that what happened in the beginning prefigures what will happen at the end of time. Events of Genesis are reenacted both in middle history, between the beginning and the end, and also at the end of times. So the traits of the tribal founders dictated the history of their families to both the here and now and also the eschatological age. Moses was shown the whole of Israel's history, past, present, future. The times of the patriarchs are reenacted in the messianic day. That shows how Israel's history runs in cycles, so that events of ancient times prefigure events now. The prophets, beginning with Moses, describe those cycles. What happens bears close ties to what is going to happen. The prophetic promises too were realized in temple times, and will be realized at the end of time.

The periods in the history of Israel, marked by the exodus and wandering, the inheritance of the land and the building of the Temple, the destruction, are all part of a divine plan. In this age Rome rules, but in the age to come, marked by the study of the Torah and the offering of sacrifices in the temple cult, Israel will be in charge. That is the fundamental pattern and meaning of history. The Holy Spirit makes possible actions that bear consequences only much later in time. The prefiguring of history forms the dominant motif in Israel's contemporary life, and the reenacting of what has already been forms a constant. Israel therefore should believe, if not in what is coming, then in what has already been. The very names of places in the land attest to the continuity of Israel's history, which follows rules that do not change. The main point is that while Israel will be punished in the worst possible way, Israel will not be wiped out.

But the cyclical character of Israel's history should not mislead. Events follow a pattern, but knowledge of that pattern, which is provided by the Torah, permits Israel both to understand and also to affect its own destiny. Specifically, Israel controls its own destiny through its conduct with God. Israel's history is the working out of the effects of Israel's conduct, moderated by the merit of the ancestors. Abraham effected a change in God's relationship to the world. But merit, which makes history, is attained by one's own deeds as well. The effect of merit, in the nation's standing among the other nations, is simple. When Israel enjoys merit, it gives testimony against itself, but when not, then the most despised nation testifies against it. But God is with Israel in time of trouble. When Israel sins, it suffers. When it repents and is forgiven, it is redeemed. For example, Israel's wandering in the wilderness took place because of the failure of Israel to attain merit. Sin is what causes the wandering in the wilderness. People rebel because they are prosperous. The merit of the ancestors works in history to Israel's benefit. What Israel does not merit on its own, at a given time, the merit of the ancestors may secure in any event. The best way to deal with Israel's powerlessness is through Torah study; the vigor of engagement with Torah study compensates for weakness.

God acts in history and does so publicly, in full light of day. That is to show the nations who is in charge. The Torah is what distinguishes Israel from the nations. All the nations had every opportunity to understand and accept the Torah, and all declined it; that is why Israel was selected. And that demonstrates the importance of both covenant and the Torah, the medium of the covenant. The nations even had a prophet, comparable to Moses. The nations have no important role in history, except as God assigns them a role in relationship to Israel's conduct. The nations are estranged from God by idolatry. That is what prevents goodness from coming into the world. The name of God rests upon Israel in greatest measure. Idolators do not control Heaven. The greatest sin an Israelite can commit is idolatry, and those who entice Israel to idolatry are deprived the ordinary protections of the law. God is violently angry at the nations because of idolatry. As to the nations' relationships with Israel, they are guided by Israel's condition. When Israel is weak, the nations take advantage, when strong, they are sycophantic. God did not apportion love to the nations of the world as he did to Israel.

The explicit propositional program of our document, summarized in its major points just now, is joined by a set of implicit ones. These comprise repeated demonstration of a point never fully stated. The implicit propositions have to do with the modes of correct analysis and inquiry that pertain to the Torah. Let me give a minor example. One may utilize reason in discovering the meaning and the rules of Scripture. Analogy for example provides adequate ground for extending a rule. There are many instances in which that same mode of reasoning is placed on display. The upshot is that while not made explicit, the systematic and orderly character of Scripture is repeatedly demonstrated, with the result that out of numerous instances, we may on our own reach the correct conclusion.

There are two implicit propositions that predominate. The first, familiar from Sifra, is that pure reason does not suffice to produce reliable results. Only through linking our conclusions to verses of Scripture may we come to final and fixed conclusions. The implicit proposition, demonstrated many times, may therefore be stated very simply. The Torah (written) is the sole source of reliable information. Reason undisciplined by the Torah yields unreliable results. The second of the two recurrent modes of thought is the more important. It is the demonstration that many things conform to a single structure and pattern. We can show this uniformity of the law by addressing the same questions to disparate cases and, in so doing, composing general laws that transcend cases and form a cogent system.

What is striking, then, is the power of a single set of questions to reshape and reorganize diverse data into a single cogent set of questions and answers, all things fitting together into a single, remarkably well-composed structure. Not only so, but when we review the numerous passages at which we find what, in the logical repertoire I called methodical-analytical logic, we find a single program. It is an effort to ask whether a case of Scripture imposes a rule that limits or imparts a rule that augments the application of the law at hand. A systematic reading of Scripture permits us to restrict or to extend the applicability of the detail of a case into a rule that governs many cases. A standard repertoire of questions may be addressed to a variety of topics, to yield the picture of how a great many things make essentially a single statement. This seems to me the single most common topical inquiry in our document. It covers most of the laws of Deut. 12-26. That conveys an impression of the dominance of this mode of logic, bearing in the deep structure of the authorship's statement its critical, if implicit, proposition within our document. The size, the repetitious quality, the obsessive interest in augmentation and restriction, generalization and limitation – these traits of logic and their concomitant propositional results form the centerpiece of the whole. And, I should maintain, that is not a merely subjective judgment, but a result that others can replicate with little difficulty.

The survey of the topical and propositional program of Sifré to Deuteronomy dictates what is truly particular to that authorship. It is its systematic mode of methodical analysis, in which it does two things. First, our authorship takes the details of cases and carefully reframes them into rules pertaining to all cases. It asks those questions of susceptibility to generalization ("generalizability") that first class philosophical minds raise. And it answers those questions by showing what details restrict the prevailing law to the conditions of the case, and what details exemplify the encompassing traits of the law overall. These are, after all, the two possibilities. The law is either limited to the case and to all cases that replicate this one. Or the law derives from the principles exemplified, in detail, in the case at hand. Essentially, as a matter of both logic and topical program, our authorship has reread the legal portions of the book of Deuteronomy and turned Scripture into what we now know is the orderly and encompassing code supplied by the Mishnah. To state matters simply, this authorship "mishna-izes" Scripture. I find in Sifra, as well as in Sifré to Numbers, little parallel to this dominant and systematic program of Sifré to Deuteronomy.

In light of this description of the documents, the results of our experiment present no surprises. Sifré to Deuteronomy stands closer to the system adumbrated by the Yerushalmi and associated writings than does any other of the four documents under study here. The conception of the salvific worth of Torah study, the definition of Israel, the role of *zekhut* – these important indicators place the document close to the Yerushalmi. More to the point, had I introduced as a principal indicator the conception of history – absent from the Mishnah, paramount for the Yerushalmi – the location of this document at the side of the Yerushalmi would have proven still more pronounced.

6. The Dating of Documents

My method yields no important results on the dating of documents. It is one thing to show how one document relates to another. When relationships prove consistent and unambiguous, we may reasonably claim that a document is prior or posterior to some other. Our results leave no reasonable doubt that Sifra and Sifré to Deuteronomy are posterior to the Mishnah. The outcome for Mekhilta Attributed to R. Ishmael is not self-evident to me, and the results for Sifré to Numbers prove inconsequential, because that document seems not to attend to issues that elsewhere have appeared to me to be indicative and typical.

But if we may say that in some ways certain compilations fall outside of the orbit of the Mishnah, or within that of the Yerushalmi, that seems to me the only conclusion, as to description, that this inquiry permits. I see no grounds in my results to permit speculation on when a given document reached closure. If after the Mishnah, how much after? For Sifra that question seems to me to yield only speculative answers, and for Sifré to Deuteronomy, only indeterminate ones. Why beyond the closure of the Mishnah it would take one hundred years, rather than a decade, to compose Sifra as we know it, I cannot say.

How about the description of the history of the formation of the Judaism of the Dual Torah? For that task, the results in hand seem to me of some modest utility. The reason is in two parts. First of all, it is important that we could not show any Tannaite Midrash to fall wholly within the orbit of the Yerushalmi, as the indicative traits examined have demonstrated. Second, we also could not demonstrate that any one of the four documents must be assigned a position, alongside of tractate Avot and Tosefta, essentially within the framework of the Mishnah.

The upshot for the comparison and location of the four documents before us is simple. Two of them, Sifra and Sifré to Deuteronomy, appear to be intermediate, at some point on the continuum that connects the Mishnah's and the Yerushalmi's system, closer to the latter than the former, but not at all within the circle of the latter. Mekhilta seems to me not to have been successfully classified by the methods used here, though some of the results may prove suggestive. And Sifré to Numbers 1-115 seems to me not to have been addressed in any important way at all.

These modest claims for what has been accomplished naturally raise the question: then what is at stake in the canonical history of ideas? And why do I maintain that this experiment has shown the usefulness of that approach, even while indicating also its limitations? These final questions require attention. For, up to this point, the reader has remained wholly within the frame of reference defined by my methods and premises, with the result that the entire inquiry by this point must appear to be an exercise in doing obvious things in obvious ways with predictable results. But in fact what in one perspective appears self-evident and even banal and trivial in another perspective presents a quite different appearance altogether. I have, in fact, framed a sustained argument with a broadly held position on these documents and how they are to be read. Let us now turn to that argument.

X

The Relevance of the Canonical History of Ideas

1. The Larger Issue of the So-Called Tannaite Midrashim

It remains to specify the reason that, despite the modest outcome, this experiment struck me as worth the time and effort. It is not only to conduct a methodological experiment, one that others can replicate. It is also to deal with important criticism of prior books of mine. Even though that criticism is phrased in an uncivil rhetoric, it is still to be taken into account, and, as always, I take seriously, and accord a respectful hearing to, the opinions of colleagues and critics.[1] In due

---

[1]The reason I think Maccoby deserves a hearing is that he is one of the few colleagues of the school opposed to me who has taken the trouble to read and review the works of which he disapproves. For that he deserves attention. The contrary position is the more common one, placed on display just now by the rather peculiar work, *The Iron Pillar – The Mishnah. Redaction, Form, and Intent.* By Dov Zlotnick (self published; produced in Jerusalem by The Bialik Institute; and distributed in North America by Ktav Publishing House, Hoboken, NJ). Zlotnick does not cite my books in his bibliography, and when he discusses subjects on which I have written books, he also does not cite them, let alone proposing to deal with their theses; and that is the case when he reproduces my results, as much as when he sets forth other positions altogether. Maccoby, to his credit, took the trouble to state his position in response to mine. But the character of Zlotnick's book shows the value of his research. Writing on the theme of "Rabbi's Mishnah and the development of Jewish law," Zlotnick argues no thesis but covers various topics, such as the editorial activity of Rabbi, memory and the integrity of the Oral Tradition, some aspects of mishnaic repetition, conservatism in the making of law; strengthening the Oral Law, the inoperative *halakah*, is the Mishnah a code, and the like. The book could have been written in 1850 by Zechariah Frankel, for Zlotnick's categories and issues ("the relation of Rabbi to his predecessors,"

course I have dealt with them all, in one way or another.[2] The reason is that criticism sets forth a position alternative to one that I have taken, and one must properly respond to propositions or positions by assessing them, even while ignoring the improper way in which contrary ideas are expressed.[3] In this book I mean to address the quite proper challenge stated by the British medievalist and playwright, Hyam Maccoby, as follows:

> Neusner argues that since the Mishnah has its own style and program, nothing outside it is relevant to explaining it....Neusner does not answer the point, put to him by E. P. Sanders and myself, that the liturgy being presupposed by the Mishnah is surely relevant to the Mishnah's exegesis. Nor does he answer the charge that he ignores the aggadic material within the Mishnah itself, e.g., Avot; or explain why the copious aggadic material found in roughly contemporaneous works should be regarded as irrelevant. Instead he insists that he is right to carry out the highly artificial project of deliberately closing his eyes to all aggadic material and trying to explain the Mishnah without it.
>
>   Hyam Maccoby[4]

As is clear, this book assesses the character of those allegedly roughly contemporaneous works that are supposed to accompany and contribute to the exegesis of the Mishnah. Is Maccoby right in supposing that these documents fall within the circle of the Mishnah

---

"the Mishnah of R. Akiba," "*halakhah*: its authority and relation to Moses" [!]) were the ones in vogue in the primitive stages of modern scholarship on the Mishnah. The book is ignorant and therefore an oddity, too eccentric to be taken seriously.

[2]Certainly the best known and most notorious of these is Saul Lieberman, whose posthumous review of some paragraphs of my translation of Palestinian Talmud tractate Horayot, in *Journal of the American Oriental Society* for July 1984, turns out to be the the the single best-known piece of writing that Lieberman did in his entire life, a compliment I cannot claim to have earned. My reading of Lieberman's oeuvre is in my "When Intellectual Paradigms Shift: Does the End of the Old Mark the Beginning of the New? *History and Theory*, October 1988, pp. 241-260.

[3]Maccoby, now cited, has the merit of reading and responding to what he reads. Zlotnick, as noted, wants the scholarly world to take seriously a book that simply ignores most of the scholarship done in the past three decades, which is mine and my students', on the subject on which he claims to make a contribution. But when Maccoby presented his picture of the same documents – the so-called tannaitic literature – in a sustained work of his own, he dismissed in half a sentence, and without a word of argument or *Auseinandersetzung*, that same corpus that Zlotnick dismissed in total silence. So we must not overestimate the man's intellectual honesty either.

[4]Hyam Maccoby, in the symposium, The Mishnah: Methods of Interpretation," *Midstream*, October 1986, p. 41.

and attest opinions held by the same authorities who produced the Mishnah? In that case a description of the system to which the Mishnah attests surely should encompass these documents and their program as well. Or is he wrong in assigning these writings to the ambience or provenance of the Mishnah? In that case these writings cannot be asked to tell us about (other) ideas held by the authorities represented in the Mishnah. For Maccoby's challenge is an interesting one and is not to be ignored. And that is so, even though he is not really a scholar, being ignorant of the literature to which he makes reference.

For one thing, his position on the relationship of Avot is eccentric, since the bulk of scholarship today concurs that tractate Avot reached closure about a generation beyond the Mishnah, that is, ca. 250. For to the point, his assumption that the so-called Tannaite Midrashim are to be classified as "aggadic" is simply ignorant, suggesting that Maccoby has only a limited knowledge of the contents and character of these documents and has never studied them, beginning to end, as I have. For to call them "aggadic" is to ignore their character, which is not "aggadic," if by *aggadah* we mean tales or narratives. They are precisely what the received tradition has called them, which is *Midrashim*, that is, exegeses of Scripture. As to the passages that are subjected to exegesis, the whole of Sifra, most of Sifré to Deuteronomy, the greater part of Sifré to Numbers, and at least half of Mekhilta Attributed to R. Ishmael, fall into the category of exegeses of legal passages, hence, as the received tradition of scholarship has it, halakhic Midrashim, and not aggadic Midrashim (to appeal to the native categories so self-evidently necessary in Maccoby"s language.) There is, as a matter of fact, very little *aggadah* – narrative and not exegesis of narrative passages of Scripture – in these documents at all. So, it is clear, Maccoby's certainty that we have in hand "copious aggadic material found in roughly contemporaneous works" is misplaced. It is devastating evidence of the man's sheer ignorance.

It is equally the fact, of course, that most scholarship has until this time not succeeded in demonstrating in detail the contents of the liturgy of Judaism(s) in the first and second century. In that matter Maccoby's confidence seems somewhat more robust than the evidence in scholarship on which it rests; no contemporary scholar of the history of liturgy takes the position he does. True, everyone concurs that the main structure seems adequately attested as to the *Shema* and the Prayer. But the details as to wording, hence contents, are not at all firm, unless we take all attributions at face value and furthermore take for granted that the wording then is pretty much the same as the wording attested only centuries later. But these suppositions require credulity beyond the powers of the generality of critical scholarship, and hence we may dismiss as just more of the familiar gullibility Maccoby's certainty on such questions.

The main point relevant to this book is a different one. It is contained in these words: "Nor does he answer the charge that he ignores the aggadic material within the Mishnah itself, e.g., Avot; or explain why the copious aggadic material found in roughly contemporaneous works should be regarded as irrelevant." The charge that I ignore "the aggadic material within the Mishnah itself" is of course nonsense, since I have composed a commentary on the entire Mishnah and skipped nothing. My various systemic descriptions, for example, *Judaism: The Evidence of the Mishnah*, have taken rich account of what Maccoby classifies as the Mishnah's "aggadah." I of course have not ignored tractate Avot, having published a translation of and commentary upon that document. I have, of course, dealt with tractate Avot in its correct and established temporal-ordinal context, as post-mishnaic by one generation, in every account I have given of the canonical history of ideas, perhaps a score in all by now. In my translations of, and introductions to, the four Tannaitic Midrash compilations discussed in this book, I have of course not ignored a line of "aggadah." But Maccoby deserves a sustained response to an interesting question that he has raised, and that is the setting, in such discourse as today passes for scholarly debate in Judaic Studies, in which I present this experiment. The question, then, is to be addressed as Maccoby has framed it.

2. Do We Really Have in Hand "Copious Aggadic Material Found in Roughly Contemporaneous Works"?

We revert to Maccoby's claim that the "roughly contemporaneous works" attest to conceptions held by contemporaries of those who produced the Mishnah, so that we must describe the system to which the Mishnah attests by appeal, also, to Mekhilta Attributed to R. Ishmael, Sifra, and the two Sifrés. Our study has uncovered little to sustain Maccoby's opinion. Sifra and Sifré to Deuteronomy are demonstrably post-mishnaic, and as we now know them, those two documents cannot have been formulated overall, not merely in detail here and there, without constant reference to the Mishnah. Sifra presented a sustained critique of the Mishnah. Sifré to Deuteronomy took as a principal problem, attested by the recurrent forms of the document as much as by its episodic statements, the question of whether cases are subject to generalization and exemplary or definitive of the law in the last detail. That effort to read Scripture as mishnaic, of "mishna-izing" Scripture, must be characterized – like the quite different focus of Sifra – as a sustained inquiry into the relationship of Scripture to Mishnah. As to Sifré to Numbers, matters at this point must be deemed indeterminate. Mekhilta, for its part, stands entirely *hors de combat*, since to begin with we cannot describe a sustaining system characteristic of the document (or characterized by the document).[5]

3. What Is at Stake in the Results of this Experiment?

Let me now make explicit what I conceive to be at stake in the results of this experiment. From the viewpoint of the study of the history of the formation of Judaism, of course, we find ourselves able to gain perspective on these documents and their position in the larger unfolding of that history. That is valuable but not critical. But from the viewpoint of the study of the history of Judaism in the first century that New Testament scholarship wishes to invoke in the exegesis of New Testament writings, particularly the Gospels, and, among them, particularly the Synoptics, and Paul, at stake is whether or not that scholarship can go on as it has. For routinely cited in that connection as attesting views held by "Judaism" (meaning, everything but the Jews who produced the Gospels and the system set forth by Paul) are these documents in particular, the only ones that can plausibly serve to tell us about views held in the first century; the later writings in the rabbinic canon, for instance, the Talmud of Babylonia or Leviticus Rabbah or the Zohar, are adduced as evidence only among the uninformed and academic outcasts, but the "critical" scholarship on early Christianity that turns to "Judaism" in its work relies very heavily upon phrases and sentences in these documents in particular.

So for that sector of New Testament scholarship, the position to which Maccoby refers (a commonplace one as is clear) is absolutely critical for the entire hermeneutic enterprise. E. P. Sanders, to whom Maccoby makes reference, simply cannot do the work he wishes to do on the characterization of first-century Judaism without access to the

---

[5]It remains to notice that the prevailing description of the Judaism of the Dual Torah as messianic finds no support whatsoever in the documents read in this study. Not only do we not find "copious aggadic material," but we also uncover no reason to suppose that the Messiah theme served any of our authorships. Quite how this squares with the descriptions of "Judaism" (meaning, everywhere, all the time) and of "the Jews" as messianic and in constant expectations of the Messiah, respectively, for instance, the representation of matters in the works on *Jesus the Jew* by Geza Vermes, is not at all clear. It seems to me unlikely that Vermes can discover in the so-called Tannaite Midrashim any support whatsoever for his theory on the character of "Judaism" and "the Jews."

Midrash compilations of later ages because the documents that pertain
and derive from a time closer to the first century, the Mishnah first of
all, simply do not deal with the subjects that Sanders wishes to treat,
for example, covenantal nomism. Hence the insistence that the so-
called Tannaitic Midrashim testify to the state of opinion in the
second, and hence perhaps also the first century. In this regard Sanders
finds himself in a difficult situation indeed, for, if we do not take as
fact that the so-called Tannaitic Midrashim are "tannaitic," that is,
speak in behalf of the same folk who produced the Mishnah, then he
cannot adduce in evidence of the state of Judaism anything that
reached closure much before 300, or even later.

And if that is so, then his description cf that Judaism is no more
critical than the description produced by promiscuous appeal to all
rabbinic sources, undifferentiated as to time and place of origin. In
describing first century Judaism, Sanders to his credit is too critical a
scholar to cite without further ado a saying that first surfaces in a
sixth or seventh century document, assigned to be sure to the name of an
authority assumed to have flourished in the first or early second
century. But then to have any "aggadic" evidence at all (that is,
evidence deemed to address in a direct way theological issues of
importance to Sanders in his work on Paul, for example, or on earliest
Christianity in general), the tannaitic classification of Mekhilta
Attributed to R. Ishmael, Sifra, and the two Sifrés, is absolutely
crucial. In my view, that enterprise of theological description of first-
century Judaism, so far as it draws on these writings, is as uncritical as
the scholarship on first century Judaism that copiously cites the Bavli
– or even the Zohar! – that that same sector (rightly) dismisses as
uncritical. *Tant pis!*

That is not to suggest the stakes in the study of the classics of the
Judaism of the Dual Torah find definition in the interests of New
Testament scholarship. The issue of the place of the so-called
Tannaite Midrashim in the canon of the Judaism of the Dual Torah –
part of the world of the Mishnah or altogether post-mishnaic – is to be
raised in its own terms. For if we wish to understand those important
writings, we have to frame a theory of the issues that impart to them
their distinctive character; we must provide for ourselves an
introduction to those documents, which will tell us, overall, how we are
to make sense of the details of any one of them. At stake is not the
parlous position of a handful of eccentrics in Gospels' research, let alone
the idiosyncratic opinion of an uninformed and cranky nonspecialist.
The correct description, analysis, and interpretation of the canonical
writings of Judaism in its formative age, the framing of a theory of the
context and character of those writings, the formation of an

appropriate hermeneutic to guide the reading of each one of them –
these fundamental tasks define the work. They moreover dictate the
importance of the results of the method I call "the canonical history of
ideas" as applied to seven indicators of the place of the so-called
Tannaite Midrashim – Mekhilta Attributed to R. Ishmael, Sifra, Sifré
to Numbers, and Sifré to Deuteronomy – in relationship to the Mishnah
and the Yerushalmi and its companion midrash compilations.

Appendix I

Testing the Method and Value of the Canonical History of Ideas.
The Case of "Rome in Talmud and Midrash"

Let me give a concrete example of how we may choose between the canonical history of ideas and the received method of setting forth the history of ideas. That method is founded on two premises, one requiring gullibility, the other affirming ignorance and a theological a priori. These are [1] the inerrancy of attributions and [2] the harmony, interchangeability, and uniformity of all documents, early and late. Let me address a familiar subject, one that has been important in this book: Rome in Talmud and Midrash.[1] The subject is familiar because we have in hand a book entirely representative of the received method, so none can allege that I invent a straw man, beat a dead horse, or otherwise misrepresent the state of scholarship when I declare it miserable. I point specifically to a highly representative work, Samuel Krauss's monograph on that subject, "Persia and Rome in the Talmud and in the Midrashim:" *Paras veRomi battalmud uvammidrashim* (repr.: Jerusalem, 1947). Hence I can call upon an example of how the subject has been treated.

---

[1]What follows is the text of my Ben Zion Bokser Memorial Lecture at Queens College (1987). I originally printed the lecture in my *Religious Study of Judaism. Description, Analysis, Interpretation* (Lanham, 1986: University Press of America), 2:161-190, under the title, "Interpretation in the Context of Accepted Opinion: The Other in General, Rome in Particular. Correcting a Major Error of Interpretation." As already noted, some of the paragraphs that follow have been utilized in Chapters One and Four. I preferred to present the essay in its original form, since the important corrections of my rather stupid errors in method refer to the paragraphs that proved important in the next context of this book.

Not only so, but in prior work of my own, done before I had developed the method illustrated in this book, I followed the received method and made a rather stupid mistake as a result, which I correct in this appendix. What follows began as the Ben Zion Bokser Lecture at Queens College. While I have set forth in Chapter One some of the ideas that are presented here, I prefer to lay out my test of falsification – specifically of my own ideas – as I originally spelled it out, begging the reader's indulgence for a small measure of repetition of some paragraphs that occur also in Chapters One and Four.

I. The Methodological Issue

The relationships between Rome and Israel in late antiquity, from the destruction of the Temple in A.D. 70 to the Muslim conquest of the Land of Israel in the mid-seventh century, have attracted attention over the years. What is at issue has not always come to the fore. What scholars have done, when approaching the rabbinic writings of the age, is to collect and organize all the sayings on Rome and to treat the resulting composite as "the talmudic," or "the rabbinic" view of Rome. In doing so they have followed the established way in which to investigate the thought of classical Judaism on any given subject. It is to collect pertinent sayings among the diverse documents and to assemble all these sayings into a composite, a portrait, for example, "*the* rabbinic view of Rome." The composite will divide up the sayings in accord with the logic of the topic at hand.

If, for example, we want to know the thought of classical Judaism about God, we collect everything and then divide up the result among such rubrics as God's attributes, God's love, or Providence, or reward and punishment, and the like. Differentiation therefore affects not the documents but the topic. That is to say, whatever we find, without regard to the document in which the saying or story occurs, joins together with whatever else we find, to form an undifferentiated aggregate, thus to illuminate a given aspect of our topic, thus God's love or Providence, as these topics are treated in a diversity of documents. How then do we organize our data? It is by allowing the topic we study to tell us its divisions, that is to say, the logic of differentiation derives from the topic, not the sources from which we draw sayings about the topic at hand.

My research for a number of years has led me to differentiate among documents and to ask each document to deliver its particular viewpoint to me. That is the foundation for the work of the present volume as well. When, therefore I wish to trace the history of an idea, it produces the representations of that idea as yielded by documents, read singly and one by one, then in the sequence of their closure. Here, of course, I further innovate by reading documents in relationship to other documents, earlier and later – the set under discussion in relationship to the Mishnah, on the one side, and the Yerushalmi, on the other, for instance. It follows that I do not join together everything I find, without regard to its point of origin in a given compilation of rabbinic sayings. Rather I keep things apart, so that I record what I find in document A, then in document B, and onward through the alphabet. What this yields is a history of the idea at hand as the documents, laid out in their sequence, tell me that history.

Now how shall we test whether the approach just now outlined proves superior to the established one? The answer is to ask what we discover if we do not differentiate among documents, as against what we find when we do. Let me spell this out, and then proceed to an examination of the issue at hand: a particular topic, sources for which are laid forth one way, then investigated and interpreted in two different ways. In the present context, I may not have to plead guilty of excessive criticism of colleagues' scholarship, since both approaches to the description and interpretation of the relationship of Rome and Israel derive from my own work, that is, the one that failed to differentiate among sources, then the one that does effect what I maintain is the required differentiation. In setting forth the positions of Neusner *versus* Neusner, I shall explain where and how I erred and why I think my revision is correct.

II. Testing the Worth of Differentiation among Documents

Let me begin by asking, *how shall we know which approach is better, or even right?* The answer to the question derives from a test of falsification: how can we show, therefore how do we know, whether we are right or wrong. One way of testing the viability of a method is to ask whether it facilitates or impedes the accurate description and analysis of data. Let me spell out this criterion.[2]

My test of the proposed approach of differentiating among documents consists in trying one approach and then its opposite to see the result: a perfectly simple experiment. Our criterion for evaluating results is simple: if we do things in two different ways, in the results of which of the two ways do we see the evidence with greater, in which lesser, perspicacity? That criterion will rapidly prove its entirely objective value. So these are the questions to be raised. If we do not differentiate among documents, then we ask what happens if we do

---

[2]I go over ground covered at the end of the Introduction.

differentiate. If we do differentiate, we ask what happens if we do not. These are simple research experiments, which anyone can replicate.

To spell them out also poses no great difficulty. If differentiating yields results we should have missed had we not read the documents one by one, then our category has obscured important points of difference. If *not* differentiating yields a unity that differentiating has obscured, so that the parts appear, seen all together, to cohere, then the category that has required differentiation has obscured important points in common. How shall we know one way or the other? Do we not invoke a subjective opinion when we conclude that there is, or is not, a unity that differentiation has obscured? I think not. In fact the operative criterion is a matter of fact and does not require subjective judgment. How so? Let me state the objective criterion with emphasis:

[1] *If we find that each one of the documents says on its own essentially what all of the documents say together, so that the parts do turn out to be interchangeable, then imposing distinctions suggests differences where there is none. The parts not only add up to the sum of the whole, as in the case of a homogenizing category. Each of the parts replicates the fundamental structure of the whole. In that case, differentiation proves misleading.*

[2] *If, by contrast, when viewed one by one, our documents in fact do not say the same thing by themselves that all of them say when read together, our category, failing to recognize differences, suggests a unity and a cogency where there is none. The parts may well add up to the sum of the whole, but each of the parts appears to stand by itself and does not replicate the statement to which, as part of a larger whole, it contributes. In that case, not effecting a considerable labor of description of the documents one by one will obscure the very center and heart of matters: that the documents, components of the whole, are themselves autonomous, though connected (if that can be shown) and also continuous (if that can be shown).*

Accordingly, the results of an experiment of differentiation where, up to now, everything has been read as a single harmonious statement, will prove suggestive – an interesting indicator of the effect and usefulness of the category at hand. At the end we shall return to these questions and answer them. In the end of this appendix, I shall revert to the stated criteria and explain why I have shown that [2] is met, and, hence, the documentary history of ideas in this test assuredly proves its value by an objective criterion.

Since, in the case of "the talmudic view of Rome," we treat all writings produced by all Jews as essentially homologous testimonies to a single encompassing Judaism, we shall now engage in a hitherto-neglected exercise of differentiation. We ask what each source produced by Jews in late antiquity, read by itself, has to say about the subject at hand. How shall we differentiate among the available writings? The simplest route is to follow the lines of distinction imposed by the writings themselves, that is, simply, to read one book at a time, and in the order in which the several books are generally held to have reached closure.

III. The Canonical Principle in Category Formation

The limns of documents then generate, form, and define our initial system of categories. That is, the document to begin with is what demands description, then analysis by comparison and contrast to other documents, then interpretation as part of the whole canon of which it forms a part.[3] In the case at hand, what we have to do is simply ask the principal documents, one by one, to tell us their picture of the topic at hand, hence, Rome and Israel's relationship to Rome. Each document, it is clear, demands description, analysis, and interpretation, all by itself. Each must be viewed as autonomous of all others. At a later stage, each document also is to be examined for its relationships with other documents that fall into the same classification (whether that classification is simply "Jewish" or still more narrowly and hence usefully defined). Then, at the end, each document is to be allowed to take its place as part of the undifferentiated aggregation of documents that, all together, constitute the evidence of a Judaism, in the case of the rabbinic kind, the canon of the Torah.

Let me spell this out. If a document reaches us within its own framework as a complete book with a beginning, a middle, and an end, we do not commit an error in simple logic by reading that document as it has reached us, that is, as a book by itself. If, further, a document contains materials shared verbatim or in substantial content with other documents of its classification, or if a document explicitly refers to some other writings and their contents, then we have to ask the question of connection. We have to seek the facts of connectedness and ask for the meaning of those connections. In the description of a Judaism, we have to take as our further task the description of the whole out of the undifferentiated testimony of all of its parts. For a Judaism does put together a set of once discrete documents and treat them as its canon. So in our setting we do want to know how a number of writings fit together

---

[3]I hasten to add, I do not take the canon to be a timeless category, as my analysis of the Mishnah and its associates indicates. Quite to the contrary, the canon itself takes shape in stages, and these form interesting categories for study.

into a single continuous and harmonious statement. In the present setting, only the part of the work is required.

IV. The Outsider in General, Rome in Particular

We come to the topic at hand: Rome and Israel. To begin with we approach the matter from its most abstract angle: Rome as representative of the outsider. The outsider in general represented a danger that took many forms, for the outsider found definition in a variety of ways. He could be an Israelite holding views other than those of sages. A perfectly loyal man, for example, who did not accept the rabbis' remarkable claims in behalf of the sanctity of what they knew, or all of their rules, posed a threat. An outsider could be a woman, simply because, in sages' view, men were normal, women abnormal. It could be a Samaritan, sharing Scripture but reading it differently. It could be a Christian, with the old Scripture and a new one, claimed to complete the old. It could be some sort of pagan, wholly outside of the frame of Israelite tradition. It could be a Roman, alien and powerful. It could be an Iranian, from the other side of the frontier, or someone still more different than that. So, in all, we may invent a hierarchy of difference, from nearest to farthest away, and we may further postulate not only degrees of difference but also differentiation among the different, and that on a polythetic basis.

Let us now proceed to review four important sources as autonomous components of a larger canon and to ask each of them to speak for itself, all by itself, on the topic at hand. These fall into two groups: the Mishnah (inclusive of tractate Abot) and a document of Mishnah exegesis, the Tosefta, and two documents of Scripture exegesis, Genesis Rabbah and Leviticus Rabbah. The former testify to the minds of compositors who flourished in the late second and third centuries (before Christianity became the state religion of the Roman empire), the later, the late fourth and fifth centuries (after the establishment of Christianity as imperial cult and faith). We shall parse the ideas at hand as they unfold in these four compilations.[4] Then we shall trace

---

[4]Since we cannot demonstrate that what is attributed to authorities within the pages of these documents really was said by them, we also cannot impute to a generation prior to that of redaction any of the ideas expressed in the several documents: what we cannot show, we do not know. And, to the contrary, what we can show, which is that the documents demonstrably speak for the authorship of the final redaction, we do know: the opinions of the ultimate, sometimes also the penultimate, redactors. That is all we know at this time. So whether or not the Mishnah or Leviticus Rabbah contains ideas held prior to the generation of redaction is not at issue. I claim here to say what the authorship at the end wished to state, in the time and circumstance of

the result, which is the canonical history of the topic at hand. Finally, we shall review the original results and show where and how they erred – and, above all, explain the reason why. In that way we shall carry out an exercise in the testing of a method. That is to say, we ask what happens when we do, and when we do not, differentiate.

V. Differentiating among Documents
1. Rome (Esau, Edom) in the Mishnah and Tractate Abot

If we ask the Mishnah, ca. A.D. 200, its principal view of the world beyond, it answers with a simple principle: the framers of the document insist that the world beyond was essentially undifferentiated. Rome to them proved no more, and no less, important than any other place in that undifferentiated world, and, so far as the epochs of human history were concerned, these emerged solely from within Israel, and, in particular, the history of Israel's cult, as M. Zeb. 14:4-9 lays matters out in terms of the cult's location, and M. R.H. 4:1-4 in terms of the before and after of the destruction.[5] The undifferentiation of the outside world may be conveyed in a simple fact. The entire earth outside of the Land of Israel in the Mishnah's law was held to suffer from contamination by corpses. Hence it was unclean with a severe mode of uncleanness, inaccessible to the holy and life-sustaining processes of the cult. If an Israelite artist were asked to paint a wall portrait of the world beyond the Land, he would paint the entire wall white, the color of death. The outside world, in the imagination of the Mishnah's law, was the realm of death. Among corpses, how are we to make distinctions? We turn then to how the Mishnah and tractate Abot treat Rome, both directly and in the symbolic form of Esau and Edom. Since the system at hand treats all gentiles as essentially the same, Rome, for its part, will not present a theme of special interest. So if my description of the Mishnah's basic mode of differentiation among outsiders proves sound, then Rome should not vastly differ from other outsiders.

As a matter of fact, if we turn to H. Y. Kosovsky, *Thesaurus Mishnae* (Jerusalem, 1956) I, II, IV, and look for Edom, Esau, Ishmael, and Rome, we come away disappointed. "Edom" in the sense of Rome

---

redaction. What else these documents contain, to what other ages and authorships they testify – these are separate questions, to be taken up on their own terms. I have done so for the Mishnah and Tosefta in various works of literary and historical study.

[5]In my *Messiah in Context, Israel's History and Destiny in Formative Judaism* (*Foundations of Judaism*, Vol. II. *Teleology*) (Philadelphia, 1983: Fortress) I dealt at some length with the larger question of the later reimagining of Israel's history. But that is not at issue here.

does not occur. The word stands for the Edomites of biblical times (M. Yeb. 8:3) and the territory of Edom (M. Ket. 5:8). Ishmael, who like Edom later stands for Rome, supplies a name of a sage, nothing more. As to Rome itself, the picture is not terribly different. There is a "Roman hyssop," (M. Par. 11:7, M. Neg. 14:6), and Rome occurs as a place name (M. A.Z. 4:7). Otherwise I see not a single passage indicated by Kosovsky in which Rome serves as a topic of interest, and, it goes without saying, in no place does "Rome" stand for an age in human history, let alone the counterpart to and opposite of Israel. Rome is part of the undifferentiated other, the outside world of death beyond. That fact takes on considerable meaning when we turn to the later fourth and fifth century compilations of scriptural exegeses. But first, we turn to the Mishnah's closest companion, the Tosefta.

VI. Differentiating among Documents
2. Rome in the Tosefta

When we come to the Tosefta, a document containing systematic and extensive supplements to the sayings of the Mishnah, we find ourselves entirely within the Mishnah's circle of meanings and values. When, therefore, we ask how the Tosefta's authors incorporate and treat apocalyptic verses of Scripture, as they do, we find that they reduce to astonishingly trivial and local dimensions materials bearing for others world-historical meaning – including symbols later invoked by sages themselves to express the movement and meaning of history. No nation, including Rome, plays a role in the Tosefta's interpretation of biblical passages presenting historical apocalypse, as we now see in the the Tosefta's treatment of the apocalyptic vision of Daniel. There we find that history happens in what takes place in the sages' debates – there alone!

T. Miqvaot

7:11

A.   A cow which drank purification water, and which one slaughtered within twenty-four hours –

B.   This was a case, and R. Yosé the Galilean did declare it clean, and R. Aqiba did declare it unclean.

C.   R. Tarfon supported R. Yosé the Galilean. R. Simeon b. Nanos supported R. Aqiba.

D.   R. Simeon b. Nanos dismissed [the arguments of] R. Tarfon. R. Yosé the Galilean dismissed [the arguments of] R. Simeon b. Nanos.

E.   R. Aqiba dismissed [the arguments of] R. Yosé the Galilean.

F.   After a time, he [Yosé] found an answer for him [Aqiba].

G.   He said to him, "Am I able to reverse myself?"

H. He said to him, "Not anyone [may reverse himself], but you [may do so], for you are Yosé the Galilean."

I. [He said to him,] "I shall say to you: Lo, Scripture states, And they shall be kept for the congregation of the people of Israel for the water for impurity (Num. 19:9).

J. "Just so long as they are kept, lo, they are water for impurity – but not after a cow has drunk them."

K. This was a case, and thirty-two elders voted in Lud and declared it clean.

L. At that time R. Tarfon recited this verse:

M. "I saw the ram goring westward and northward and southward, and all the animals were unable to stand against it, and none afforded protection from its power, and it did just as it liked and grew great (Dan. 8:4) –

N. "[This is] R. Aqiba.

O. "'As I was considering, behold, a he-goat came from the west across the face of the whole earth, without touching the ground; and the goat had a conspicuous horn between his eyes.

P. "'He came to the ram with the two horns, which I had seen standing on the bank of the river, and he ran at him in his mighty wrath. I saw him come close to the ram, and he was enraged against him and struck the ram and broke his two horns' – this is R. Aqiba and R. Simeon b. Nanos.

Q. "'And the ram had no power to stand before him' – this is R. Aqiba.

R. "'But he cast him down to the ground and trampled upon him' – this is R. Yosé the Galilean.

S. "'And there was no one who could rescue the ram from his power' – these are the thirty-two elders who voted in Lud and declared it clean."

I cite the passage here only to underline the contrast between the usage at hand and the one we shall find in the late fourth or early fifth century composition.

Since, in a moment, we shall take up writings universally assigned to the later fourth or early fifth century, when Rome had turned definitively Christian, we do well to ask the Tosefta to tell us how it chooses to speak of Christianity. Here, too, the topic (if it is present at all) turns out to produce a trivial and not a world-historical comment, a fact that in a moment will strike us as significant. To the first-century authority, Tarfon is attributed the angry observation that there were people around who knew the truth of the Torah but rejected it:

Tosefta Shabbat

13:5

The books of the Evangelists and the books of the minim they do not save from a fire [on the Sabbath]. They are allowed to burn up where they are, they and [even] the references to the Divine Name that are in them....

> Said R. Tarfon, "May I bury my sons if such things come into my hands and I do not burn them, and even the references to the Divine Name which are in them. And if someone was running after me, I should escape into a temple of idolatry, but I should not go into their houses of worship. For idolators do not recognize the Divinity in denying him, but these recognize the Divinity and deny him. About them Scripture states, 'Behind the door and the doorpost you have set your symbol for deserting me, you have uncovered your bed' (Isa. 57:8)."

This statement has long persuaded scholars that the rabbinic authority recognized the difference between pagans and those minim under discussion, reasonably assumed to be Christian. I see no reason to differ from the established consensus. The upshot is simple: when Christians came under discussion, they appear as a source of exasperation, not as Israel's counterpart and opposite, let alone as ruler of the world and precursor to Israel's final triumph in history. We stand a considerable distance from deep thought about Israel and Rome, Jacob and Esau, this age and the coming one. What we witness is a trivial dispute within the community at hand: heretics who should, but do not, know better. And when we hear that mode of thought, we shall look back with genuine disappointment upon the materials at hand. They in no way consider the world-historical issues that would face Israel, and the reason, I maintain, is that, at the point at which the document in which the passage occurs was brought to closure, no one imagined what would ultimately take place: the conversion of the empire to Christianity, the triumph of Christianity on the stage of history.

We turn, finally, to the usage of the words Esau, Edom, Ishmael, and Rome, which in just a moment will come to center stage. Relying on H. Y. Kosovsky [here: Chaim Josua Kasowski], *Thesaurus Thosephthae* (Jerusalem, I: 1932; III: 1942; VI, 1961), we find pretty much the same sort of usages, in the same proportions, as the Mishnah has already shown us. Specifically, Edom is a biblical people, T. Yeb. 8:1, Niddah 6:1, Qid. 5:4. Ishmael is a proper name for several sages. More important, Ishmael never stands for Rome. And Rome itself? We have Todor of Rome (T. Bes. 2:15), Rome as a place where people live, for example, "I saw it in Rome" (T. Yoma 3:8), "I taught this law in Rome" (T. Nid. 7:1, T. Miq. 4:7). And that is all.

If we were to propose a thesis on "Rome and Christianity in the Talmud and Midrash" based on the evidence at hand, it would not produce many propositions. Rome is a place, and no biblical figures or places prefigure the place of Rome in the history of Israel. That is so even though the authors of the Mishnah and the Tosefta knew full well who had destroyed the Temple and closed off Jerusalem and what these events had meant. Christianity plays no role of consequence; no one takes the matter very seriously. Christians are people who know the truth but deny it: crazies. To state the negative: Rome does not stand for Israel's nemesis and counterpart, Rome did not mark an epoch in the history of the world, Israel did not encompass Rome in Israel's history of humanity, and Rome did not represent one of the four monarchies – the last, the worst, prior to Israel's rule. To invoke a modern category, Rome stood for a perfectly secular matter: a place, where things happened. Rome in no way symbolized anything beyond itself. And Israel's sages did not find they had to take seriously the presence or claims of Christianity.[6]

VII. Differentiating among Documents
3. Rome in Genesis Rabbah

So much for books brought to closure, in case of the Mishnah, at ca. A.D. 200, and, in the case of the Tosefta, about a hundred years later (no one knows). We come now to the year 400 or so, to the documents produced in the century after such momentous events as, first, the conversion of Constantine to Christianity, second, the catastrophe of Julian's failure in allowing the Temple to be rebuilt, the repression of paganism and its effect on Judaism, the Christianization of the Holy Land, and, it appears, the conversion of sizable numbers of Jews in the Land of Israel to Christianity and the consequent Christianitzation of Palestine (no longer, in context, the Land of Israel at all). We turn first to Genesis Rabbah, generally assigned to the year 400. What do we find there?

In Genesis Rabbah sages read the book of Genesis as if it portrayed the history of Israel and Rome – and Rome in particular. Now Rome plays a role in the biblical narrative, with special reference to the counterpart and opposite of the patriarchs, first Ishmael, then Esau, and, always, Edom. For that is the single obsession binding sages of the document at hand to common discourse with the text before them. Why Rome in the form it takes in Genesis Rabbah? And how come the obsessive character of sages' disposition of the theme of Rome? Were their picture merely of Rome as tyrant and destroyer of the Temple, we should have no reason to link the text to the problems of the age of redaction and closure. But now it is Rome as Israel's brother, counterpart, and nemesis, Rome as the one thing standing in the way of Israel's, and the world's, ultimate salvation. So the stakes are different, and much higher.

---

[6]The dogma that Christianity never made a difference to Judaism confused me too, as I shall point out presently.

Let us begin with a simple example of how ubiquitous is the shadow of Ishmael/Esau/Edom/Rome. Wherever sages reflect on future history, their minds turn to their own day. They found the hour difficult, because Rome, now Christian, claimed that very birthright and blessing that they understood to be theirs alone. Christian Rome posed a threat without precedent. Now another dominion, besides Israel's, claimed the rights and blessings that sustained Israel. Wherever in Scripture they turned, sages found comfort in the iteration that the birthright, the blessing, the Torah, and the hope – all belonged to them and to none other. Here is a striking statement of that constant proposition.

LIII:XII

1. A.   "[So she said to Abraham, 'Cast out this slave woman with her son, for the son of this slave woman shall not be heir with my son Isaac.'] And the thing was very displeasing to Abraham on account of his son" (Gen. 21:11):

   B.   That is in line with this verse: "And shuts his eyes from looking upon evil" (Isa. 33:15). [Freedman, p. 471, n. 1: He shut his eyes from Ishmael's evil ways and was reluctant to send him away.]

2. A.   "But God said to Abraham, 'Be not displeased because of the lad and because of your slave woman; whatever Sarah says to you, do as she tells you, for through Isaac shall your descendants be named'" (Gen. 21:12):

   B.   Said R. Yudan bar Shillum, "What is written is not 'Isaac' but 'through Isaac.' [The matter is limited, not through all of Isaac's descendants but only through some of them, thus excluding Esau.]"

3. A.   R. Azariah in the name of Bar Hutah: "The use of the B, which stands for two, indicates that he who affirms that there are two worlds will inherit both worlds [this age and the age to come]."

   B.   Said R. Yudan bar Shillum, "It is written, 'Remember his marvelous works that he has done, his signs and the judgments of his mouth' (Ps. 105:5). I have given a sign , namely, it is one who gives the appropriate evidence through what he says. Specifically, he who affirms that there are two worlds will be called 'your seed.'

   C.   "And he who does not affirm that there are two worlds will not be called 'your seed.'"

No. 1 makes "the matter" refer to Ishmael's misbehavior, not Sarah's proposal, so removing the possibility of disagreement between Abraham and Sarah. Nos. 2, 3 interpret the limiting particle, "in," that is, *among* the descendants of Isaac will be found Abraham's heirs, but not all the descendants of Isaac will be heirs of Abraham. No. 2 explicitly excludes Esau, that is Rome, and No. 3 makes the matter doctrinal in the context of Israel's inner life. As the several antagonists of Israel stand for Rome in particular, so the traits of Rome, as sages perceived them, characterized the biblical heroes. Esau provided a favorite target. From the womb Israel and Rome contended.

LXIII:VI

1. A. "And the children struggled together [within her, and she said, 'If it is thus, why do I live? So she went to inquire of the Lord. And the Lord said to her, 'Two nations are in your womb, and two peoples, born of you shall be divided; the one shall be stronger than the other, and the elder shall serve the younger']" (Gen. 25:22-23):

   B. R. Yohanan and R. Simeon b. Laqish:

   C. R. Yohanan said, "[Because the word *struggle* contains the letters for the word *run*,] this one was running to kill that one and that one was running to kill this one."

   D. R. Simeon b. Laqish: "This one releases the laws given by that one, and that one releases the laws given by this one."

2. A. R. Berekhiah in the name of R. Levi said, "it is so that you should not say it was only after he left his mother's womb that [Esau] contended against [Jacob].

   B. "But even while he was yet in his mother's womb, his fist was stretched forth against him: 'The wicked stretch out their fists [so Freedman] from the womb' (Ps. 58.4)."

3. A. "And the children struggled together within her:"

   B. [Once more referring to the letters of the word *struggled*, with special attention to the ones that mean *run*,] they wanted to run within her.

   C. When she went by houses of idolatry, Esau would kick, trying to get out: "The wicked are estranged from the womb" (Ps. 58:4).

   D. When she went by synagogues and study houses, Jacob would kick, trying to get out: "Before I formed you in the womb, I knew you" (Jer. 1:5)."

4. A. "...and she said, "If it is thus, why do I live?"

   B. R. Haggai in the name of R. Isaac: "'This teaches that our mother, Rebecca, went around to the doors of women and said to them, 'Did you ever have this kind of pain in your life?'"

   C. "[She said to them,] "'If thus:" If this is the pain of having children, would that I had not gotten pregnant.'"

   D. Said R. Huna, "If I am going to produce twelve tribes only through this kind of suffering, would that I had not gotten pregnant."

5. A. It was taught on Tannaite authority in the name of R. Nehemiah, "Rebecca was worthy of having the twelve tribes come forth from her. That is in line with this verse:

   B. "'Two nations are in your womb, and two peoples, born of you, shall be divided: the one shall be stronger than the other, and the elder shall serve the younger. When her days to be delivered were fulfilled, behold, there were twins in her womb. The first came forth red, all his body like a hairy mantle, so they called his name Esau. Afterward his brother came forth' (Gen. 25:23-24).

   C. "'Two nations are in your womb:' thus two.

   D. "'and two peoples:' thus two more, hence four.

   E. "'...and one shall be stronger than the other:' two more, so six.

   F. "'...and the elder shall serve the younger:' two more, so eight.

G.   "'When her days to be delivered were fulfilled, behold, there were twins in her womb:' two more, so ten.

H.   "The first came forth red:' now eleven.

I.   "Afterward his brother came forth:' now twelve."

K.   There are those who say, "Proof derives from this verse: 'If it is thus, why do I live?' Focusing on the word for *thus*, we note that the two letters of that word bear the numerical value of seven and five respectively, hence, twelve in all."

6.   A   "So she went to inquire of the Lord:"

B.   Now were there synagogues and houses of study in those days [that she could go to inquire of the Lord]?

C.   But is it not the fact that she went only to the study of Eber?

D.   This serves to teach you that whoever receives an elder is as if he receives the Presence of God.

Nos. 1-3 take for granted that Esau represents Rome, and Jacob, Israel. Consequently the verse underlines the point that there is natural enmity between Israel and Rome. Esau hated Israel even while he was still in the womb. Jacob, for his part, revealed from the womb those virtues that would characterize him later on, eager to serve God as Esau was eager to worship idols. The text invites just this sort of reading. No. 4 and No. 5 relate Rebecca's suffering to the birth of the twelve tribes. No. 6 makes its own point, independent of the rest and tacked on. In the next passage Rome appears as a pig, an important choice for symbolization, as we shall see in Leviticus Rabbah as well:

LXV:I

1.   A   "When Esau was forty years old, he took to wife Judith, the daughter of Beeri, the Hittite, and Basemath the daughter of Elon the Hittite; and they made life bitter for Isaac and Rebecca" (Gen. 26:34-35):

B.   "The swine out of the wood ravages it, that which moves in the field feeds on it" (Ps. 80:14).

C.   R. Phineas and R. Hilqiah in the name of R. Simon: "Among all of the prophets, only two of them spelled out in public [the true character of Rome, represented by the swine], Asaf and Moses.

D.   "Asaf: 'The swine out of the wood ravages it.'

E.   "Moses: 'And the swine, because he parts the hoof' (Deut. 14:8).

F.   "Why does Moses compare Rome to the swine? Just as the swine, when it crouches, puts forth its hoofs as if to say, 'I am clean,' so the wicked kingdom steals and grabs, while pretending to be setting up courts of justice.

G.   "So Esau, for all forty years, hunted married women, ravished them, and when he reached the age of forty, he presented himself to his father, saying, 'Just as father got married at the age of forty, so I shall marry a wife at the age of forty.'

H.   "'When Esau was forty years old, he took to wife Judith, the daughter of Beeri, the Hittite, and Basemath the daughter of Elon the Hittite.'"

How long would Rome rule, when would Isarael succeed? The important point is that Rome was next to last, Israel last. Rome's triumph brought assurance that Israel would be next – and last:

LXXV:IV

2.   A.   "And Jacob sent messengers before him:"

      B.   To this one [Esau] whose time to take hold of sovereignty would come before him [namely, before Jacob, since Esau would rule, then Jacob would govern].

      C.   R. Joshua b. Levi said, "Jacob took off the purple robe and threw it before Esau, as if to say to him, 'Two flocks of starlings are not going to sleep on a single branch' [so we cannot rule at the same time].'"

3.   A.   "...to Esau his brother:"

      B.   Even though he was Esau, he was still his brother.

Esau remains Jacob's brother, and that Esau rules before Jacob will. The application to contemporary affairs cannot be missed, both in the recognition of the true character of Esau – a brother! – and in the interpretation of the future of history.

To conclude: Genesis Rabbah reached closure, people generally agree, toward the end of the fourth century. That century marks the beginning of the West as we have known it. Why so? Because in the fourth century, from the conversion of Constantine and over the next hundred years, the Roman Empire became Christian – and with it, the West. So the fourth century marks the first century of the history of the West in that form in which the West would flourish for the rest of time, to our own day. Accordingly, we should not find surprising sages' recurrent references, in the reading of Genesis, to the struggle of two equal powers, Rome and Israel, Esau and Jacob, Ishmael and Isaac. The world-historical change, marking the confirmation in politics and power of the Christians' claim that Christ was king over all humanity, demanded from sages an appropriate, and, to Israel, persuasive. response.

VIII. Differentiating among Documents
4. Rome in Leviticus Rabbah

What we see in Leviticus Rabbah is consistent with what we have already observed in Genesis Rabbah: how sages absorb events into their system of classification. So it is sages that make history through the thoughts they think and the rules they lay down. In such a context, we find no interest either in the outsiders and their powers, or in the history of the empires of the world, or, all the more so, in redemption and the messianic fulfillment of time. What is the alternative to the use of the sort of symbols just now examined? Let us turn immediately to the relevant passages of Leviticus Rabbah:

XIII:V
1. A.   Said R. Ishmael b. R. Nehemiah, "All the prophets foresaw what the pagan kingdoms would do [to Israel].

    B.   "The first man foresaw what the pagan kingdoms would do [to Israel].

    C.   "That is in line with the following verse of Scripture: 'A river flowed out of Eden [to water the garden, and there it divided and became four rivers]' (Gen. 2:10). [The four rivers stand for the four kingdoms, Babylonia, Media, Greece, and Rome]."

2. A.   R. Tanhuma said it, [and] R. Menahema [in the name of] R. Joshua b. Levi: "The Holy One, blessed be He, will give the cup of reeling to the nations of the world to drink in the world to come.

    B.   "That is in line with the following verse of Scripture: 'A river flowed out of Eden' (Gen 2:10), the place from which justice [DYN] goes forth."

3. A.   "[There it divided] and became four rivers" (Gen 2:10) – this refers to the four kingdoms.

    B.   "The name of the first is Pishon (PSWN); [it is the one which flows around the whole land of Havilah, where there is gold; and the gold of that land is good; bdellium and onyx stone are there]" (Gen. 2:11-12).

    C.   This refers to Babylonia, on account [of the reference to Babylonia in the following verse:] "And their [the Babylonians'] horsemen spread themselves (PSW)" (Hab. 1:8).

    D.   [It is further] on account of [Nebuchadnezzar's being] a dwarf, shorter than ordinary men by a handbreadth.

    E.   "[It is the one which flows around the whole land of Havilah" (Gen. 2:11).

    F.   "This [reference to the river's flowing around the whole land] speaks of Nebuchadnezzar, the wicked man, who came up and surrounded the entire Land of Israel, which places its hope in the Holy One, blessed be He.

    G.   That is in line with the following verse of Scripture: "Hope in God, for I shall again praise him" (Ps. 42:5).

    H.   "Where there is gold" (Gen. 2:11) – this refers to the words of Torah, "which are more to be desired than gold, more than much fine gold" (Ps. 19:11).

    I.   "And the gold of that land is good" (Gen. 2:12).

    J.   This teaches that there is no Torah like the Torah that is taught in the Land of Israel, and there is no wisdom like the wisdom that is taught in the Land of Israel.

    K.   "Bdellium and onyx stone are there" (Gen. 2:12) – Scripture, Mishnah, Talmud, and lore.

4. A.   "The name of the second river is Gihon; [it is the one which flows around the whole land of Cush]" (Gen. 2:13).

    B.   This refers to Media, which produced Haman, that wicked man, who spit out venom like a serpent.

C. It is on account of the verse: "On your belly will you go" (Gen. 3:14).

D. "It is the one which flows around the whole land of Cush" (Gen. 2:13).

E. [We know that this refers to Media, because it is said:] "Who rules from India to Cush" (Est. 1:1).

5. A. "And the name of the third river is Tigris (HDQL), [which flows east of Assyria] (Gen. 2:14).

B. This refers to Greece [Syria], which was sharp (HD) and speedy (QL) in making its decrees, saying to Israel, "Write on the horn of an ox that you have no portion in the God of Israel."

C. "Which flows east (QDMT) of Assyria" (Gen. 2:14).

D. Said R. Huna, "In three aspects the kingdom of Greece was in advance (QDMH) of the present evil kingdom [Rome]: in respect to shipbuilding, the arrangement of camp vigils, and language."

E. Said R. Huna, "Any and every kingdom may be called 'Assyria' (ashur), on account of all of their making themselves powerful at Israel's expense."

F. Said R. Yosé b. R. Hanina, "Any and every kingdom may be called Nineveh (NNWH), on account of their adorning (NWY) themselves at Israel's expense."

G. Said R. Yosé b. R. Hanina, "Any and every kingdom may be called Egypt (MSRYM), on account of their oppressing (MSYRYM) Israel."

6. A. "And the fourth river is the Euphrates (PRT)" (Gen. 2:14).

B. This refers to Edom [Rome], since it was fruitful (PRT), and multiplied through the prayer of the elder [Isaac at Gen. 27:39].

C. Another interpretation: "It was because it was fruitful and multiplied, and so cramped his world.

D. Another explanation: Because it was fruitful and multiplied and cramped his son.

E. Another explanation: Because it was fruitful and multiplied and cramped his house.

F. Another explanation: "Parat" – because in the end, "I am going to exact a penalty from it."

G. That is in line with the following verse of Scripture: "I have trodden (PWRH) the winepress alone" (Isa. 63:3).

7. A. [Gen. R. 42:2:] Abraham foresaw what the evil kingdoms would do [to Israel].

B. "[As the sun was going down,] a deep sleep fell on Abraham; and lo, a dread and great darkness fell upon him]" (Gen. 15:12).

C. "Dread" ('YMH) refers to Babylonia, on account of the statement, "Then Nebuchadnezzer was full of fury (HMH)" (Dan. 3:19).

D. "Darkness" refers to Media, which brought darkness to Israel through its decrees: "to destroy, to slay, and to wipe out all the Jews" (Est. 7:4).

E. "Great" refers to Greece.

F. Said R. Judah b. R. Simon, "The verse teaches that the kingdom of Greece set up one hundred twenty-seven governors, one hundred and twenty-seven hyparchs and one hundred twenty-seven commanders."

G. And rabbis say, "They were sixty in each category."

H. R. Berekhiah and R. Hanan in support of this position taken by rabbis: "'Who led you through the great terrible wilderness, with its fiery serpents and scorpions and thirsty ground where there was no water]' (Deut. 8:15).

I. "Just as the scorpion produces eggs by sixties, so the kingdom of Greece would set up its administration in groups of sixty."

J. "Fell on him" (Gen. 15:12).

K. This refers to Edom, on account of the following verse: "The earth quakes at the noise of their [Edom's] fall" (Jer. 49:21).

L. There are those who reverse matters.

M. "Fear" refers to Edom, on account of the following verse: "And this I saw, a fourth beast, fearful, and terrible" (Dan. 7:7).

M. "Darkness" refers to Greece, which brought gloom through its decrees. For they said to Israel, "Write on the horn of an ox that you have no portion in the God of Israel."

O. "Great" refers to Media, on account of the verse: "King Ahasuerus made Haman [the Median] great" (Est. 3:1).

P. "Fell on him" refers to Babylonia, on account of the following verse: "Fallen, fallen is Babylonia" (Isa. 21:9).

8. A. Daniel foresaw what the evil kingdoms would do [to Israel].

B. "Daniel said, I saw in my vision by night, and behold, the four winds of Heaven were stirring up the great sea. And four great beasts came up out of the sea, [different from one another. The first was like a lion and had eagles' wings. Then as I looked, its wings were plucked off....And behold, another beast, a second one, like a bear....After this I looked, and lo, another, like a leopard....After this I saw in the night visions, and behold, a fourth beast, terrible and dreadful and exceedingly strong; and it had great iron teeth]" (Dan. 7:3-7).

C. If you enjoy sufficient merit, it will emerge from the sea, but if not, it will come out of the forest.

D. The animal that comes up from the sea is not violent, but the one that comes up out of the forest is violent.

E. Along these same lines: "The boar out of the wood ravages it" (Ps. 80:14).

F. If you enjoy sufficient merit, it will come from the river, and if not, from the forest.

G. The animal that comes up from the river is not violent, but the one that comes up out of the forest is violent.

H. "Different from one another" (Dan. 7:3).

I. Differing from [hating] one another.

J. This teaches that every nation that rules in the world hates Israel and reduces them to slavery.

K. "The first was like a lion [and had eagles' wings]" (Dan. 7:4).

L. This refers to Babylonia.

M. Jeremiah saw [Babylonia] as a lion. Then he went and saw it as an eagle.

N. He saw it as a lion: "A lion has come up from his thicket" (Jer. 4:7).

O. And [as an eagle:] "Behold, he shall come up and swoop down as the eagle" (Jer. 49:22).

P.   People said to Daniel, "What do you see?"

Q.   He said to them, "I see the face like that of a lion and wings like those of an eagle: 'The first was like a lion and had eagles' wings. Then, as I looked, its wings were plucked off, and it was lifted up from the ground [and made to stand upon two feet like a man and the heart of a man was given to it]' (Dan. 7:4).

R.   R. Eleazar and R. Ishmael b. R. Nehemiah:

S.   R. Eleazar said, "While the entire lion was smitten, its heart was not smitten.

T.   "That is in line with the following statement: 'And the heart of a man was given to it' (Dan. 7:4)."

U.   And R. Ishmael b. R. Nehemiah said, "Even its heart was smitten, for it is written, 'Let his heart be changed from a man's' (Dan. 4:17).

V.   "And behold, another beast, a second one, like a bear. [It was raised up one side; it had three ribs in its mouth between its teeth, and it was told, Arise, devour much flesh]" (Dan. 7:5).

W.   This refers to Media.

X.   Said R. Yohanan, "It is like a bear."

Y.   It is written, "similar to a wolf" (DB); thus, "And a wolf was there."

Z.   That is in accord with the view of R. Yohanan, for R.Yohanan said, "'Therefore a lion out of the forest [slays them]' (Jer. 5:6) – this refers to Babylonia.

AA.   "'A wolf of the deserts spoils them' (Jer. 5:6) refers to Media.

BB.   "'A leopard watches over their cities' (Jer. 5:6) refers to Greece.

CC.   "'Whoever goes out from them will be savaged' (Jer. 5:6) refers to Edom.

DD.   "Why so? 'Because their transgressions are many, and their backslidings still more' (Jer. 5:6)."

EE.   "After this, I looked, and lo, another, like a leopard [with four wings of a bird on its back; and the beast had four heads; and dominion was given to it]" (Dan. 7:6).

FF.   This [leopard] refers to Greece, which persisted impudently in making harsh decrees, saying to Israel, "Write on the horn of an ox that you have no share in the God of Israel."

GG.   "After this I saw in the night visions, and behold, a fourth beast, terrible and dreadful and exceedingly strong; [and it had great iron teeth; it devoured and broke in pieces and stamped the residue with its feet. It was different from all the beasts that were before it; and it had ten horns]" (Dan. 7:7).

HH.   This refers to Edom [Rome].

II.   Daniel saw the first three visions on one night, and this one he saw on another night. Now why was that the case?

JJ.   R. Yohanan and R. Simeon b. Laqish:

KK.   R. Yohanan said, "It is because the fourth beast weighed as much as the first three."

LL.   And R. Simeon b. Laqish said, "It outweighed them."

MM.   R. Yohanan objected to R. Simeon b. Laqish, "'Prophesy, therefore, son of man, clap your hands [and let the sword come down twice; yea, thrice. The sword for those to be slain; it is the sword for the great slaughter, which encompasses them]' (Ezek.

	21:14-15). [So the single sword of Rome weighs against the three others]."
NN.	And R. Simeon b. Laqish, how does he interpret the same passage? He notes that [the threefold sword] is doubled (Ezek. 21:14), [thus outweighs the three swords, equally twice their strength].
9. A	Moses foresaw what the evil kingdoms would do [to Israel].
B.	"The camel, rock badger, and hare" (Deut. 14:7). [Compare: "Nevertheless, among those that chew the cud or part the hoof, you shall not eat these: the camel, because it chews the cud but does not part the hoof, is unclean to you. The rock badger, because it chews the cud but does not part the hoof, is unclean to you. And the hare, because it chews the cud but does not part the hoof, is unclean to you, and the pig, because it parts the hoof and is cloven footed, but does not chew the cud, is unclean to you" (Lev. 11:4-8).]
C.	The camel (GML) refers to Babylonia, [in line with the following verse of Scripture: "O daughter of Babylonia, you who are to be devastated!] Happy will be he who requites (GML) you, with what you have done to us" (Ps. 147:8).
D.	"The rock badger" (Deut. 14:7) – this refers to Media.
E	Rabbis and R. Judah b. R. Simon.
F.	Rabbis say, "Just as the rock badger exhibits traits of uncleanness and traits of cleanness, so the kingdom of Media produced both a righteous man and a wicked one."
G.	Said R. Judah b. R. Simon, "The last Darius was Esther's son. He was clean on his mother's side and unclean on his father's side."
H.	"The hare" (Deut 14:7) – this refers to Greece. The mother of King Ptolemy was named "Hare" [in Greek: lagos].
I.	"The pig" (Deut. 14:7) – this refers to Edom [Rome].
J.	Moses made mention of the first three in a single verse and the final one in a verse by itself [(Deut. 14:7, 8)]. Why so?
K.	R. Yohanan and R. Simeon b. Laqish:
L	R. Yohanan said, "It is because [the pig] is equivalent to the other three."
M.	And R. Simeon b. Laqish said, "It is because it outweighs them."
N.	R. Yohanan objected to R. Simeon b. Laqish, "'Prophesy, therefore, son of man, clap your hands [and let the sword come down twice, yea thrice]' (Ezek. 21:14)."
O.	And how does R. Simeon b. Laqish interpret the same passage? He notes that [the threefold sword] is doubled (Ezek. 21:14).
10. A	[Gen. R. 65:1:] R. Phineas and R. Hilqiah in the name of R. Simon: "Among all the prophets, only two of them revealed [the true evil of Rome], Assaf and Moses.
B.	"Assaf said, 'The pig out of the wood ravages it' (Ps. 80:14).
C.	"Moses said, 'And the pig, [because it parts the hoof and is cloven-footed but does not chew the cud]' (Lev. 11:7).
D.	"Why is [Rome] compared to a pig?
E	"It is to teach you the following: Just as, when a pig crouches and produces its hooves, it is as if to say, 'See how I am clean [since I have a cloven hoof],' so this evil kingdom takes pride, seizes by

violence, and steals, and then gives the appearance of establishing a tribunal for justice."

F.   There was the case of a ruler in Caesarea, who put thieves, adulterers, and sorcerers to death, while at the same time telling his counsellor, "That same man [I] did all these three things on a single night."

11. A.   Another interpretation: "The camel" (Lev. 11:4).

B.   This refers to Babylonia.

C.   "Because it chews the cud [but does not part the hoof]" (Lev. 11:4).

D.   For it brings forth praises [with its throat] of the Holy One, blessed be He. [The Hebrew words for "chew the cud" – bring up cud – are now understood to mean "give praise." GRH is connected with GRWN, throat, hence, "bring forth [sounds of praise through] the throat."

E.   R. Berekhiah and R. Helbo in the name of R. Ishmael b. R. Nahman: "Whatever [praise of God] David [in writing a psalm] treated singly [item by item], that wicked man [Nebuchadnezzar] lumped together in a single verse.

F.   "'Now I, Nebuchadnezzar, praise and extol and honor the King of Heaven, for all his works are right and his ways are just, and those who walk in pride he is able to abase' (Dan. 4:37).

G.   "'Praise' – 'O Jerusalem, praise the Lord' (Ps. 147:12).

H.   "'Extol' – 'I shall extol you, O Lord, for you have brought me low' (Ps. 30:2).

I.   "'Honor the King of Heaven' – 'The Lord reigns, let the peoples tremble! He sits enthroned upon the cherubim, let the earth quake' (Ps. 99:1).

J.   "'For all his works are right' – 'For the sake of thy steadfast love and thy faithfulness' (Ps. 115:1).

K.   "'And his ways are just' – 'He will judge the peoples with equity' (Ps. 96:10).

L.   "'And those who walk in pride' – 'The Lord reigns, he is robed in majesty, the Lord is robed, he is girded with strength' (Ps. 93:1).

M.   "'He is able to abase' – 'All the horns of the wicked he will cut off' (Ps. 75:11)."

N.   "The rock badger" (Lev. 11:5) – this refers to Media.

O.   "For it chews the cud" – for it gives praise to the Holy One, blessed be He: "Thus says Cyrus, king of Persia, 'All the kingdoms of the earth has the Lord, the God of the Heaven, given me" (Ezra 1:2).

P.   "The hare" – this refers to Greece.

Q.   "For it chews the cud" – for it gives praise to the Holy One, blessed be He.

R.   Alexander the Macedonian, when he saw Simeon the Righteous, said, "Blessed be the God of Simeon the Righteous."

S.   "The pig" (Lev. 11:7) – this refers to Edom.

T.   "For it does not chew the cud" – for it does not give praise to the Holy One, blessed be He.

U.   And it is not enough that it does not give praise, but it blasphemes and swears violently, saying, "Whom do I have in Heaven, and with you I want nothing on earth" (Ps. 73:25).

12. A. Another interpretation [of GRH, cud, now with reference to GR, stranger:]

B. "The camel" (Lev. 11:4) – this refers to Babylonia.

C. "For it chews the cud" [now: brings up the stranger] – for it exalts righteous men: "And Daniel was in the gate of the king" (Dan. 2:49).

D. "The rock badger" (Lev. 11:5) – this refers to Media.

E. "For it brings up the stranger" – for it exalts righteous men: "Mordecai sat at the gate of the king" (Est. 2:19).

F. "The hare" (Lev. 11:6) – this refers to Greece.

G. "For it brings up the stranger" – for it exalts the righteous.

H. When Alexander of Macedonia saw Simeon the Righteous, he would rise up on his feet. They said to him, "Can't you see the Jew, that you stand up before this Jew?"

I. He said to them, "When I go forth to battle, I see something like this man's visage, and I conquer."

J. "The pig" (Lev. 11:7) – this refers to Rome.

K. "But it does not bring up the stranger" – for it does not exalt the righteous.

L. And it is not enough that it does not exalt them, but it kills them.

M. That is in line with the following verse of Scripture: "I was angry with my people, I profaned my heritage; I gave them into your hand, you showed them no mercy; on the aged you made your yoke exceedingly heavy" (Isa. 47:6).

N. This refers to R. Aqiba and his colleagues.

13. A. Another interpretation [now treating "bring up the cud" (GR) as "bring along in its train" (GRR)]:

B. "The camel" (Lev. 11:4) – this refers to Babylonia.

C. "Which brings along in its train" – for it brought along another kingdom after it.

D. "The rock badger" (Lev. 11:5) – this refers to Media.

E. "Which brings along in its train" – for it brought along another kingdom after it.

F. "The hare" (Lev. 11:6) – this refers to Greece.

G. "Which brings along in its train" – for it brought along another kingdom after it.

H. "The pig" (Lev. 11:7) – this refers to Rome.

I. "Which does not bring along in its train" – for it did not bring along another kingdom after it.

J. And why is it then called "pig" (HZYR)? For it restores (MHZRT) the crown to the one who truly should have it [namely, Israel, whose dominion will begin when the rule of Rome ends].

K. That is in line with the following verse of Scripture: "And saviors will come up on Mount Zion to judge the Mountain of Esau [Rome], and the kingdom will then belong to the Lord" (Ob. 1:21).

To stand back and consider this vast apocalyptic vision of Israel's history, we first review the message of the construction as a whole. This comes in two parts, first, the explicit, then the implicit. As to the former, the first claim is that God had told the prophets what would happen to Israel at the hands of the pagan kingdoms, Babylonia,

Media, Greece, Rome. These are further represented by Nebuchadnezzar, Haman, Alexander for Greece, Edom or Esau, interchangeably, for Rome. The same vision came from Adam, Abraham, Daniel, and Moses. The same policy toward Israel – oppression, destruction, enslavement, alienation from the true God – emerged from all four.

How does Rome stand out? First, it was made fruitful through the prayer of Isaac in behalf of Esau. Second, Edom is represented by the fourth and final beast. Rome is related through Esau, as Babylonia, Media, and Greece are not. The fourth beast was seen in a vision separate from the first three. It was worst of all and outweighed the rest. In the apocalypticizing of the animals of Lev. 11:4-8/Deut. 14:7, the camel, rock badger, hare, and pig, the pig, standing for Rome, again emerges as different from the others and more threatening than the rest. Just as the pig pretends to be a clean beast by showing the cloven hoof, but in fact is an unclean one, so Rome pretends to be just but in fact governs by thuggery. Edom does not pretend to praise God but only blasphemes. It does not exalt the righteous but kills them. These symbols concede nothing to Christian monotheism and biblicism. Of greatest importance, while all the other beasts bring further ones in their wake, the pig does not: "It does not bring another kingdom after it." It will restore the crown to the one who will truly deserve it, Israel. Esau will be judged by Zion, so Obadiah 1:21. Now how has the symbolization delivered an implicit message? It is in the treatment of Rome as distinct, but essentially equivalent to the former kingdoms. This seems to me a stunning way of saying that the now-Christian empire in no way requires differentiation from its pagan predecessors. Nothing has changed, except matters have gotten worse. Beyond Rome, standing in a straight line with the others, lies the true shift in history, the rule of Israel and the cessation of the dominion of the (pagan) nations.

To conclude, Leviticus Rabbah came to closure, it is generally agreed, around A.D. 400, that is, approximately a century after the Roman Empire in the east had begun to become Christian, and half a century after the last attempt to rebuild the Temple in Jerusalem had failed – a tumultuous age indeed. Accordingly, we have had the chance to see how distinctive and striking are the ways in which, in the text at hand, the symbols of animals that stand for the four successive empires of humanity and point towards the messianic time, serve for the framers' message.

IX. The Result of Differentiating:
Issues of Symbolization among Documents

When the sages of the Mishnah and the Tosefta spoke of Edom and Edomites, they meant biblical Edom, a people in the vicinity of the land of Israel. By Rome they meant the city – that alone. That fact bears meaning when we turn to documents produced two centuries later, and one hundred years beyond the triumph of Christianity. When the sages of Genesis Rabbah spoke of Rome, it was not a political Rome but a messianic Rome that is at issue: Rome as surrogate for Israel, Rome as obstacle to Israel. Why? It is because Rome now confronts Israel with a crisis, and, I argue, Genesis Rabbah constitutes a response to that crisis. Rome in the fourth century became Christian. Sages responded by facing that fact quite squarely and saying, "Indeed, it is as you say, a kind of Israel, an heir of Abraham as your texts explicitly claim. But we remain the sole legitimate Israel, the bearer of the birthright – we and not you. So you are our brother: Esau, Ishmael, Edom." And the rest follows.

By rereading the story of the beginnings, sages discovered the answer and the secret of the end. Rome claimed to be Israel, and, indeed, sages conceded, Rome shared the patrimony of Israel. That claim took the form of the Christians' appropriation of the Torah as "the Old Testament," so sages acknowledged a simple fact in acceding to the notion that, in some way, Rome too formed part of Israel. But it was the rejected part, the Ishmael, the Esau, not the Isaac, not the Jacob. The advent of Christian Rome precipitated the sustained, polemical, and, I think, rigorous and well-argued rereading of beginnings in light of the end. Rome then marked the conclusion of human history as Israel had known it. Beyond? The coming of the true Messiah, the redemption of Israel, the salvation of the world, the end of time. So the issues were not inconsiderable, and when the sages spoke of Esau/Rome, as they did so often, they confronted the life-or-death decision of the day.

When we come to Leviticus Rabbah, we find ourselves several steps down the path explored by the compilers of Genesis Rabbah. The polemic represented in Leviticus Rabbah by the symbolization of Christian Rome, therefore, makes the simple point that, first, Christians are no different from, and no better than, pagans; they are essentially the same. Second, just as Israel had survived Babylonia, Media, Greece, so would they endure to see the end of Rome (whether pagan, whether Christian). But of course the symbolic polemic rested on false assumptions, hence conveyed a message that misled Jews by misrepresenting their new enemy. The new Rome really did differ from the old. Christianity was not merely part of a succession of undifferentiated modes of paganism. True, the symbols assigned to Rome attributed worse, more dangerous traits than those assigned to the earlier empires. The pig pretends to be clean, just as the Christians give the signs of adherence to the God of Abraham, Isaac, and Jacob. That much the passage concedes. But it is not enough. For out of symbols should emerge a useful public policy, and the mode of thought represented by symbols in the end should yield an accurate confrontation with that for which the symbol stands.

This survey of four documents read one by one, then in pairs, yields a simple result. A striking shift in the treatment of Rome does appear to take place in the formative century represented by work on Genesis Rabbah and Leviticus Rabbah. In earlier times Rome symbolized little beyond itself, and Edom, Esau (absent in the Mishnah, a singleton in Tosefta), and Ishmael were concrete figures. In later times these figures bore traits congruent to the fact of Christian rule. The correspondence between the modes of symbolization – the pig, the sibling – and the facts of the Christian challenge to Judaism – the same Scripture, read a new way, the same messianic hope, interpreted differently – turns out to be remarkable and significant when we compare what the earlier compilers of canonical writings, behind the Mishnah and the Tosefta, produced to the writings of the later ones, behind the two Rabbah compilations. When we differentiate one document from the next, the details of each document turn out to cohere to the systemic traits of the document as a whole. And, furthermore, what a document says about the common topic turns out to bear its own messages and meanings. That, in a single sentence, justifies the route of canonical differentiation I advocated at the outset.

X. The Result of Not Differentiating:
Missing a Distinction that Makes a Difference

When I originally worked on this problem, I took the view that the rabbinic canon, from beginning to end, fails to effect differentiation when it treats the outsider.[7] I maintained that the recognition of the outsider depends upon traits that, so far as the framers of the writings at hand are concerned, remain not only constant but uninteresting. The

---

[7] I refer to "Stable Symbols in a Shifting Society: The Delusion of the Monolithic Gentile in Documents of Late Fourth-Century Judaism," *History of Religions* 1985, 25: 163-175. Cf. also Jacob Neusner and Ernest S. Frerichs, eds., *"To See Ourselves as Others See Us:" Christians, Jews, "Others" in Late Antiquity* (Atlanta, 1985: Scholars Press Studies in the Humanities), pp. 373-396.

outsider is just that – not worthy of further sorting out. And, as a result of that premise, in the unfolding of canonical doctrine on the outsider, I did not discern substantial change from one document to the next. So, I concluded, people put out of mind that with which they cannot cope, and the outsider stood for the critical fact of Israelite life, the nation's weak condition and vanquished status. So for the same fundamental cause that accounts for the persistence among the founders of the Mishnah's system of the priestly conception of Israelite life, so too a single tight abstraction masked the detailed and concrete features of the other. All "others" looked alike – and posed a threat. The less response to that threat, the more comforting the illusion of inner control over an outer world wholly beyond one's power. Ignoring what could not be sorted out and focusing upon what could, the sages' Israelite kept at a distance a hostile world and retained command of a universe of rule and order. But I believe that in approaching matters as I did, I failed to see the traits stressed by the two Rabbah collections, traits specific to Rome as Christian and irrelevant to all other outsiders. I missed the message because I failed to compare what the Mishnah and the Tosefta say about Rome/Esau/Ishmael/Edom with what the two Rabbah-compilations say about the same matter. And the reason was that it never entered my mind that Christianty would make much difference to Judaism – a point to which I shall come back at the end.

Now to return to the methodological question. I can display the repertoire of results attained by a labor of harmonization simply by citing my own uncomprehending words. By seeing things without distinguishing among sources, what conclusions did I draw? Here, alas, are my *ipsissima verba*:

> What demands attention is the failure of people to reimagine a symbol that no longer corresponds to, or conveys, perceived reality. When, to be specific, people continue to speak in the same language about something that has in fact produced drastic change, we must ask why. For reason suggests symbols serve to construct an imaginary world that, for the structure to serve, must in some way correspond to the world out there. When, therefore, a critical area of social experience undergoes vast transformation, the symbols also should undergo metamorphosis. The one thing that should change is the character of the symbols through which people portray in their minds what is going on in that world that their minds and imaginations propose to mediate and to interpret.
>
> ...I point out that the mode of symbolization of the outsider, perceived as a nation and great power equivalent to Israel, remained stable during that period that marked Israel's complete transformation from one thing to something else.

As we have seen, this is simply not true. The opposite is the case. The movement from the Mishnah and its companion to the two Rabbah compilations suggest no failure to reimagine a symbol, but a careful reconsideration of Scripture to find and appropriate a useful symbol to make sense of perceived reality. Scripture supplied the rules of history as much as the laws of society, and in Genesis sages found those rules, hence, Jacob and Esau told them the historical laws governing the relationship of Israel and Rome. In consequence, we see not a failure but an enormously imaginative and successful intellectual initiative.

At the outset of the period at hand, before A.D. 70, Israel in its land constituted a small political entity, a state, like many others of its time and place. It was subordinate to a great empire but was a distinct and autonomous unit, a part of the political structure of that empire. It had working institutions of self-government and politics. At the end of the same period, by the seventh century, Israel in no way constituted a political entity. Such institutions of a political or juridical character that it had had, had lost the recognition and legitimacy formerly conferred upon them.

Moreover, when Israel looked outward, toward the world beyond its limits, the changes proved no less stunning. At the outset, Rome, and at the end, Rome, but what a different Rome! In the first three centuries, Rome was what it had always been, what its predecessors in the Middle East had always been: pagan, essentially benign toward Israel in its land. From the fourth century, Rome became something unprecedented: a kind of Israel and a kin to Israel, a knowledgable competitor, a powerful and canny enemy, a brother.

The modes by which the Jews, or, more to the point, the rabbis whose writings survive, proposed to symbolize the world had therefore to take up two contradictory worlds. On the one hand these "symbols of the stranger," of Israel's history and destiny, and of Israel's relationship to the outsider, dealt with a world in which Israel was like the outsider: a nation among nations, a political entity confronting another such entity, thus history among other histories. At the end, these symbols had to convey the reality of .an Israel that was essentially different in genus from the outsider: no longer a nation in the sense in which other groups constituted a nation, no longer a political entity like others, no longer standing at the end of a history essentially consubstantial with the history of the nations.

What we shall see is the surprising fact that, so far as we are able to tell, the modes of political and social symbolization remained essentially stable in a world of change. More to the point, the outsider remained what he had always been, a (mere) pagan, part of a world demanding from Israel no effort whatsoever at differentiation. The "nations" were all alike, and Israel was still not essentially different from them all: consubstantial, thus judged by the same standards, but to be sure guiltless while the rest were guilty. What makes so puzzling the stability of the modes of symbolization of Israel and the nations,

Israel's history and destiny, and the substance of Israel's doctrine, is a simple fact. In the interval, Christianity had not only come to full and diverse expression, it also had reached power.

But the modes of symbolization as revealed by the canonical writings read one by one show enormous and surprising change. Imagination, an act of extraordinary daring – these characterize the later fourth- and fifth-century thinkers. They confronted an unprecedented challenge, and they responded in an unprecedented way, by determing the equivalence of the two great powers of the world, Israel and Rome. Of course there was nothing equivalent about the two, either in Heaven (from sages' viewpoint on God's view) or on earth (from everyone else's viewpoint). But that is part of the amazing work at hand. Once more, therefore, we observe: the preceding statement is simply false. I missed the difference among the sources, therefore I saw everything as pretty much the same thing when it was not. And, to proceed:

> In coming to power, Christianity drew upon essentially the same symbolic heritage to which Israel had long had access. To Christianity as much as to Judaism the pagan was a pagan, not differentiated; history began in Eden and led through Sinai to the end of time; the Messiah stood at the climax and goal of this world's history; revelation ("Torah") came from one God to unique Israel. True, for all forms of Christianity, the values assigned to the repertoire of symbols at hand hardly corresponded to those imputed by the Jews. But the symbols remained the same, and so Israel now resorted to what had become a shared symbolic system and structure to express its history and politics.
>
> Under such circumstances, who would be surprised to learn that deep thought went into the revision of the available symbols, a restatement in such wise as to differentiate what had been treated as uniform, to redefine what had been grasped as settled? Surely the Christian, in the symbolic system of Judaism, should look like something other than the pagan, maybe worse but at least different. Certainly history as a mode of social symbolization should proceed on a somewhat different path from the one it had taken when the one God had not yet come to rule, when Israel's ancient Scriptures had not yet come to define the nature and destiny of humanity. Reckoning with the profound political changes at hand, we might imagine, should lead at least some profound thinkers to reconsider the symbolic system that had formerly prevailed or, at the very least, the nature and definition of symbols that had gone forward into the new age and remained vivid. After all, social change should generate symbol change, political change should make its mark upon the symbols of politics and society.

I now see that the thinkers at hand did reconsider the available symbolic system and effect considerable revisions of it – at precisely the right points. And what follows also is simply wrong, for the reasons now amply spelled out:

> But if that is what reason dictates we should expect, it is not how things actually happened....It would take the rabbis of the canon of Judaism nearly a millenium to take seriously the specific character and claims of Christianity and to begin to counter in a systematic way the concrete assertions of that religious tradition. Before the High Middle Ages, Judaism would have nothing to say about, let alone to, Christianity. More probative, Jewish thinkers would maintain the fantastic pretense that nothing important happened in either the first or the fourth century, that is, in either the supernatural or the political world at hand. As we shall now see, one important indicator of that fact is the unwillingness of the rabbinic exegetes of the fourth and early fifth centuries to concede that Christians were different from pagans. On the contrary, the rabbinic sources treat all pagans as essentially faceless, and Christianity not at all, except as part of that same blank wall of hostility to God (and, by the way, to Israel).

When we consider the movement from the first two documents we examined to the third and the fourth, we realize that every word in the preceding discussion is wrong. In fact the documents brought to closure in the fourth century say something entirely different from those concluded earlier.

XI. Conclusion
The Methodological Upshot

What went wrong? The answer is simple. I began my research with perfect faith in a dogma of Judaism and therefore also of scholars of Judaism. It is that Christianity never made any difference to Judaism. So I took for granted, without knowing it, that I too would find that Christianity never made any difference. My original results then conformed to the premise with which I had commenced work. That is how I could earlier conclude, reflecting a consensus I myself simply took for granted instead of questioning:

> In fact it would be many centuries before Jews would take seriously, and in its own terms, the claim of Christianity to constitute a kind of Judaism, and not a kind of paganism. It would take a long time for Jews to distinguish the Christian from other outsiders. When that differentiation began to emerge, it would be in Christian Europe, on the part of Joseph Kimhi and Moses Nahmanides and others who had no choice. By that time, to be sure, "paganism" had long disappeared from the world of Israel's residency, on the one hand, and any expectation that Roman rule would give way to Israelite hegemony had lost all worldly credibility. Then, but only then, we find Jews confronting in a systematic way and with solid knowledge of the other side the facts of history that had emerged many centuries earlier.

Whether a different symbolic system would have produced a more realistic and effective policy for the confrontation with triumphant Christianity we shall never know. For so long Israel had pretended nothing happened of any importance, not in the first century, not in the fourth. By the time people came around to concede that, after all, Christianity was here to stay and was essentially different from anything Israel had earlier encountered, it was an awareness too late to make such a difference in Israel's framing of its picture of the outsider and its policy toward the alien."

We now recognize that this statement is not only wrong, it is wrongheaded. The error is not niggling and it is not inconsequential. It is fundamental, because it is methodological. The methodological error is both general and specific. In general I erred by believing other people instead of asking how people knew the things they took for granted. I took over a prevailing attitude of mind – and I did not even realize it. The specific error was that I failed to work along lines I myself had already discovered. I homogenized what should be analyzed and differentiated. I gave "the talmudic view of...," having spent many years trying to show that there is no such thing.

Let me in conclusion return to the questions with which we began and answer them:

[1] *If we find that each one of the documents says on its own essentially what all of the documents say together, so that the parts do turn out to be interchangeable, then imposing distinctions suggests differences where there is none....In that case, differentiation proves misleading.*

The outcome is that failing to differentiate among documents and to listen to the message of each on its own, I missed what in fact was a striking and fresh trait in one set of compilations. Not having heard the evidence of one canonical statement, I did not recognize the originality, the unprecedented nature, of another. So harmonization misled me. Now to turn to the opposite:

[2] *If, by contrast, when viewed one by one, our documents in fact do not say the same thing by themselves that all of them say when read together, our category, failing to recognize differences, suggests a unity and a cogency where there is none....In that case, not effecting a considerable labor of description of the documents one by one will obscure the very center and heart of matters: that the documents, components of the whole, are themselves autonomous, though connected (if that can be shown) and also continuous (if that can be shown).*

Clearly, the documents read one by one do yield insight that combining all their statements on a given topic does not bring to light. So, in sum, differentiating among documents shows us things that not differentiating among them obscures. Not seeing the books as individual statements obscured for me those shifts and turnings that now appear to respond to the movement of the wheel of history. And, it follows, the thinking at hand, concerning both the outsider in general and Rome in particular, the history of humanity but especially the history and destiny of Israel – that thinking turns out, properly analyzed, to respond in a deep and systematic way to the single most considerable challenge the Jewish people in the Land of Israel was to face for the next fifteen hundred years: the rise of the Christian West as brother and enemy to Israel, the Jewish people. We who stand at the other side of the abyss mark the first generation to know that the siblings, Jacob and Esau, Israel and Rome, Judaism and Christianity, may learn to exchange the kiss of peace. And, as in the time of the meeting and reconciliation of the first Jacob and the first Esau, so today, it is at the very moment that Jacob, having labored in exile for so long, once more enters upon the land and the patrimony that is his.

Appendix II

David Weiss Halivni on the Tannaite Midrashim

David Weiss Halivni, in his *Midrash, Mishnah, and Gemara. The Jewish Predilection for Justified Law* (Cambridge, 1986: Harvard University Press), deals with the same documents as are treated here, and his thesis should not be ignored. Halivni observes that the Mishnah and associated materials consist "almost entirely of fixed law; they contain very little discursive material." In their view "law was to be officially transmitted only in the apodictic form." Argument and discussion would be neglected and not preserved. He further maintains that "this state also prevailed throughout the Amoraic period (200-427), until the redactors of the Talmud...came to the aid of the discursive material and affirmed it worthy to be preserved."

The role of the redactors of the Talmud, called by Halivni "Stammaim," was "to provide lengthy explanatory notes, complete defective statements, supplement the text with passages of their own." These conclusions, reached in his commentary to half of the Talmud of Babylonia, led Halivni to suppose that in casting matters as they did, the *Stammaim* reverted to the practice of the authorship of collections of biblical commentaries on legal passages of Scripture.

Specifically, Halivni inquires into what he calls "midrashic form," "the form used when law is tied to Scripture." Using as the subtitle of his book "the Jewish predilection for justified law," he argues that there is a Jewish "proclivity for vindicatory law, for law that is justified, against law that is autocratically prescribed." This distinction leads him to take the view that what he calls Mishnaic form, that is, law without exegetical foundation linking law to Scripture, was exceptional: "Mishnaic form initially emerged as a response to the particular political and religious conditions that prevailed in Palestine during the period following the destruction of the Temple." He further maintains that there is a "Jewish inclination for the vindicatory. The discovery that Jewish apperception since the time of the Bible favored justificatory law was an unexpected result of this study." The book then is divided by periods: biblical, post-biblical, mishnaic, amoraic, stammaitic, then the Gemara as successor of Midrash, and the legacy of the Stammaim. The work rests on three premises.

First, Halivni takes for granted the unity of all sources in a single "Judaism," joined to the axiom that the talmudic literature speaks for all Jews of the time and the postulate of a cogent "Jewish mentality." That is why he can fabricate a single "Jewish apperception."

Second, he takes for granted the reliability of all attributions of sayings.

Third, Halivni takes as historical fact the accuracy of what is attributed.

Each of the premises on its own renders null the author's use of evidence to demonstrate his theses. The first is undemonstrated and as a matter of fact racist. The second is uncritical, the third, gullible and credulous. Whether a differentiated and critical reading of the same sources would lead to the same conclusions no one can say. In all, Halivni's book is rather naive and intellectually retrograde. Very, very learned, if not very critical or persuasive, the book has led nowhere and is likely to mark a dead end. The approach to intellectual history offered in this book presents the alternative, and I think the sole right, critical way to conduct research into the Tannaite Midrashim.

Appendix III

Dov Zlotnick on the Mishnah

THE IRON PILLAR – THE MISHNAH. REDACTION, FORM, AND INTENT. By Dov Zlotnick. Produced by The Bialik Institute, Jerusalem. 1988. 273 pp. (N.p.). Distributed in North America by Ktav Publishing House, Hoboken, NJ.

The Bialik Institute claims credit only for "producing" the book – presumably setting type and printing and binding it. Ktav admits only to distributing it in North America, and the firm's owner denies any other part in publishing it. The Jewish Theological Seminary of America, where Zlotnick has taught for decades, did not include the book in its Moreshet Series. So it appears no one wishes to claim credit for sponsoring this pathetic item.

I cannot say I blame Ktav, Bialik Institute, or The Jewish Theological Seminary of America. For, writing on the theme of "Rabbi's Mishnah and the development of Jewish law," Zlotnick argues no thesis. Through a process of jejune free association, rather, he manages to pass his opinion on this and that. He covers various topics, such as the editorial activity of Rabbi, memory and the integrity of the Oral Tradition, some aspects of mishnaic repetition, conservatism in the making of law; strengthening the Oral Law, the inoperative *halakah*, is the Mishnah a code, and the like.

The book could have been written in 1850 by Zechariah Frankel, for Zlotnick's categories and issues ("the relation of Rabbi to his predecessors," "the Mishnah of R. Akiba," "*halakhah:* its authority and relation to Moses" [!]) were the ones in vogue in the primitive stages of modern scholarship on the Mishnah. The book is ignorant and therefore an oddity, too eccentric to be taken seriously. It is an example of what, by publishing only a single book, it means for an author to "publish too much."

Index

DATE DUE

2/19/95			

HIGHSMITH   # 45220